ILLEGAL ALPHABETS AND ADULT BILITERACY

When people today argue about "illegal aliens," the last question on their minds may be the one explored in this book: how do "illegal aliens" chart the speech-sounds of colloquial English? The book is timeless in offering an unusually direct entry into how a group of Mexican fruit pickers analyze their first encounter with local American speech in a tiny rural Midwestern community in the United States. The level of concrete detail is distinctive among the current discussions on the hot topic of unauthorized immigration. Readers see close up how intelligently migrant workers help each other use what they already know—the alphabetic principle of one letter, one sound—to teach each other, from scratch, at the very first contact, a language which none of them can speak. They see how and why the strategies adult immigrants actually use in order to cope with English in the real world seem to have much in common with those used by missionaries and linguists to write down hitherto unwritten languages, but little in common with those used in publicly funded bilingual and ESL classrooms.

What's new in this expanded edition of Tomás Mario Kalmar's landmark *Illegal Alphabets and Adult Biliteracy* are in-depth commentaries from six distinguished scholars—Peter Elbow, Ofelia García, James Paul Gee, Hervé Varenne, Luis Vázquez León, and Karen Velasquez—who bring to it their own personal, professional, and (multi)disciplinary viewpoints. These commentaries sharpen the socioeconomic, political, and educational implications of the book for the fields of New Literacies Studies, anthropology, and sociolinguistics, and extend its relevance to readers in Latin American Studies and the new and rapidly expanding fields of Migrant Studies and Border Studies.

Tomás Mario Kalmar organized Paulo Freire's visit to Sydney in 1974 and served as his interpreter. He has helped design a wide variety of innovative educational pr[...] from Su Casa Migrant Head Start in southe[...]y Monterey Bay. Currently, he is Co-Dire[...]nter, International Sonoran Desert Alliance[...]

ILLEGAL ALPHABETS AND ADULT BILITERACY

Latino Migrants Crossing the Linguistic Border

Second Expanded Edition

Tomás Mario Kalmar

With commentaries by

Peter Elbow
Ofelia García
James Paul Gee
Hervé Varenne
Luis Vázquez León
Karen Velasquez

Routledge
Taylor & Francis Group

NEW YORK AND LONDON

First published 2015
by Routledge
711 Third Avenue, New York, NY 10017

and by Routledge
2 Park Square, Milton Park, Abingdon, Oxon OX14 4RN

Routledge is an imprint of the Taylor & Francis Group, an informa business

© 2015 Taylor & Francis

First edition published by Lawrence Erlbaum Associates, Inc. 2001

Library of Congress Cataloging in Publication Data
Kalmar, Tomás Mario, 1942– Illegal alphabets and adult biliteracy: Latino
  migrants crossing the linguistic border, expanded edition/Tomas Mario
  Kalmar.—Second editon.
  pages cm
  Includes bibliographical references and index. 1. English language—
  Study and teaching—Spanish speakers. 2. English language—Study and
  teaching—United States. 3. Languages in contact—United States.
  4. English language—Self-instruction. 5. Adult education—United
  States. 6. Hispanic Americans—Education. 7. Hispanic Americans—
  Languages. 8. Bilingualism—United States. 9. English language—
  Alphabet. I. Title.
  PE1129.S8K28
  2015428.0071′073—dc232014034711

ISBN: 978-1-138-80427-2 (hbk)
ISBN: 978-1-138-80429-6 (pbk)
ISBN: 978-1-315-75312-6 (ebk)

Typeset in Bembo and Stone Sans
by Florence Production Ltd, Stoodleigh, Devon, UK

para mamacita
bruja letrada

CONTENTS

GRACIAS/ACKNOWLEDGMENTS

Into this book I have poured 20 years of life shared with friends and strangers. As it goes to press, I celebrate *con mucho cariño y respeto* the memory of my dear friend, the late Alfred Schenkman. In 1983, just before he died, Alfred published 500 copies of *The Voice of Fulano*.

It took 12 more years to legitimize the conversion of that slim volume of miscellaneous bilingual field notes into the doctoral dissertation which—with barely any changes—you, dear Reader, now hold in your hand. I thank the many communities who taught me to value the intellectual labor of *alfabetización*, and I thank the various institutions that helped legitimize the tale I tell.

At the Harvard Graduate School of Education, Joe Maxwell taught me integrity. Carol Chomsky persuaded me not to omit the technical linguistic details. Jim Gee persuaded me to Discourse the Harvard way. Donaldo Macedo helped exorcise my reluctance to do so. And when the rites of passage got tough, Hanna Fingeret nourished my courage.

The Spencer Foundation blessed the production of this book with a generous Doctoral Dissertation Fellowship. Deepest gratitude to Catherine Lacey!

The *Illinois Times*, the St. Louis Mercantile Library at the University of Missouri-St. Louis, and the *Southern Illinoisan* kindly granted permission to reproduce the articles on pp. 11, 24–25, and 26–33, respectively. Dover Publications granted permission to reproduce the glossary on p. 97, and MIT Press the glossaries on pp. 104–105.

Lifelong gratitude to Silja Kallenbach, to Beatriz McConnie Zapater, and to Barbara Newman. And *gracias* to all the other folks in the original 14 ALIPs of the Boston Adult Literacy Initiative, and to the people at Umass/Boston and Roxbury Community College who supported the work of the Boston Adult Literacy Resource Institute in its first five years. Also to the Lawrence Literacy Coaltion, and to Luis Prado of Alianza Hispana, and all the folks there.

Peg and Steve Falcone and Joe Liberto first welcomed my family and me to Carbondale. Jennifer FauntLeRoy provided a home for my two sons and me—and Pobblesquatch—and, while tornados whirled us around, delivered babies in the backwoods. The good people of Cobden and Anna and Carterville taught me what it takes to desegregate a community *poco a poco*, one move at a time. Kaye Weatherford persuaded me that I could choose to see what others see.

Alex Paull, Steve Baker, Cathy Signorelli, and the rest of the Carbondale Leonard Peltier Support Group taught me solidarity. And Patti and Kevin and Hugh and Bob and Dave and the Oakland Avenue gang kept me yodeling. Y más que nunca, sueño con todos los compadres y todos sus familiares, tanto en Cherán como en Illinois. Primeramente con Kim y Steve Titus, y don Fidel y doña Concepción Bartolo y mi ahijadita Margarita, y también Garth Gillan, y Pánfilo y Sara Queriapa y sus familiares, y las familias de Catalina Román, de don José Gomez, y de todas las pioneras de Su Casa Migrant Head Start Day Care Center, y Salvador Tehandón, y Margarita García, y muchos muchos más que aquí no se puede ni nombrar.

I thank three Pauls for their support of this work: Paul Friedrich, Paulo Freire, and Paul Simon.

As I kiss this book goodbye, my heart sings for my family, especially my dear brother Jorge, who, when he was 6, taught his little brother the *abecedario* of Spanish and whose faith in this book has never wavered, and my sons Christopher and Dmitri, who, when they were 10 and 6 years old, donated their pocket money to help xerox the *diccionario mojado*—a copy of which they one day sold for a dollar to the Bishop of Belleville. And most of all, my pearl of great price, my wife Bridget Suárez O'Hagin.

NOTE ON THE SECOND EDITION

What is new about this edition of *Illegal Alphabets and Adult Biliteracy* is the addition of six substantive commentaries written from a variety of viewpoints. The commentators offer their own personal, professional, and (multi)disciplinary reflections, sharpening the socioeconomic, political, and educational implications of the book, clarifying its relevance and extending its scope.

PROLOGUE

This book begins with a true story about "illegal aliens" who, in the summer of 1980, in the little town of Cobden, Illinois, decided to help each other write down English *como de veras se oye*—the way it really sounds. Why and how they did this, what they actually wrote down, and what happened to their texts makes up the plot of the story.[1]

The middle of the book[2] is about how even progressive educators in the United States don't seem to know what they're talking about when the topic is "illegal aliens." The strategies adult immigrants actually use in order to cope with English out in the real world seem to have little in common with those used by students in publicly funded bilingual and English as a second language (ESL) classrooms.

And the end of the book is about the ideal of a universal alphabet, about the utopian claim that anyone can use a canonical set of, say, 26 letters to reduce to script any language, ever spoken by anyone, anywhere, at any time. This claim is so familiar to us that we easily overlook how much undocumented intellectual

---

1. For an overview of the situation in and around Cobden in 1980, see the excellent newspaper articles by Jim Orso and Bridget Walsh, pp. 24–33, below. Of the 2,000 Mexican migrant workers who harvested the crops in and around Cobden in 1980, about 800 were Tarascans from Cherán, Michoacán. Readers of this book may perhaps be unaware of the impressive and remarkable role played by the Tarascan people not only in the history of Mexico from pre-Columbian times to the present, but also in the history of both Christian and revolutionary adult biliteracy campaigns worldwide since the late 1930s. At the end of Chapter 4, I propose further research into the history of the Tarascan Project within the postmodern theoretical framework offered here.

2. To help readers who enjoy a nonlinear trajectory through a book, I have supplied numerous cross-references in footnotes such as this one. You might regard these cross-references as if they were hypertext links. For example, at this point, those who want to begin reading in the middle might like to look at pp. 62–68 below.

labor was invested over the centuries by those who successfully carried the alphabet across the border from one language to the next. From this undocumented labor, without which none of us would now be able to read, we all, today, profit.

As far as possible, I have tried to steer clear of technical terminology that might look like jargon to the uninitiated. Readers familiar with any of the postmodern discourses now available on the social construction of symbolic forms should have no trouble bringing such discourses to bear on what I have to say about the *game*, the *discourse*, and the *scene of writing*, which constitute the focus of my theoretical analysis.

The *game* is played with letters of the Roman alphabet and the speech-sounds of one or more languages. The aim of this game is to establish a consistent relationship between a letter and a sound. The challenge is to decide what counts as a single sound in a language you don't yet know. The game begins in Chapter 1 with a surprising way of writing *where d'you live?* and ends with 180 ways of writing *the law doesn't protect us.* Chapter 2 spells out the rules of the game and describes how it spread and grew in Cobden in 1980, producing a handwritten set of English–Spanish glossaries. Chapter 3 explains why, upon first looking at these glossaries, monolingual teachers have trouble understanding the point of the game. Chapter 4 discusses how, since the 1930s, professional linguists working worldwide for the Army, the Academy, the Church, and the Revolution have played the game for high stakes to produce official glossaries that are legitimate, institutionalized versions of the same genre as the humble-looking "illegal" Cobden glossaries. And the epilogue suggests that the game, though unfamiliar to monolingual adults in the United States, may in fact be as old as the alphabet itself.

The *discourse* is a way of talking about the game, talking about what counts as a valid move, a good move, the best move possible. The Mexican migrant workers in Chapters 1 and 2 talk about the game in a way that makes sense to them, makes no sense to the teachers in Chapter 3, and yet is surprisingly similar to the way anthropologists, linguists, missionaries, and revolutionary educators talk about the game in Chapter 4.

The *scene of writing* is not what we are used to. The Cobden glossaries, which are the protagonist of my narrative, look the way they do because they were written not in the familiar scene that we call "the classroom," but in the field— that is to say, in an "institutional no-man's land between two legal systems, two economies, two sovereign states, two languages, and, ultimately, between two institutionalized forms of alphabetic literacy."[3] It is the space in which "illegal aliens" dwell, and which I myself have gone in and out of for the 20 years that it has taken this book to legitimize its present shape.

> *The Rio Grande is a boundary*
> *drawn between real and imaginary.*

---

3. See pp. 77, 90 below.

To calculate its length requires complex analysis.
Many backs have got wet, baptized in the big Texan river
whose length can be charted in miles or kilometers.
Many necks have got red, inflamed by nightmares
and visions of apocalyptic terror.
There is a real river, and there is an imaginary one.
The wetbacks know one river, the rednecks another.
The Rio Grande runs right through the center of the United States;
it courses through the little town of Cobden, Illinois.
It runs between the applicant's pen and
the bureaucrat's form in the office of
every government-funded agency.
It runs between the pews in church.
It runs along the telephone wires.
Deep river.

When people today argue about "illegal aliens" in the United States, probably the last question on their minds is the one I have chosen to devote this book to: How do "illegal aliens" use an alphabet which they already know in order to chart the speech-sounds of colloquial English? My hope is that readers who bear with me all the way through to the end will interpret my story as a parable with serious political implications.

The value of the alphabet, like that of gold,
has to be guaranteed by the state and its agencies
through its apparatus of laws, regulations and customs
that set the standard, that determine the formal structure
of the alphabet and regulate its distribution.
Inventing your own coding system,
like minting your own coins,
challenges the monopolistic
tendencies of the state.
The authors of these diccionarios
forged new linguistic tokens,
following ad-hoc,
pragmatic criteria—just as
the local police
instituted new paralegal customs
to control the gray no-man's-land
between God-fearing illegal aliens,
and law-breaking legal citizens.[4]

---

4. Kalmar (1983: 106, 93)

1

NO MAN'S LAND

Quasi captivos sensus in suam linguam victoris
iure transposuit.

—Jerome

I

Líricamente

On Monday, July 7, 1980, the temperature in Cobden, Illinois rose, as it had for
the past week, to 110° in the shade. No one could remember it ever being this
hot before. Many blamed it on atmospheric changes caused by the eruption of
Mt. St. Helens in Washington state.

The 2,000 people who picked the apples in the orchards around Cobden on
that Monday did not, of course, work in the shade. When the day's work was
done, some of the Mexicans gathered on the porch of Su Casa Grocery Store,
as usual, to chat with one another and with their new Anglo friends. The Anglos
were locals from Union and Jackson counties who came to Su Casa Grocery
Store on weekday evenings in the hope of picking up a little Spanish in return
for teaching a little English. That, at least, was how they first explained their
reason for coming, when these gatherings had first begun about six weeks earlier.
Week by week, the character of the meetings had gone through changes. People
began gathering every weeknight (except Friday). Some, on each "side" of the
language barrier, came only once or twice. Others came often, and brought their
friends. Sometimes there were only half a dozen of us, sometimes 30 or 40.
Gradually, shyly, people who could not speak each other's language exchanged

bits and pieces of ordinary speech, the common coin of each other's social customs. Gradually, face-to-face encounters between Anglos and Mexicans, between legal citizens and illegal migrant laborers, became less embarrassing. Under the guise of lowering the language barrier, in the "neutral territory" of the Mexican grocery store, people were, as the Mexicans put it, *ganando confianza*: building trust across the social (and legal) gulf that divided locals and migrants. Very quietly, almost invisibly, Cobden was beginning to desegregate itself.

On that Monday, July 7, 1980, people felt too hot, and too numerous, to crowd into the store. A few strolled down to the little park down the street, and others joined them. By around 7 p.m., I counted about 80 people in the park, locals and migrants, half and half. Little kids were on the swings, teenagers on the basketball court, and more mature adults on the bench or in the shade of the tree. This was more people than I had seen in the park before. The park, in fact, was usually empty.

On the basketball court, two teams had formed. It was not Mexicans *versus* Anglos. Each team was mixed. But the game was pure basketball. Mexicans tend to regard basketball as quintessentially Mexican. It was played in pre-Columbian Mexico. North Americans tend to regard it as quintessentially Yankee. Despite the language barrier, the rules of the game were common knowledge. Players and spectators kept up a supportive banter of phrases in English and Spanish. From time to time, to comment on a good or bad shot, players or spectators tried out some rather mild cusswords in each other's language. Much laughter.

While Mexican and Anglo body rhythms playfully contested possession of the ball on the court according to the well-known rules of the game, a group of us older, or at least less energetic, men shared the rhythms of Mexican and North American music, country and western and ranchera, bluegrass and corridos, sitting or standing in the shade of a tree that had lost a couple of branches to the recent tornado. We shared soft drinks and Kentucky Fried Chicken. Jim had brought his banjo; I had brought my guitar. Constantino, Pancho, Antonio, and some of the other men were from Los Altos de Jalisco and sang the old corridos—*La carcel de Cananea, Valentín de la Sierra, El veinticuatro de junio, Rosita Alvirez*[1]—in the old traditional style which demands that two men sing in such close harmony and with such complete recall of the entire text that you cannot tell who is leading and who is following, which is *la primera voz*, which *la segunda voz*—which is the first voice, which the second. To maintain concentration, you gaze into each other's eyes throughout all the verses, keeping your voices always a third apart (never, as in bluegrass harmony, an open fourth or fifth). These corridos are invariably learned *líricamente*—"lyrically," that is to say by heart, by "word of mouth," orally, not from written texts.

---

1. For these, and for corridos in general, see the classic work by Mendoza (1984).

Jim tried to accompany the corridos on his banjo, without much luck. His banjo licks fit in much better with the polka rhythms of the norteño style, especially this song, as sung by Pancho and Antonio on that day:

1. Porque somos los mojados
   siempre nos busca la ley
   porque andamos ilegales
   y no sabemos inglés
   la migra terca a sacarnos
   y nosotros a volver.

   Si unos sacan por Laredo
   por Mexicali entran diez
   por Ciudad Juárez, Tijuana,
   y por Nogales también
   ¿qiuen puede sacar la cuenta
   cuantos entramos al mes?

   (Chorus:)
   El problema de nosotros

1. *Because we are "wetbacks"*
   the law is always after us
   because we go round illegal
   and don't speak English
   the INS is bent on throwing us out
   and we're bent on coming back

   For each one thrown out at Laredo
   ten get in through Mexicali,
   Ciudad Juárez, Tijuana,
   and Nogales as well.
   Who can keep score
   how many of us come per month?

   (Chorus:)
   Our problem

facil se puede arreglar
que nos den una gringuita
para poder emigrar
en cuanto nos den la mica
la mandamos a volar

can easily be solved
let them give us a little gringa
so that we can emigrate
as soon as they give us our green card
we'll tell her to split

2. ¿Si se acabara el mojado
   de quién podrán depender?
   ¿Quién piscara el jitomate,
   lechuga, y el betabel?
   El limón, uva, y toronja—
   todo se echara a perder.

2. If there were no wetbacks
   on whom could they depend?
   Who'd pick the tomatoes,
   the lettuce, the beet?
   The lemons, grapes, grapefruit—
   it would all go to waste.

Y los salones de baile
todos tendrán que cerrar
porque si se va el mojado
¿quienes van a ir a bailar?
y las que viven de welfare
¿quién las irá a consolar?

And all the dance halls
will have to close down
because if the wetback leaves
who's going to go dancing?
And the women on welfare—
who's going to console them?

Then Jim and his friend Simon sang *Cold Cold Heart* and other old Hank Williams songs, in close country harmony, often in parallel thirds, which sounded, in this context, somewhat Mexican in flavor. When Jim sang *If You've Got the Money, I've Got the Time*, Alfredo and Raúl joined in. They were two of the most highly respected men in the Tarascan community. Alfredo was in his early fifties, Raúl—who had distinguished himself on the basketball court—in his late forties. Both men had traveled from Cherán to various regions of the United States and back again many times.

Later, Raúl and Alfredo decided to write down *toda la letra*—the whole text, the complete lyrics—of *You Picked a Fine Time to Leave Me Lucille*, which had been sung more than once that night. They already knew it *líricamente*—they sang along with everyone else every time it got sung. They wanted to write it down so they could remember it on their own. Jim and Simon could remember the opening lines, the rest they "faked." Two lines satisfied Raúl. Alfredo wanted the whole thing. He went around collecting bits of it here and there, from one person, and another until finally he had the whole thing down pat. He looked at his score and sang it just like on the record.

Raúl	Alfredo	(Spanish version)
YO PICTI FAY TAIYO	LLU PICT FANY TAM	ME ABANDONASTE
TU LIVE MI LUCI	TO LIMI LUSIO	MUY PRONTO MUJER
FORR JANDRI CHOUREN	FOR JAGRE CHILDON	CON LA COSECHA,
HENE CROOF ENDI FIIL	EN COROP IN FIL	LOS HIJOS Y YO
	AYFRD SAN BE TAMS	
	LIBT TRU SAN SE TAMS	
	BAT DIS TAM	
	DU JORTN GUANT JIOL	
	LLU PICT FANY TAM	
	TO LIMI LUSIO	

Working together, Raúl and Alfredo and Jim and Santiago and me came up with a Spanish version. We had to keep counting syllables in each language, to make sure it fit the tune. It took about 15 minutes to translate just two lines. But these two lines sounded almost like a corrido:

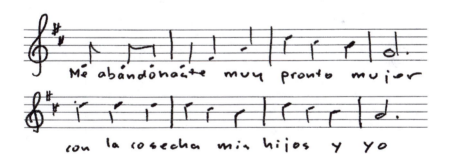

While his elders were making field transcriptions of local oral texts, Panchito was learning his first words in English. Panchito, about 15 years old, was probably the youngest Tarascan man in the area. He had been in the United States less than a week and this was his first social encounter with friendly locals. He had been active in the basketball game, and was now hanging out with Cipriano and Alfonso, two older teenagers from Los Altos de Jalisco (i.e., not Tarascans). Cipriano and Alfonso had formed a friendship with Renée, a 14-year-old white picker who often came to the meetings with her mother. Tonight, Renée had brought her friend Stephanie, a young woman her own age. Panchito kept looking at Stephanie. Finally, he came over to where we were singing. In the softest possible voice, he asked, "¿Como se dice en inglés ¿donde vives??" How do you say *donde*

vives in English? Panchito listened closely to Jim, Simon, and some of the other men saying *where d'you live?* He mimicked them until he got it off by heart, *líricamente.* He borrowed a ballpoint pen and a scrap of paper from Alfredo. He wrote JUELLULIB.

He kept looking at his piece of paper and trying it out. "La lengua tiene que doblarse donde uno la maneja," said Alfredo—your tongue has to fold the way you tell it to. To my ears, Panchito was wrapping his tongue around the southern twang just fine. He echoed, I thought, Jim's local intonation and rhythm perfectly. "Tiene la musiquita de la voz," said Raúl—he's caught the melody of the voice. Panchito even pronounced the final *v* in *live* (represented by the final B in his JUELLULIB). Monolingual Spanish speakers have trouble hearing this sound at the end of a word or phrase—and therefore have trouble saying it—because the rhythms of spoken Spanish don't end that way. Panchito, Alfredo, and Raúl, however, were not monolingual. They were bilingual in Tarascan and Spanish. And they were musicians.

Panchito looked across at Stephanie. Doubt flickered on his face, I urged him to practice on Martha, who was standing nearby. A long silence, during which he gazed at Martha, gazed pensively at his piece of paper. Finally, something overcame his shyness. He stepped up to Martha and touched her elbow. When she turned to him, he said, softly, "JUELLULIB?" "Carbondale," said Martha. The smile that flowered on his lips as he crossed the language border was the first smile I had seen on his face since the day he arrived from Cherán.

From that day on, he smiled more and more often, and by the end of the summer he had become something of a leader among his compañeros, some of whom were a good deal older than he was.

I copied JUELLULIB into my own notebook and it made me smile in turn. Panchito had a lot to learn. But so did I. JUELLULIB struck me, at the time, as funny, and it took a number of subsequent experiences to convert my amusement into respect unmixed with condescension.

II

The Death of Leonardo

At the end of that week, on Friday, July 11, the Chief of Police convened a meeting in Cobden. Present at the meeting were Gustavo, a bilingual South American law student who was working as an intern for the Illinois Migrant Legal Assistance Program, based in Chicago; Rafael, a Puerto Rican, María, an upper-class Mexican, and Maximo, a bilingual middle-class Mexican student at Southern Illinois University, who together made up the Anti-Alcoholism Project; and me wearing my "hat" as the Illinois Migrant Council's regional Education Director.

Body finally identified
THU NOV 6 1980
as migrant worker

By H. B. Koplowitz
Of The Southern Illinoisan

The body of a man found dead July 12 on U.S. 51 south of Cobden has at last been positively identified.

According to Union County State's Attorney William Ballard, the Mexican Department of Defense identified the man last week as Leonardo Valdez, 21, of Michoacan Province, Mexico. The identification was made from fingerprint samples sent to Mexico by the state's attorney's office. X *murder list*

Valdez died July 12, apparently as the result of a late night hit-and-run accident. According to Union County deputy Jim Ray, three and perhaps four vehicles hit Valdez. Two cars stopped at the scene, but lab tests of paint chips found on the body indicated that those cars probably hit Valdez after he was already dead and lying along the highway.

There had been rumors of foul play concerning the incident, rumors partially fueled by a lack of information. Because the body was not positively identified immediately, an obituary was never printed. And, because the incident is still an open case, the Union County sheriff's department did not report it.

According to information compiled through the sheriff's department, the state's attorney's office and the Illinois Migrant Council, on the night of Valdez's death, he had been drinking at the Country Cafe in Cobden. There had been a disturbance at the

bar and a Cobden policeman took Valdez to a migrant camp north of Cobden.

One of the mysteries about the incident is how Valdez got from the migrant camp north of Cobden to south of Cobden where his body was found.

Ballard said Valdez was probably standing when he was fatally injured because bones in his chest were broken. After that, his head was run over by a second car. The head was severely injured, which gave rise to reports of decapitation, Ballard said.

Valdez was apparently an illegal alien because no papers were found on him, Ballard said. Other migrants were able to identify Valdez, but it took several months to get an official identification from fingerprints.

The migrant community held a Mass for Valdez several months ago. He was buried in the Anna Cemetery.

Some people have suggested that Union County officials did not pursue their investigation of the incident as vigorously as they might have if Valdez had not been a migrant, a charge that Ballard pointedly denies.

"We didn't ignore the incident," said Ballard. "That's not our attitude down here at all."

Deputy Ray said the sheriff's department has followed up on about a dozen leads in the past four months, including two leads two weeks ago. But there still are no suspects in the case, which is still open.

The Death of Leonardo

The Police Chief began by explaining that he had called the meeting because people were saying that the Mexicans were taking over the town. "You gotta keep your boys in line," he told us.

He was referring to the *de facto* desegregation of the little village park that had been under way for a week. Where I saw people simply strolling over to the park because it was too hot and crowded in the store basement, he saw Mexicans crossing an invisible line that had never been crossed before. If what had impressed me was the way Raúl, Alfredo, and little Panchito used the alphabet to notate what they had already learned *líricamente*, what had impressed the Police Chief was the way they played basketball every night. He explained that as nephew of the largest grower in the region, he felt some responsibility for keeping things under control and making sure they didn't get out of hand.

My notes for the meeting record that the Police Chief went on to say that he himself was grateful to these hard-working Mexicans as long as they made no trouble; that during the heat wave one of the Mexicans had passed out on the street, been jailed, and, on being released, had passed out again; and that this was the *only* case in which he, the Chief of Police, had taken the steps necessary to have a Mexican deported. "What was he charged with?" asked Gustavo, the legal intern. "Improper use of the highway," explained the Chief of Police.

The meeting ended with Gustavo asking, "What, precisely, is your policy towards the Mexicans in this area?" and the Chief of Police answering, "Our policy is very simple: we are here to enforce the law."

★   ★   ★

That night, around midnight, the bartender at the Country Cafe took a baseball club and attacked three of his Mexican customers: Enrique, 17, Leonardo, a man in his forties, and Calixto, also 17. There are two versions of what happened next. The unofficial version is that the police arrived and took Enrique and Leonardo home to their respective camps, leaving Calixto, who was relatively unscathed, to get home by himself. Enrique they left bleeding on his camp bed, with his scalp split open and his right eye injured; Leonardo they left, no one knows how badly injured, at a different camp north of Cobden. The next day, Enrique's uncle, Miguel, brought Enrique to my house in Carbondale. Enrique was in critical medical condition. (He was looked after by my housemate, Dr. Jennifer FauntLeRoy, and was not well enough to return to work until two weeks later.) Leonardo's body, meanwhile, had been found at 4:00 a.m. (Saturday, July 12) lying on the main highway, US51, south of Cobden. His head had been severed from his body. The unofficial version was silent on the question of how Leonardo's body had got from his camp north of Cobden to the highway south of Cobden.

The official version was eventually published in the *Southern Illinoisan* on Thursday, November 6, 1980—almost four months later (see above, p. 7).

Officially, Leonardo was the victim of a hit-and-run accident. The Illinois Bureau of Investigation analyzed flecks of paint found on the body and concluded that three "or maybe four" cars had run over Leonardo—hence the decapitation. Scientific evidence showed that Leonardo was already dead when at least two of the cars hit him. When the first car hit him, he was officially still alive: he "was probably standing when he was fatally injured because bones in his chest were broken." The unofficial Mexican version suggests that Leonardo may have been already dead before the first car hit him; the official version does not allow for this possibility.

As far as I could tell, the law was not enforced. The bartender at the Country Cafe was never charged with any crime, not even selling liquor to minors. (He eventually offered Enrique some money to make up for the two weeks' earnings Enrique had missed.) None of the Mexican witnesses were interviewed. Nor were the drivers of the three or four cars in the "hit-and-run" business ever publicly identified.

Since no documents of any sort had been found in Leonardo's empty pockets, he was "apparently an illegal alien," and no identification of the deceased was officially possible—until the Mexican army finally identified his fingerprints, months later.

Leonardo was, as far as I know, the only Tarascan in the area who was not from Cherán: he was said to be from Azajo. This was his first summer in Cobden. Unlike the Tarascans from Cherán (such as Calixto and Enrique), Leonardo seems to have had no friends or family in the United States.

Following Leonardo's death, Cobden was quiet for three weeks. Mexicans aimed for invisibility. The basketball court stood empty. Anglos stopped coming to Su Casa Grocery Store. Meanwhile, Leonardo's body was not buried.

On Wednesday, July 30, a small group gathered again in the basement of Su Casa Grocery Store. This was (as far as I know) the first such "public" meeting since the death of Leonardo Valdez. I wasn't there, but I heard about it from Evaristo. As a "legal" Mexican-American (from Texas), Evaristo had been hired by the Illinois Migrant Council, on Department of Labor money, to manage the Su Casa Grocery Store. He often knew the latest word-of-mouth news. He told me people were planning to meet again a week later, on August 6. I decided to join them.

III

Doló Dasn't Protect As

Breaking the Ground: Burying Leonardo

On Wednesday, August 6, 1980, when I arrived at Su Casa Grocery Store at around 6:30 p.m., there was no one there.

Some minutes later, Evaristo drove up, with María. María and I had not seen each other since the July 11 meeting with the Chief of Police. Evaristo and María explained that "everyone" was going to Anna.

Going to Anna was very unusual. People said the last black man in Anna had been lynched in 1948.

María, who had aristocratic Catholic connections, had persuaded the Catholic priest in Anna to say a *misa para el difunto*—a Mass for the deceased Leonardo. There was a Catholic church right in Cobden, but for some reason a mass in Cobden was out of the question. After the mass in Anna, Leonardo was, at long last, going to be buried. In the lily-white Anna cemetery.

Maria invited me to come too. I decided to stay and pass the word on to anyone who hadn't yet heard. A few minutes later, the Román family drove by, Calixto at the wheel. They hadn't heard about the funeral. They decided to go. Then Rob Tate showed up. He had been coming over from Carterville ever since the very first "language exchange" meetings[2] and he was the only Anglo who, after Leonardo's death, continued to come. He expressed no interest in attending a Catholic mass, and the two of us sat around waiting to see if anyone else would show.

The funeral in Anna was attended by 60 Mexicans, certainly the largest public gathering of illegal aliens ever seen in the region. María was firmly in control and delivered a homily in Spanish on the perils of drink. Leonardo was buried in an unmarked grave.

After the funeral, about a dozen men drove back from Anna to the grocery store in Cobden, mainly men who had come to many previous meetings, old-timers such as the Jalisco clan, Alfonso, Cipriano, and Constantino, but also a couple of men who had never come before: Juan, known as El Peligroso, and Esequiel. No Tarascans. Neither Renée nor her friend Stephanie showed up. Nor did Martha. Perhaps they didn't know the meeting was taking place. By 8:00 p.m., no *gringuitas* had come. It looked as if maybe everyone might just call it a day and go home.

Breaking the Taboo: Covering the Topic

Then a car pulled up and two women stepped out. Two new *gringuitas* who had never come before. Bridget and Danon, freelance reporters working for the *Illinois Times* on an article about migrant workers in Illinois. Their arrival cast me in the role of interpreter, at least initially. I introduced them formally to each of the men in turn. Danon asked me if it would be all right to take photos. I translated her question into Spanish, and translated the positive response back into English.

---

2. Monday, May 5; see Kalmar (1983: 16–17).

Whenever local Anglos talked face to face with local mojados for the first time, there was an inevitable sense, on the side of the Anglos, of a taboo being broken. If I was present at such initial encounters, my mediation as an interpreter lent a modicum of legitimacy to the ritual drama of breaking the taboo. By and large, the mojados themselves welcomed the witness of any local Anglos who crossed the no man's land between "legal" and "illegal," documented and undocumented, discourse and silence. On this night, having buried Leonardo, they especially welcomed the witness of these two female reporters from Springfield, the state capital.

Previously, before July 12, Anglos who arrived at the grocery store around 8:00 p.m. walked in on a lively scene and could join in conversations that were already going on. Bridget and Danon did not know, of course, that people tonight were much more somber than usual. About Leonardo's burial in Anna they knew nothing. They seemed surprised that the mojados trusted them immediately. Everyone looked at each other in thoughtful silence and then Constantino suggested that we go down into the basement after all.

Three months later (on November 7, 1980), Bridget's incisive article and Danon's photos appeared in the *Illinois Times*.[3] The informal encounter between these two freelance reporters and a group of mojados illuminates the paradoxical process of documenting the undocumentable. Many middle-class citizens in southern Illinois, especially intellectuals affiliated with Southern Illinois University, Carbondale, assumed they were doing the mojados a favor by letting silence cover the topic of their existence, their presence in the area, the economic importance of their work. All the same, there has long been a national public discourse on the topic of "illegal aliens." From time to time, the local media "covered" this topic. In the summer and fall of 1979, the local radio station, WSIU, and the local daily, the *Southern Illinoisan*, had reported, in detail, on the epidemic of Giardia Lamblia, a tropical disease that spread through the migrant camps and was at first blamed on the unsanitary toilet practices of the Mexicans, but was ultimately traced to the contaminated water in nearby Alto Pass. In the fall of 1980, the *St. Louis Globe-Democrat* carried an excellent article by Jim Orso under the headline "One grower says they're the best in the business." (The grower is quoted as saying "It would take 60 people to do what these [three dozen] boys are doing." The article is reproduced below, pp. 24–25.) And in October 1980, *North Pass News*, a type-written six-page newspaper published and distributed in Makanda, the home town of then congressman Paul Simon, devoted an issue to "The Tarascan People: Their Present and Future."

---

3. Reproduced, with permission, on pp. 26–32 below.

No Man's Land

The newspaper articles also exemplify the difficulty of categorizing the meetings that took place in the basement of the grocery store. Jim Orso called them "dialogue sessions." Bridget and Danon seem to have imagined that what they witnessed on August 6 was a legitimate "class," authorized by the Illinois Migrant Council.

It was not a class in the ordinary sense of the word, and it was not sponsored by the Illinois Migrant Council or any other legitimate institution. These meetings were not constrained to play by the rules of the game that govern legitimate classroom activities, and the implications of this fact are worth spelling out in detail for the light they throw on what actually happened in the basement on August 6.

In that basement, that night as on other nights, there was no timetable, no agenda, no curriculum, no textbook. Gatherings began and ended at no fixed time, and were never the same twice. There was no gatekeeping mechanism. No one was paid to perform the role of teacher. No one claimed the gatekeeper's authority to admit some people and deny entry to others. No one kept public records of who was present and who was absent. No one knew in advance what direction any given gathering might take. No one played the role of student in return for 30 dollars a week. In short, no one was officially in control. I certainly wasn't. Which is surely why the meetings were perceived by the Police Chief as a threat to the status quo, and why he instructed me to keep "my" boys in line. If it had been a "normal" class, under the auspices of the Illinois Migrant Council, it would have posed no such threat.

For the past 10 years, the Illinois Migrant Council had been conducting Adult Basic Education classes (including English as a Second Language, GED, and Pre-Vocational Education) throughout the state of Illinois. None of these classes were perceived as posing a threat to existing power structures. Their stated goal was to help seasonal and migrant farmworkers settle out into the main-stream of the U.S. economy. The classes were funded (at more than $2,000,000 per year) by the U.S. Department of Labor. "Illegal aliens" were therefore *not* eligible to attend. These legitimate classes followed the rhythms of "government time" and reproduced the normal Discourse[4] of public education. The federal funds were used to rent classrooms, buy texts and educational materials, pay a salary to the teachers, and above all to pay a CETA stipend to the students. Teachers were paid to teach. Students were paid to learn—or, at least, to attend. Teachers were responsible for handing out the weekly CETA checks to the students. The size of the check depended on the student's documented attendance. Roles were clear. Gatekeeping was firm. Record-keeping was adequate and, in principle, public.

---

4. On which, see Chapter 3.

If 1980 had been like previous years, the Illinois Migrant Council would, as usual, have run one such class in Cobden from mid-June to mid-September, with a total budget of about $10,000. This covered the costs of a small part-time ABE class for 10 adults, meeting from 6:00 p.m. to 9:00 p.m., Monday through Wednesday, for 15 weeks. In previous years, these summer classes had served as a gate through which the 10 eligible migrants (and their local wives) could get on the escalator leading from English as a Second Language to Adult Basic Education to a GED to Vocational Education to legitimate job placement. Migrant workers who were not "illegal" and were still showing up in class at the height of the picking season in mid-September were regarded as having *terminated positively* and were recruited to participate in the Illinois Migrant Council's full-time winter classes as a first step in the process of settling out of the migrant stream and joining the mainstream labor force of the United States.

But in 1980 normal conditions were not met. By May 1980, the Illinois Migrant Council's central office in Chicago found it was "over budget" and therefore no one would be receiving CETA stipends ($27.90 per nine-hour week) to attend the summer class in Cobden. Hitherto, the stipend had been perceived by Illinois Migrant Council personnel as an incentive, without which it would be difficult to persuade pickers to put in three evenings a week after picking apples and peaches all day long. Would anyone attend classes on a regular basis for free?

The central office, however, wanted formal documentation to be submitted as if conditions were normal. In particular, they wanted to report to the Department of Labor, for the sake of appearance, 10 names of legal and eligible migrant workers in the region—as if the 10 were receiving stipends. Simply put, they wanted to document a fiction as if it were fact.

As Education Coordinator for the local (Delta) region of the Illinois Migrant Council, it was my responsibility to compile the necessary formal documentation. My strategy for dealing with this situation was twofold. On the one hand, I maintained, through thick and thin, that I was under no obligation to report to the Federal Government, or any other authority, the names of people, Anglos or Mexicans, "legal" or "illegal," who chose, for whatever private reason, to assemble freely in Cobden, at the grocery store or in the park. I therefore refused to produce the formal but fictitious documentation requested by the central office. On the other hand, I maintained it was in everyone's best interest to be upfront about what was really happening in Cobden, and as the summer progressed, I circulated, within and without the Illinois Migrant Council, various informal working papers, reporting on what I saw as a collective effort by locals and migrants to lower the language barrier that was preventing communication on shared concerns.[5]

---

5. Some of these working papers were subsequently published by Schenkman in Kalmar (1983).

It seemed to me immoral to pretend that 10 migrant workers were sitting in a classroom doing classroom exercises when in fact well over 200 people,[6] all told, including many local Anglos who would never have come to a regular ESL class, were engaged in a freewheeling, unstructured give and take in the informal gatherings in Cobden.

Much more went on at the meetings than merely "teaching a little Spanish, learning a little English." Of those who came regularly, Alfonso and Cipriano were two who enjoyed playing the role of student for free, at least when Renée did not show up. Renée was a white migrant worker in her early teens.[7] She and her mother had, in May and June, frequently joined the meetings. Her mother had stopped coming after a while, but Renée had formed a close friendship with Alfonso and Cipriano, and the three of them would go off into a corner, or walk outside, and have long conversations in Spanish and English, which they were picking up from each other *líricamente* (i.e., without writing anything down). Renée had picked up quite a lot of Spanish in the field, while picking the apples and peaches. Alfonso and Cipriano were not Tarascans. They were cousins, part of the Gomez clan from Los Altos de Jalisco. Alfonso was the only Mexican in the area who had stayed in school past sixth grade. (Many had not made it past second or third grade.) Alfonso was the most literate member of the group: he had recently graduated from high school in Mexico.[8]

On the nights when Renée did not show up, Alfonso and Cipriano, and a varying group of other young men, had enjoyed playing the role of student for free, with Martha, who enjoyed playing the role of teacher for free. It was Martha who, under normal circumstances, would have been the teacher of the part-time summer class, receiving a modest salary. This year, however, she came, from time to time, of her own free will, as a private individual like anyone else (including me). Whenever Martha arrived, she would soon be surrounded by a group of young men doing traditional classroom exercises out of a book under her guidance, while other people engaged in other activities.

On August 6, neither Renée nor Martha had come. As I followed Bridget, Danon, Constantino, and the others into the dark basement with the dirt floor and the bare light bulb, neither I, nor, as far as I could tell, anyone else, was in control. I felt, as often before, that we were entering a learning environment situated in no man's land. Anything could happen. I was prepared to go with the flow.

---

6. Counting those who only came once or twice.

7. Renée and her friend Stephanie were socializing with Alfonso and Cipriano at the Village Park on Monday, July 7 (see p. 5 above).

8. For sample texts written by Renée, Cipriano, and Alfonso, see below, pp. 45 #8, 45 #10 a–c, 51–53.

Un silencio muy largo

Everyone sat down. Some on milk crates, others on the row of seats that had once belonged to a movie theater. Above our heads, as usual, the loud hum of the refrigerator in the grocery store. Otherwise, silence. No one spoke. I felt that I should be translating the mojado silence into English for the Anglos, and maybe the Anglo silence into Spanish for the mojados. But I preferred the silence and had no desire to break it.

The silence with which this meeting began, or now began again, may carry within it the true answer to my questions: Why did these men, gathered together on this night, decide to produce their own diccionarios?

One of the hardest things to interpret about cultures is, surely, their silences. And yet, of all that we observe, silences often seem the most pregnant, charged with meaning, crying out to be interpreted.

Meditating and reflecting on language, one tends to forget, over and over again, that silence is the background, the vanishing point of the landscape in which language (as Halliday[9] would say) *does its job*. Or, as Quakers say, silence is *where words come from*. Silence is not a given, it calls for interpretation. Silence, too, is socially constructed.

And on that night, in that basement, we shared a silence that we ourselves "socially constructed," a bilingual, hybrid silence situated simultaneously in two languages at the same time—and in the no man's land between the two languages, the unmarked grave.

A legal and an illegal silence.

A male and a female silence.

We sat waiting to see what words would come from that untranslatable, unspeakable void: what job that situation called what language to do.[10]

Breaking the Silence

None of the previous gatherings had begun with a long, spontaneous silence. But then none had begun with a funeral, either. Martha would probably have felt comfortable playing the teacherly role and initiating some activity to break the silence. But Martha was not there, and no one took her place.

The silence went on and on. It lasted 10, 15, maybe 20 minutes. Whose voice would finally break it?

It was an Anglo voice that, at last, broke the silence—Rob Tate's. "What are we going to do?" It was not immediately clear whom he was addressing: who was included, who excluded, in his *we*.

---

9. Halliday (1975, 1978, 1989).
10. Tyler (1987).

An innocuous question, asked often enough on other nights, in other situations, in Spanish as often as in English. But on this night, on this occasion, the question rang out in the silence with new force. To my ears, it resonated with Lenin's "What is to be done?"

What is to be Done?

Silence followed Rob Tate's question. Silence followed, at first, each subsequent utterance. One at a time, people broke their personal, individual silence, and said something—in Spanish. Gradually, various themes emerged, various topics, a line of argument. It was not, at first, clear whether this was in response to Rob's question, suggesting possible things to do.

One of the first topics was: tenemos que dominar el inglés, *we have to master English*. On previous nights, it had been "let's learn *each other's* language." Tonight, Juan said that, in his opinion, helping gringos speak Spanish was futile, and others agreed with him. "We've got to concentrate on mastering *their* way of speaking."

Constantino said "Tenemos que razonar."

I translated this for Danon and Bridget as "We've got to strategize." *Razonar* is a normal Spanish word, cognate, of course, with *reason*. Constantino tended to use this word to name the activity of sitting or standing around in a group, thinking things out collectively, proposing a course of action, arguing the pros and cons, and coming to some shared conclusion.

Esequiel introduced another topic: yo sí conozco palabras sueltas, lo que no me lo sé es pegarlas. [I do know isolated words, what I can't do is stick 'em together.] Others agreed that this was their main problem with English. (To help me translate this idiom for Bridget, Danon, and Rob, Juan explained that when you ask a girl to dance in Mexico, she can choose whether to dance suelta or pegada: unattached or clasped in your arms.)

The main difficulty with learning English, said Constantino, was *la escritura de inglés*. (I still didn't grasp that by *escritura*, Constantino meant not only what English teachers mean by *spelling*, but also what the French mean by *écriture*—writing "in the larger sense.") Constantino wanted his compañeros to understand that the *escritura* of English was quite unlike what they imagined, quite different from the *escritura* of Spanish,[11] quite unlike what they thought of as *escritura*, period. Constantino said the challenge was to *alfabetizar los sonidos*. No one seemed to understand what he was talking about.

He appealed to me to help him make his point. Implicitly, he invoked the series of conversations he and I had had at previous meetings. He would take me aside and ask me to please just tell him *el abecedario de inglés*. Thinking he was

---

11. Or the *escritura* of Tarascan.

referring to the alphabet, I would always reply that the abecedario of English and the abecedario of Spanish were one and the same, *igualitos*. The only difference was little details such as the *ñ* and the *ll*. After the meetings in the park, however, Constantino had argued with me. The abecedarios of English and Spanish, he had claimed, are not at all the same: the alfabetos are, but the abecedarios are not.

By *alfabeto*, Constantino meant a set of letters, by *abecedario* a set of sounds. The letters of the alphabet are the same for English and Spanish, but the relation between letters and sounds, between script and speech, are very different. I had finally got it, and I had told him that I'd been to university, but I could not stand there and alfabetizar los sonidos de inglés: I could not recite the abecedario of English, the phonemes in lexical order. Nor did I know anyone who could.

Breaking the Ice: JUELLULIB

Thinking about the problem of making words stick, and the way the *escritura* of English misrepresents the blank spaces between words, and trying to explain to Bridget and Danon what the heated conversation in Spanish was all about, I walked to the easel and wrote down, with no comment, the first English words that Panchito had written, in the park, two days after he arrived from Cherán:

JUELLULIB

Cipriano asked me to say it. I didn't want to. I told him: you can read, *you* say it. They laughed. Danon asked, "Why're they laughing? What's it say?" Cipriano asked me to ask Danon to say it. She looked at it and said "I can't read this." I translated her response into Spanish. They asked, "Why can't she read this?" I said, "Tal vez es analfabeta"—maybe she's illiterate. More laughter, at the notion that a newspaper reporter is analfabeta and can't read as simple a phrase as JUELLULIB.

Tomás (in English): They want to know why you can't read this—are you illiterate?

Now the gringuitas laughed. The joke was shared.

Danon: I don't know Spanish—that's why I can't read it!

When I translated this, there was more laughter, at the notion that JUELLULIB is Spanish.

As people wrestled more and more seriously with the paradox that was actually no joke,[12] the conversation became even more lively. Juan and others called JUELLULIB a rompecabezas—a mind-bender, a brain-teaser. Someone else called

---

12. Cottom (1989)—see below, pp. 58ff.

it a trabalenguas, a tongue-twister. Neither Cipriano nor Danon are analfabetas yet neither can read this word, Cipriano because it's English, and he doesn't speak English, Danon because it's Spanish, and she doesn't speak Spanish.

What *is* this word? ¿Es inglés? ¿Es español? Both? Neither?

More and more laughter was shared as people conversed in twos and threes, trying to solve this puzzle, this riddle. I heard Constantino's terms—*escritura, abecedario, alfabeto, ortografía*—being taken up and explored by one group after another. Finally, after much teasing, Cipriano got his nerve up and risked reading the word aloud (sight-reading the score). He pronounced the LL as [dʒ] and did not pronounce the final B. Alfonso understood what Cipriano was saying, and smiled. Alfonso turned to Bridget and repeated what Cipriano had just said (i.e., without looking at the easel), addressing it as a bona fide question to Bridget: he really wanted to know where she lived. She in turn had no trouble understanding his question and replied, "In Carbondale. Where do *you* live?"

It was the first face-to-face gringo–mojado exchange of the evening, unmediated by an interpreter. It broke the ice.

Inverting the Hierarchy: DONDEVIVIS

Bridget, Danon, and Rob now wanted to know how to say *where d'you live* in Spanish. People got up from their seats, and rapidly, as on many previous evenings, groups formed with one gringo per group. Cipriano and Alfonso helped Bridget practice ¿*donde vives?* Esequiel, Froilán, and Pascual helped Danon; Constantino and Juan helped Rob (who really had learned this phrase in the past already—more than once).

When Constantino heard Bridget asking Cipriano to write it down, he intervened and suggested that Bridget learn the phrase *líricamente* (like Jacinto in the park, and like Alfredo and his song) and then write it down in her own *escritura*.

Bridget and Danon conferred, jotted down some attempts on paper, and then Bridget wrote on the easel:

DONDEVIVIS[13]

First some men expressed polite surprise that two reporters could make such simple spelling errors. Others then said that although it was not correcto, it was bueno. All the men (except Alfonso) had had less than six years of schooling in

---

13. That is, they wrote it as one word, not two, and although the E in DONDE and the E in VIVES represent allophones of one Spanish phoneme, Bridget and Danon represented the first and second vowels in VIVIS as allophones of the phoneme represented by I.

Mexico. But this was sufficient for them all to feel sure that there should be a space between E and V (DONDE · VIVES) *porque no es una sola palabra, sino dos*— because it's not just one word, it's two. And that the last vowel *se escribe con la e*—is written as E, not I. Juan concluded that Bridget and Danon's problem with Spanish was the same as his problem with English: *como se pegan las palabras*, how words stick to one another.

Alfonso, who had so far said much less than usual and had been watching the proceedings pensively, now explained that there are five *vocales* (vowels) in Spanish but that there are many more in English and they're not the same as the Spanish *vocales*, and that this was probably why Bridget and Danon failed to distinguish between the first and second *sílabas* (syllables) of *vives*. Constantino said no, it's the other way around, VIVIS had too few *vocales*, not too many. The problem, he argued, was that the *escrituras* of English and Spanish are *dos sistemas distintos*, two different systems. He asked Bridget and Danon how many vowels there are in English. Bridget and Danon said they didn't know. Rob said he didn't either. Constantino looked at me and I felt that I could read in his eyes that he finally believed me that gringos, even newspaper reporters, could not recite the *abecedario* of English.

Constantino was Alfonso's *tío político* (roughly, uncle-in-law, as distinct from *tío carnal*, uncle by blood). Alfonso had finished high school but he maintained a modest demeanor of *respeto* in Constantino's presence. The two of them now had a quiet conversation together and then Alfonso asked Bridget, in English, "How many words?" pointing to JUELLULIB.

Bridget wrote down WHERE DO YOU LIVE? under JUELLULIB:

JUELLULIB

WHERE DO YOU LIVE?

"Cuatro palabras," said Alfonso to Constantino. Everyone stared in silence at the surprising contrast between two *escrituras*, two ways of writing the same thing, one *bueno* but not *correcto*, the other *correcto* but not *bueno*.

The Dictionary is Useless

At this point, Juan pulled out a paperback Spanish–English dictionary. Half a dozen people started talking at once, telling Juan he was wasting his time. They were part of a group that, back in June, had looked pretty systematically at five different paperback dictionaries, brought in by various people, including Anglos. They had finally concluded that *el diccionario no sirve*, the dictionary doesn't work.

Every time Juan tried to speak, someone interrupted him. There are too many words in the dictionary. If you do find a Spanish word, you still don't know how to *say* it in English, you only know how to *write* it. Speaking English is one thing, writing it is something else. And if you know how to say a word in English, *líricamente*, you still can't find it in the dictionary. Alfonso pointed to JUELLULIB and said, "Así se oye." It sounds like this. He pointed to WHERE DO YOU LIVE? and said, "Y así se escribe en el diccionario." And in the dictionary it's written like this.

While all this was going on, Rob was showing Bridget and Danon Juan's dictionary. It had no pronunciation guide at all. Rob explained that few dictionaries had pronunciation guides and these were all written in a special code, not the same for each dictionary. He told Bridget and Danon how everyone had decided it was useless to try to learn a special alphabet, with weird symbols, that was used nowhere except in this or that dictionary, and which he, Rob, certainly couldn't read.

Constantino Calls for a Show of Hands

By now, Constantino was standing up and addressing the whole group. Like many of the men, he had a mode of speech (a register, a tone of voice) that he used to reason in public (*razonar*). His oratory was sometimes pretty fancy, but always directed and focused. The gist of his discourse was as follows:

> We need to find our own way out of this situation. *Nos hace muy trabajoso aprender las dos cosas de un solo viaje, la nueva pronunciación y la nueva escritura:* it's a lot of work for us to learn the two things at the same time, the new pronunciation and the new spelling system. There are 26 letters in the alphabet, but English has more than 26 sounds. So a letter is worth (*vale*) more than one sound. And that's why you don't know how to say it.
>
> Forget the dictionary. And forget *la escritura*. What we need to study is the *abecedario* of English. We need to figure it out for ourselves, our way. Otherwise they'll never understand us, even when we speak English. If you, Juan, want to stick words together you need to know the *abecedario*, not the *escritura*, of English. For us, this (pointing to JUELLULIB) *is better than that* (pointing to WHERE DO YOU LIVE?). Son dos sistemas distintos, *they are two different systems. We cannot study both at the same time.* O la una o la otra, *it's one or the other. We have to decide which of the two comes first for us.*

Constantino ended his speech by proposing that everyone work together to study *primero la pronunciación, luego la escritura*, first the pronunciation, then the [correct] spelling system. And he called for a vote. Those who want to start with the *escritura*, raise your hand. Only one hand went up—Alfonso's. Those who want to start with *la pronunciación*. Everyone's hand went up, including Alfonso's. People laughed. Alfonso explained that he had spent years studying English in high school in Mexico and already knew *mucha escritura*—a lot of spelling—but that none of his teachers had ever pronounced English the way gringos spoke in

Cobden, and he, Alfonso, wanted to study both *ortografías* at the same time. People replied fine, be that way, we'll stick to *la ortografía mexicana*, the Mexican way of writing.

EVRI BARI GUANTS TULEM

I stepped out of the room for a cigarette and a breath of fresh air. When I came back, someone was saying "La cosecha empieza con la primera uva." The harvest starts with the first grape.

They chose *todo el mundo quiere estudiar* (everybody wants to study) as their "first grape," their first attempt to write English *como de veras se oye*, the way it really sounds. The bet was that *todo el mundo quiere estudiar* could be written in English using *la ortografía mexicana*, one letter one sound. A couple of people already knew how to say *todo el mundo* in English. Everybody said it well, intelligibly, with only a slight accent. Rob, Danon, and Bridget understood, and practiced saying *todo el mundo*, but couldn't get the vowels right, and couldn't get the first *d* right. They had a thick gringo accent. Everyone smiled. They wanted me to pronounce *everybody* correctly. I alluded to the recurrent motif at these meetings: that my pronunciation of English tended to sound *británico*. "¿Quieren hablar como la reina de inglaterra?" I asked them—do you want to speak like the Queen of England? Laughter. They got the joke.

"Cada región tiene su propia musiquita, su propio ritmo," said Juan—every region has its own intonation, its own rhythm. "Su propio tiple," added Constantino—its own twang.

Rob, Bridget, and Danon agreed to serve as models for the local pronunciation. Everyone (including me) echoed them to get the *tiple* right: the Southern drawl, the rhythm, the intonation, and the allophones.

People worked on writing down the sounds that they themselves were saying. Everyone except Juan (who was there for the first time) had their little notebook and pen in their back pocket.

Froilán went to the easel and wrote EVRI. Underneath it, Cipriano wrote EBRI. Above these two words, Alfonso wrote EVERY:

EVERY

EVRI

EBRI

As discussion proceeded, Alfonso stood in front of the group like a teacher and noted the main points on the easel.[14] He circled the two vs and the B, because in Mexico these are two ways of writing the same sound. He put a line through

---

14. See Danon's photo, p. 33.

the second E in EVERY, because "así se escribe pero no se oye"—that's how it's written, but it's not heard (i.e., it's "silent"). And he circled the Y and the IS because, according to him, in English spelling, Y can be a vowel, the same as I.

The consensus was that EVRI was the best of the three. There was no discussion about *body*, because it turned out everyone had written it the same way: BARI.

The second half of the sentence, *quiere estudiar*, caused a lot of trouble and laughter. The translation was easy, *wants to study*,[15] but the pronunciation was a tongue-twister. *Se traba la lengua*. The cluster of consonants around the neutral vowel (wa*nts to s*tudy) stumped everyone. And no one could stop themselves from saying "estudi" (inserting an [e] before the initial *st* and saying [u] instead of [ʌ]). (The pronunciation of a cognate is often trickier than that of a non-cognate.)

Someone called out, "¡Todos quieren aprender, pero muchos no quieren estudiar!"—everyone wants to learn, but no one wants to study.

The target sentence was changed to *todo el mundo quiere aprender* (i.e., from everybody wants to study to everybody wants to learn).

But *wants to learn* caused further headaches. They didn't like the way I said *to learn*. They wanted to hear Rob say it, over and over, because he had the local *tiple*, the local dialect. They worked hard on mimicking his vowels, his "dark" /l/, his very liquid, semi-vowel /r/ and his final /n/.

People worked in small groups, or alone. Some wandered around looking at what others were writing. When everyone was done, it turned out that *wants* and *to learn* had each been transcribed in three different ways. In *wants*, the only question was what to do about the initial /w/:

GUANTS

HUANTS

UANTS

Each version had its advocates. They wanted me to referee, to say which was the best. Not the most correct, but the closest to the way it really sounds. I declined. But I wrote WANTS underneath the three versions on the easel. Rob Tate suggested a vote. Almost everyone voted for GUANTS.

The three transcriptions of *to learn* surprised Rob, Bridget, Danon, and me:

TULONT

TULEM

TULURN

I expected everyone to choose the third version, TULURN, but in fact they all said the second one was the shortest, and therefore the best, even though (as far as I could hear) no one was pronouncing the word with a final /m/.

---

15. Too easy. *Estudiar* means more than *study*.

So everyone had learned, everyone was very happy, and very tired. By now it was about 10:30 p.m. Everyone was writing down the complete sentence in their little notebooks:

> EVRI BARI GUANTS TULEM.
> TODO EL MUNDO QUIERE APRENDER.

Murder

There came a lull.

It was time to call it a day.

Danon looked at her watch.

No one moved.

Quiet conversations ended. Silence. An echo of the silence with which the evening had begun.

Suddenly, Juan spoke one word, loudly and clearly, in English: "murder."

"¿Y qué?" said Esequiel.

"The law," said Juan, again in English.

"La ley," said Froilán.

"Siempre nos busca la ley,"[16] sang Esequiel.

And Antonio, who had not spoken up all night, said, "La ley no nos ampara."

The law does not protect us. This sentence promptly became the second grape of the harvest. They followed the same process as for the first sentence. The variant transcriptions for each part of the sentence were as follows:

(The law	doesn't	protect	us)
DOLOR	DATSUN	PORTEX	AS
DOLOD	DASUNT	PORTEEX	
DOLOC	DATSNT	PROTKT	
DOLÓ	DANTS	PROTEKT	
TOLOON	DASN'T	PROTEEKT	
	DSNT	PROTECT	

And the final vote was for:

DOLÓ	DASN'T	PROTECT	AS

And we called it a day.

---

16. The second line of the song *Los mojados* (see above, p. 3), where I translate it as *the law is always after us.*

One grower says they're the best in the business

SEP 6 - 1980

By JIM ORSO
Globe-Democrat Staff Writer

COBDEN, Ill. — Three dozen Mexicans moved silently — but at a blistering pace — among the peach trees that dotted a gentle hillside near Cobden, about 100 miles southeast of St. Louis.

Grower Ed Flamm looked on in fascination.

"It started as a gradual thing, the Mexicans doing the work. And then it went completely that way, because these boys are just natural at this. It would take 60 people to do what 30 of these boys are doing," Flamm said.

"All you have to do is keep them in water."

Down among the rows of trees, deep-brown Mexican men stooped and reached to fill their half-bushel canvas bags with fruit, then rushed to a nearby wagon to dump the load.

As their bags emptied, the men reached quickly for a white chip issued by a worker and representing 30 cents.

Words were rarely exchanged. The language barrier here between Spanish-speaking workers and their English-speaking bosses seems to add to the quickened pace. No one can ask questions.

"I know 'mucho verde' (too green) and 'rojo' (red). That's all I need," Flamm said.

The need for bilingualism is only one of many sides of the phenomenon as Southern Illinois' multimillion dollar fruit industry grows increasingly dependent on Spanish-speaking migrant workers.

There is also the issue of the state's huge employment rates in this territory where thousands of migrant workers come each summer.

And cultural differences between migrants and residents in small towns near the orchards sometimes produce clashes.

Finally, there is the matter of illegal aliens among Illinois' 32,000 migrant workers. No one knows for sure how many of the the Mexican laborers are not registered to work here legally, but many assume the number is very high.

"The wages the guy accepts are prima facie evidence that he is in the U.S. illegally," said Jack Parks, an agent with the U.S. Immigration and Naturalization Service at St. Louis.

"No one else would work for the wages set by some of the growers," he said.

FOR MANY GROWERS, illegal aliens answer the need for a stable yet temporary work force to meet the needs of high demands of fruit picking in the heat of summer.

"Why should I ask the workers about their legal status?" Flamm said, adding that it makes no difference to him if his workers are registered.

For Cobden Police Chief Art Pender, illegal aliens are a minor nuisance, only because some of them are unlicensed drivers.

"The one area that they're really deficient in is driver licenses. They just plain don't have 'em," Pender said of the Mexicans sometimes cited for traffic violations as they travel to and from Cobden from nearby camps.

U.S. Rep. Paul Simon, D-Illinois, said illegal aliens in the farm labor force are both a "liability and an asset" to the economy of the region.

Simon said he would favor legislation creating "temporary work cards" for non-U.S. citizens who cross the border in search of work.

Simon said high unemployment rates in Southern Illinois are not eased by farm jobs partly because "our present employment policies do not encourage good work habits, and the migrant workers are willing to put in long hours and do some of the work that others might not do."

Those who work closely with the migrants say there are more "local" laborers than normal this year because of lack of work elsewhere. But there also are more migrant workers in Illinois — because of crop failures elsewhere, according to Illinois Job Service officer Virginia Ortega Avery.

Mrs. Avery's employment office in the Union-Jackson Farm Labor Camp near Cobden functions somewhat like a trade union hall. Area growers come to the office looking for prospective workers who have registered with Mrs. Avery in search of employment.

Most migrant workers live in camps on the growers' property that must be licensed by the Illinois Department of Public Health. But the Union-Jackson camp was opened about 10 years ago to provide housing for laborers whose employers were attempting to cut out the high cost of state-approved housing.

THE CAMP HOUSES ABOUT 180 persons and includes a day care center and health clinic funded by federal grants.

Mrs. Avery said about 80 percent of the near 1,000 workers in Union and Jackson Counties speak Spanish as their native language — as their only language, usually.

At the Su Casa grocery store in Cobden, an education coordinator for the Illinois Migrant Council has been bringing the Mexicans and local residents together in recent months for dialogue that he hopes will lead to much more than verbal understanding between the groups.'

"It's time to face the, fact that the Mexicans are here to stay," Tomas Kalmar said over coffee in Flamm's Cafe at Cobden.

Kalmar started the language exchange program in part to bring Mexicans and Cobden residents together on a common footing.

He hopes the program will bring a better understanding of the Mexican migrant workers. But Cobden isn't expected to transform into a bilingual haven over night.

Pender said he and other police officers have enrolled in fall courses in the Spanish language at the local college. They bypassed the weekly Su Casa dialogue, Pender said, because "it's for the Mexicans ."

At a recent dialogue session in Cobden, about a dozen Mexicans and about three "Anglos" came to Kalmar's class.

One of them, Eduardo, told a reporter that "trust" is the byword for Mexicans on the road year-round in an alien country.

"I am always working some place, then I go to the next place," he said, saying his next stop will be the orange groves of Florida.

"The travelers have a knack for establishing trust quickly, because you need to make good friends," he said through an interpreter. "The people who grow up together, in one place, do not make friends so fast."

Eduardo, 35, said "the money I earn here and there" is sent to his family in Mexico City, to benefit his parents, two brothers and three sisters he last saw in 1973 when he left Mexico for the life of the migrant worker.

It is simple economics, said Eduardo. "The pay is better here for the same work." But the life is hard, he said, and many Mexicans return home soon.

"Some Mexicans can do this, some can't stand it any more an go back, others stay and forget their families."

Eduardo said he returns each year to work for Flamm, who he said "is good for me."

And Flamm says the Mexicans are good for him. His peach pickers can make up to $60 a day, he said, when the conditions are right for picking 100 bushels in a day.

"You just can't get pickers around here that will work like this" he said, as the silent men marched relentlessly to the wagon that began to fill with tree-ripened peaches.

"You ought to see 'em when I really get 'em going."

Migrants in the Midwest

In southern Illinois life is better but still hard

by Bridget Walsh

Peach pickers at Flamm's Orchard drop fruit into wagon crates and receive a token worth 30 cents for each bag picked

THE 1980 HARVEST season has set records for the number of migrants following the crops. The Midwest migrant stream has brought more than 200,000 piece workers, pushed out of Texas by drought, to compete for fewer jobs in the north central states. By June the Texas-based Mexican Americans have picked the Florida orange groves and head up Route 75. Mexicans with and without papers have crossed under border points at Nueva Loredo, Reinosa, and Villa Acuna; many pay a "coyote" to smuggle them into this country and to a destination where there may or may not be work. Other Mexicans are easily recruited in the Rio Grande Valley by crewleaders; they pack into trucks for the haul to the northern canneries.

However diverse the migrant's route, his purpose is a common one. Part of a cycle of mutual need, the migrant travels to earn a wage by picking fruits and vegetables for the American grower so that the public's demand for cheap food can be maintained.

AS THE GATEWAY of the Midwest, Illinois brings the migrants out of the Ozarks and the Southeast. The Illinois Migrant Council's Emergency Center greets the traveler at Cairo, where Route 51 winds north. The flat concrete building lacks any amenity of an official welcome center. A two-by-four props up the sink where faucets run constantly, and a leaky roof requires that the director shift his desk when it rains. Nevertheless, the way station is open twenty-four hours a day, powered by eight bilingual workers who consider it their "privilege to serve" the working poor who come by truck and carload. Migrants can shower here, cook a meal, hook their vehicles to the auto diagnostic center, and sleep in the seven trailers that surround the center. Writes Jane Moreno, a Mexican-American from Kerrville, Texas: "To some people this place might not look like much, but when you've been traveling for two or three days in the cold or in the heat, hungry, dirty, completely exhausted, then this place looks like heaven. Thank you all very much."

Up the road from Cairo, in the hills that are sometimes called the Illinois Ozarks, lie the southern Illinois fields that siphon thousands of workers from this migrant stream. These peach and apple orchards unite Black, Anglo, and Hispanic migrants with small, independent growers in high-risk odds against the vagaries of the weather. Blacks pick in diminishing numbers, while Anglos account for 30 percent of the work force in southern Illinois because of their preference for fruit-picking. The Anglos, found at the bottom end of the American social scale, are generally less stable than Mexicans in their work efforts, hopelessness often erupts in hostility toward the more ambitious Mexicans who threaten their jobs. It is Mexicans, more than 80 percent of them illegal aliens, who constitute the majority of pickers. They are preferred by the farmers, who respect their work ethic. "The Mexicans do a better job," says one grower. "They care more."

Most of these illegal aliens are Mexicans with first loyalty to their Tarascan Indian culture. Transplanted from the town of Cheran in the state of Michoacan, the Tarascans form an extended family network. Besides Spanish, they speak a native tongue which the Mexican government seeks to preserve by requiring that it be taught in the state schools. The Tarascans were never conquered by their Aztec neighbors, or the invading Spaniards and Catholic missionaries. Their ancient tribal system, based on collective public works and religious ceremony laced with music and mime, has withstood absorption since the 13th century. Tarascan migrants, many of them single men who cannot find work in the rural interior of Mexico, arrive in southern Illinois under the protection and guidance of a tribal elder with years of experience as the connection with growers. "This is labor contracting at its informal best," says one observer, who adds that the choice of work locale by such gentle, dignified, and self-contained people is a compliment to the region.

"The migrant knows that the money he makes here is worth more in his own country," says a Department of Labor employee. It is common for workers, particularly married men whose families have stayed behind in Mexico, to send wages home for their survival until the next harvest season. Grower Leonard Flamm tells of migrants who come on Monday morning with addressed envelopes filled with cash from last week's check. He converts the money at a local bank and mails the envelopes to Mexico for the migrants. "I didn't keep up on the outflow of money this year like I intended, but it's a lot. And they deserve it. You don't make money sitting on the bottom of the ladder."

Leonard Flamm, a partner in the family operation of Flamm Orchards, is one of the "patrons" who finds himself wedged between environmental concerns, financial demands of crop yield, and treatment of migrants. He manages a field crew of about fifteen pickers, and drives between the tree rows with a tractor that pulls a flatbed containing three crates. Each migrant carries his own ladder from tree to tree. The workers climb on the wagon's running board to open the bottom of the picking bag. Peaches roll into the crates in a cloud of fuzz. "It's hot, dirty, itchy work," agrees Leonard Flamm. "You just got to like to do it." He shakes his head in dismay at American work attitudes, the labor force's refusal to do piece work in the fields. "Anyone drawing the aid check can earn more sitting at home. I have a stack of work applications two inches thick from people who say, 'I know you're not hiring, but can I use your name?' If they do come out, they want you to fire them so they can draw the check again."

Growers like Leonard Flamm openly recognize that illegal aliens are needed to take up the slack of the American labor-force; moreover, they say the country's immigration laws aren't working. "Immigration and Naturalization Service makes a show of order along the border," says one observer. "But the INS has had budget cutbacks, and they are absorbed with the Cubans. And if a raid happens, you can bet it will come at the end of the harvest." While it is illegal for an undocumented alien to be in the United States, state and federal law also says that it is only illegal for an employer to "knowingly" hire a migrant without papers. "I don't ask," says one grower. "I don't know if any of my workers are illegal or not. They give me their name and social security number."

Word spreads quickly in the Mexican-Tarascan communication network; the alien learns to make up a 3-2-4 patterned social security number for the grower. Besides social security, the undocumented worker pays taxes; no welfare benefits are available to the illegal alien. Because an alien fears being counted, he remains mute when an employer "forgets" the number of hours the migrant has worked. Such inequities occur at small orchards where only a handful of migrants live in a building behind a small grower's house. Before the Illinois Department of Health will inspect the premises, ten workers or four families must reside in one building. If a grower strings the migrants along in slack periods, that worker can earn just enough to eat until the full harvest. While many migrants understand when they are unfairly taken advantage of, they are reluctant to come forward. Yet some migrants have begun to speak up. Provided with temporary visa cards by the Immigration and Naturalization Service, nineteen workers, some of them illegal, will remain after the season to testify in a civil suit filed on their behalf at the federal court at Benton by the Illinois Migrant Legal Assistance Project. The suit charges a local grower with payment of less than $2 per hour for harvesting of a crop during the slow time, between peach and apple picking. Such violation of the minimum wage law, which states that a worker's piece work must equal the hourly minimum wage, has presented a no-win situation for workers in the past. Migrant is pitted against migrant in a degrading competition for sparse work.

IN AN ATTEMPT to control inequities and meet government regulations, southern Illinois growers banded together in 1971. With the help of the Farmers' Home Administration, they built the Union-Jackson Farm Labor Camp. These 180 workers, who must have a job with one of the growers before moving into the camp, live with their families in thirty-six concrete-block apartments along Route 51 near Cobden. Each migrant pays a $20 deposit and a dollar per working day to stay at the camp; his employer contributes $2.50 per migrant for each working day as a share of lodging expense.

Rows of barracks stack the hillside at the farm labor camp. Workers lounge in the shade of the walls, trying to escape the heat. A car, tailpipe dragging, disgorges a group of migrants who have come from the fields. Over the past five years, the camp has evolved from a violent ghetto, where local police dreaded to come, to a migrant service center with increasing community ties. Social workers involved with migrants in other states call it "The Hilton" now; Union County Sheriff Larry Tripp cites the day care center, alcohol prevention program, and medical clinic as major factors in reducing tensions within the camp. "People are providing guidelines so the migrant doesn't feel so lost and isolated."

At Su Casa Day Care Center, situated at the bottom of the camp's hillside, there is laughter, rainbow colors, and the shuttling of toys. Staff members bathe, rock, and feed forty-three children, the maximum allowable according to square footage. Director Kay Weatherford describes how travel is strenuous and intense for the children, whose parents arrive in an unknown locale to look for work. "Their needs are great. Travel saps them and makes them vulnerable to disease. We do what we can when we can do it." Adaptability is the key to survival at the day care center. When children couldn't eat American food, Kay Weatherford instituted a parent involvement program, where camp mothers prepared a favorite Mexican meal each noon. After it became apparent that the staff and children had difficulty in mixing, Mexican women following a husband or father in the migrant stream were hired. "The

Children at the Union-Jackson Farm Labour Camp.

children go to their own kind," says a staff member. "They are a more affectionate culture. It's the touch, the inflection, the Spanish word, that we didn't know."

The interface of two cultures reveals areas that chafe and strain. Some staff workers have found the children's need to touch offensive, the sanitation problems and culture shock overwhelming. "It's a burnout job," agrees intern Sue Carmel, as she scrubs Caesar in a tub. "This is the underbelly of the United States that people don't see. They don't want to see." She disinfects the diaper table and sets Caesar on it, explaining that each child gets bathed in the morning. "The water cools them. It calms them and helps them sleep." Caesar was one of the children first carried into the center screaming and kicking, Sue explains. New arrivals gawk, become withdrawn, and don't play with toys for the first week. "But the change in a child is my reward," says Sue. "When Caesar finally laughed, it was the nicest sound. Now he leaps into my arms, unaware that his mother is gone." Sue is amazed that her peers who have been raised with advantages cannot cope with the reality of migrant life. She has a new-found respect for the durability of the Mexicans, who survive in a foreign culture where "everything" is different.

When a child arrives at the day care center with bruises, investigation often leads to a drinking father. Because a 1976 study indicated that crimes, car accidents, and physical abuse stemmed from alcohol usage by migrants, the Illinois Department of Mental Health set up a recreation and alcohol prevention program at the labor camp. Raphael de Torres, director of the Fellowship

House program, sees drinking as a family illness. The physical exertion, low wages, and transient lifestyle create frustration in the migrant. The father goes on a "cerveza" binge with the family's money; the children suffer, and the wife becomes upset. "Mexicans look to each other for identity and support, so I recruit the whole family," says Raphael of his alcohol education and counseling program.

While most Mexican women deny having been beaten, physical evidence can be overwhelming. Angela Lecaros is a recently battered wife, and her options are limited. She bailed her husband out of the Cobden, Illinois jail with the family savings. "How can a woman with three kids, who doesn't drive and speaks little English, get back to Mexico by herself?" asks a social worker. Early in the season, a *Self-Help Guide for Battered Women* was translated into Spanish, but the staff discovered that Mexican women often don't read their language well. Now, specially trained staff members demonstrate, with the "here and now" approach that is more graphically effective with uneducated migrant women, how to ward off an attacker. This "Passive Self-Defense" class helps the woman protect herself without seeming aggressive to an inebriated husband.

Explanation of U.S. laws on drinking is another aspect of the farm labor camp's alcohol prevention program. Because young migrants are bored and isolated during off-work hours, an extensive sports program has been established to distract would-be drinkers. Nightly and on weekends, boxing, soccer, baseball, and volleyball games lure migrants to playing fields below the labor camp.

BEHIND FELLOWSHIP HOUSE and Su Casa Day Care Center stands a long white trailer that houses the Migrant Clinic. Operated out of an old bus in earlier days, the federally-funded clinic treats an average thirty workers per day. "There are more workers and fewer jobs," says administrative director Carolyn Garcia. "Stress is higher, so we have more nutritional problems." The staff provides diagnosis, treatment of disease, immunizations, pre- and post-natal care. Birth control information is available also. "We cannot push," says a clinical assistant. "There is often resistance for religious reasons. We merely present options." The Migrant Clinic stays open at night to serve workers who have been in the fields all day. The maladies are what one might expect for farm laborers: a toe slashed by a hoe, skin infections like "granitos" from peach fuzz, insect bites, lower back pain, ear infections from swimming in local ponds, and heat exhaustion. "This is a clinic for the working poor. There is no charity here," says director Garcia. "The migrants pay for services on a sliding scale. They want to pay. This year we have heard 'No tengo dinero' [I have no money] for the first time. But they are proud. They come back and pay what they can."

Parents wait with their one-year-old son for the day care center to open. Both parents must work in the fields for the child to qualify for day care.

The migrants accept Dr. Jennifer FauntLeRoy as the equivalent of their modern healing woman, a "curandera." Dr. FauntLeRoy finds the Hispanic workers well-mannered, shy, and cleaner than the other migrants. "They know their bodies, even though a doctor would differ with their choice of cure." She looks forward to the time when a "model" migrant clinic like this one will be the rule rather than the exception. It takes a special type of migrant to tire of following the crops and join the Illinois Migrant Council's "Settle Out" program, which is intended to prepare the Mexican workers to join mainstream American life. In a twenty-week period the migrants who participate can receive vocational training and earn a "general education" diploma. The Tarascan Indians are unlikely "Settle Out" candidates because they are anxious to cross back over the border after the seasonal picking. Most often a Chicano (Mexican-American) family seeks more stability than harvesting allows; they will have lived in Texas for years and become acculturated to American ways. But even then, after years of working in factories or the trades, former migrants will return to the harvest. "It's in their blood," one Migrant Council staff member says. "They like working out of doors, their dark skins adjust to the heat, and they miss the communication with fellow Hispanics." The staff member questions the value of encouraging migrants to settle out. "You build up their hopes and promise them the American Dream. Then you wonder if you can deliver."

More relevant to the Mexicans' needs has been the Illinois Migrant Council's English classes, taught in the basement of a grocery store on the main thoroughfare of Cobden. Word has spread through the migrants'

After work, migrants meet in the basement of the Cobden grocery store to study English.

communication network that growers prefer workers who return each year, and who can act as translators for new arrivals in the fields. So the migrants gather after work to participate in a "language dialogue." They file slowly downstairs, all men, with slicked-back hair and tired eyes. Guided by Tomás Kalmar of the IMC, the migrants teach each other, bringing English words heard in the fields to be pronounced and defined in Spanish. The *Wetback Dictionary*, or *Diccionario Mojado* as the migrants named their collection, grows weekly and has been made portable by photocopying. A quick learning device which bypasses the eccentricities of English spelling, the *Wetback Dictionary* (example: Jeit [hate]—odio) "beats anything coming out of academia," according to Tomás.

The mayor of Cobden has offered the use of city hall for the English classes; the county sheriff and his deputies have begun Spanish classes at a local college. These official responses indicate a recognition that the migrants are here to stay. But friendships between migrants and locals are harder to come by. Most townspeople are reluctant to state their feelings about the migrants' presence. Economics bind them together now; the town, the growers, and the migrants benefit from the harvest. Beyond that, in the movement toward bilingualism, all is flux.

Bridget Walsh *is a freelance writer living in Carbondale.*[17]

17. This article appeared in the *Illinois Times*, November 7, 1980—see p. 11, above.

2

THE COBDEN GLOSSARIES

> What the lever did for physics, the chess move promises
> to do for sociology.
>
> —Geertz

The discourse on letters and sounds that began in the basement of the grocery store on August 6 continued in and around Cobden until the migrants left the area in late October. On Thursday, August 21, a group of 15 Anglos and migrant workers, meeting in Cobden's Village Hall, collectively produced what they playfully called a *diccionario mojado*—a "wetback glossary" (see pp. 48ff below). This chapter narrates events leading from those narrated in the preceding chapter up to and beyond the crucial meeting in the Village Hall, with particular attention to the formal structure of the handwritten texts produced by the developing discourse on letters and sounds.

After the August 6 meeting, the basement of the grocery store became, once again, a place where Mexicans could gather clandestinely—with or without friendly Anglos. The men who decided, on August 6, to figure out how to write English the way it sounds never again met as a unit. On different evenings, different groups of people conversed about different topics. One night, for example, the conversation was about fines collected by the local police for odd traffic violations. Paying the police $70 in cash every time you were caught driving through Cobden was routine, but Santiago being "fined" $70 when he pulled up on the side of Highway 51 because he'd run out of gas was noteworthy. So was Juan's story of a policeman walking into his trailer and "fining" him for driving without a license right there at his kitchen table. "Fined" is in quotes because the $70 cash handed over on the spot was technically a bond, forfeited when you didn't show up in court. One day, I took it on myself to go to the county seat in Jonesboro and look up the records. The records showed that each summer for the past two years, the police had collected $3,000 this way. With some of this cash, they had bought a computer for their office.

One night, Santiago borrowed a little accordion that I'd bought at a local pawnshop for $20. He stayed up all night figuring out one tune after another, by himself. The next night, his friends said they hadn't slept a wink. (I didn't have the heart to reclaim the accordion.) I watched Santiago's fingers hunt for the right keys on the keyboard by trial and error, as he "spelled out" the notes of a tune he knew *líricamente*.

And from time to time, someone, or a group of people, would have occasion to write down a bit of English the way it sounds, bringing to bear on the topics of these other discourses their discourse on *alfabetos* and *abecedarios*.

Meanwhile, this way of coding English speech-sounds moved out of the basement into other environments. The basement of the store was no longer the only, or even the typical, "scene of writing." While working in the field, drinking in the bar, chatting with friends at home, individuals would play with letters and sounds to transcribe bits of spoken English, with or without Spanish glosses. Putting pen to paper transformed ordinary social situations into scenes of writing.

The practice of carrying a notebook and a pen in one's back pocket spread from person to person along and across social networks. The little blank spiral notebooks had colored flowers on the cover and cost 29 cents. Jacinto bought himself one after bringing his first word home from the field. He had written it on the palm of his hand: LIMISI (*let me see*). He copied it into his notebook, along with a gloss in Spanish, DEJAMEVER. (For Jacinto's first glossary, see p. 51, below.)

I

Constructing a Hybrid Alphabet

To the eyes of many monolingual North Americans, these specimens of spoken English coded in "Mexican orthography" look, at first sight, odd and unfamiliar.[1] The knowledge of letters and sounds needed to read—and write—texts such as these appears novel, even to literacy experts. Therefore, before presenting more texts, in various stages of development, from various contexts, I consider some of the obvious and not so obvious formal features of the texts that we have already seen in Chapter 1.

Writing something down "the way it sounds," whether in your own language or someone else's, is not a simple mechanical operation, especially if the language in question has not hitherto been written down this way.

---

1. This is the theme of Chapter 3, below.

"Strictly speaking, phonetic transcription records not an utterance but an *analysis of an utterance*"[2] and therefore variant transcriptions of a given utterance (e.g., DOLOR, DOLOD, DOLOC, DOLÓ, TOLOON, *the law*) record variant *analyses* of that utterance. Each such analysis can be fruitfully interpreted as a strategy chosen by a player in a game.[3] Furthermore, at the meeting on August 6, the various players were not playing different games: they were all playing one game together, a game with sufficient room for play to allow for many possible strategies. Out of 180 possible ways of transcribing *The law doesn't protect us*—five for *the law* times six for *doesn't* times six for *protect*—they chose one as the best. By what criteria?

Anyone attempting to transcribe an utterance in a hitherto unwritten language "the way it sounds" has to begin by solving many little puzzles, many *rompecabezas* and *trabalenguas*.[4] Is this one sound or two? Are these two sounds the same or different? If I let this letter stand for this sound here, can I let it stand for a different sound there? Must the value of a letter be fixed, or can it vary on a "sliding scale?"[5] What if my answers to these questions differ from yours? Can we read each other's transcriptions? If I let this letter stand for this sound, can you let it stand for a different sound? How do these puzzles interconnect? Are we connecting moves in a single game? Or are we playing unconnected, possibly incompatible, games?

It's in the minute details that the problem of making up what I call a *hybrid alphabet* arises. This is my shorthand term for Constantino's project of using one *alfabeto* to code two different *abecedarios*, two different sound systems. It's a problem because, strictly speaking, the sound patterns of two different languages are structurally incommensurate. What is impossible in pure theory becomes possible in practice only by "fudging" the application of the code's basic ground rule: one letter, one sound.[6]

Consider, for example, the following details in the decisions that produced the texts written in the basement on August 6:

1.   The use of puns such as DOLOR and DATSUN.
2.   The choice between GUANTS, HUANTS, and UANTS for the initial sound of *wants*.
3.   The choice between O, E, and U for the vowel in *learn*: TULONT, TULEM, TULURN.
4.   The choice between NT, M, and RN for the final consonant in *learn*: TULONT, TULEM, and TULURN.

---

2. Abercrombie (1967: 127), emphasis added. On Abercrombie's important distinction between impressionistic and systematic transcriptions, see Chapter 4 below, especially pp. 94–95.
3. See Chapter 4 below for a detailed treatment of this interpretation.
4. On *rompecabezas* and *trabalenguas*, see pp. 17–18 above.
5. The phrase "sliding scale" comes from Pike's first published article, Pike (1938); see epigraph to Chapter 4, p. 83 below.
6. This "fundamental theorem" of structural linguistics was proved by Sapir in his classic 1925 paper. I discuss it in more detail in Chapter 4, pp. 85–90.

5.   The choice between ᴛ and ᴅ for the initial consonant of *the*: ᴅᴏʟᴏʀ, ᴅᴏʟᴏᴅ,
     ᴅᴏʟᴏᴄ, ᴅᴏʟó, ᴛᴏʟᴏᴏɴ.
6.   The choice between ᴏʀ, ᴏᴅ, ᴏᴄ, ó, and ᴏᴏɴ for the final vowel of *the law*:
     ᴅᴏʟᴏʀ, ᴅᴏʟᴏᴅ, ᴅᴏʟᴏᴄ, ᴅᴏʟó, and ᴛᴏʟᴏᴏɴ.
7.   The use of ᴅ for the initial sounds of both *the* and *doesn't*: ᴅᴏʟó ᴅᴀsɴ'ᴛ.

Hybrid Units: The Strategic Use of Puns Such as ᴅᴏʟᴏʀ and ᴅᴀᴛsᴜɴ

ᴅᴏʟᴏʀ and ᴅᴀᴛsᴜɴ were puns intended to provoke laughter. ᴅᴏʟᴏʀ means "the law" in English but it means "grief" in Spanish. It was Juan himself who wrote this, just after he had said (in English) "murder" and "the law" (above, p. 23). The laughter provoked by letting this one string of letters mean two such different things released some of the tension around the tacit allusion to Leonardo's death and burial.

   In the case of ᴅᴀᴛsᴜɴ, it was the absurd incongruity that made them laugh. This string of six letters was familiar from billboards and TV ads on both sides of the border. It's not English. It's Japanese. ᴅᴀᴛsᴜɴ was a playful move in the game. It has the right letters in almost the right order (compare ᴅᴀsᴜɴᴛ).

   The strategy that produced these puns can be laid out as a three-step algorithm. First, pick a speech unit in English that you want to write the way it sounds. (The harvest is gathered one grape at a time.) Then pick a speech unit in Spanish (or, in the case of ᴅᴀᴛsᴜɴ, Japanese–Spanish) that is "most like" the target speech unit. Write the Spanish speech unit the way it sounds, and let the string of letters have the value of the target speech unit in English *despite the difference in meaning*.

   Schematically: Let *A* be a language whose *abecedario* is unknown. Let *B* be a language whose *abecedario* is known (i.e., already coded on the principle of one letter one sound).

   To create a hybrid unit that is "in" both *A* and *B*:

1.   Find a unit [x] in *A*.
2.   Given [x] in *A*, find a unit [y] in *B* that "sounds like" [x]. (If [y] and [z] in
     B both "sound like" [x] in *A*, decide which of the two is closer to [x].)
3.   Given a string of letters ʏ which take the value [y] in *B*, let ʏ take the value
     [x] in *A*. Look at ʏ and say [x].

   Juan looked at ᴅᴏʟᴏʀ and said "the law." (Who knows whether he thought "grief?")

   This three-step schema will prove helpful as my narrative and my argument proceed.[7]

---

7. See pp. 41, 85ff below.

The Choice Between GUANTS, HUANTS, and UANTS for the Initial Sound of wants

In conventional Spanish spelling, no word begins with *ua* and only a handful of foreign loanwords begin with *wa*. *Hua* is always, and *gua* often, pronounced [wa]—e.g., *huapango*, *guarache* (often spelled *huarache*). Thus, although the Roman alphabet offers two choices for a single letter, W or U, the majority voted to let a pair of letters GU take the value of an English speech-sound similar to one of the values that GU already has in Spanish.

The Value of Schwa: The Choice Between O, E, and U for the Vowel in learn: TULONT, TULEM, TULURN

O, E, and U do not represent three different sounds; they do not represent different pronunciations of *to learn*, all equally wrong. They represent three different *strategies* for recording one and the same sound: the neutral vowel "schwa," IPA [ə]. This sound is alien to Spanish. There is no vowel in the *abecedario* of Spanish that is close to [ə].[8] The Spanish values of O, E, and U are more or less equally close to—and equally far from—[ə]. When the authors of these three transcriptions (and their readers) pronounced what they had written, they said [ə], not [e], [o], or [u]. They gave O, E, and U the value of the vowel sound heard in *learn*. In short, the choice between O, E, and U does not represent a choice between three Spanish accents, caused by "interference" of Spanish speech habits, although it can easily be misinterpreted that way if taken out of context. The choice is between three strategies for coping with one of the consequences of sticking to the Roman alphabet used in *la ortografía mexicana*: how to assign values to A, E, I, O, U to transcribe much more than five vowels in the *abecedario* of English.

Occam's Razor: The Choice Between NT, M, and RN for the Final Consonant in learn: TULONT, TULEM, and TULURN

Likewise, they voted for TULEM not because they mispronounced the final consonant of *learn* as a bilabial, but because TULEM was *shorter* than the alternatives. The final M in TULEM, like the T in TULONT, was an ad hoc *mnemonic device* (marking the final consonant as not an ordinary dental [n], but as alveolar or palatal). In choosing the shortest transcription as the best, they seem to have regarded the final consonant of *learn* as one sound, not two.

---

8. Tarascan does have such a vowel, and since 1939 it has been represented in Cherán by the ʌ (called a "wedge" or "turned v") taught to the Tarascans in the Tarascan Project by Morris Swadesh—see below, pp. 108–113.

Legal Moves: The Choice Between т and ᴅ for the Initial Consonant of the: ᴅOLOR, ᴅOLOD, ᴅOLOC, ᴅOLÓ, тOLOON

"In order to understand what a knight 'means' in chess one needs to know its role in the game . . . To ask how the piece moves on the board *is* to ask for an elucidation of the concept 'chess knight'."[9] By the same token, to understand what ᴅ "means" in one of these texts, one needs to know its role in the game, how ᴅ "moves on the board."

In ᴅOLÓ, ᴅ "means" the first sound in *the law*. It is to be looked upon as the symbol standing for a voiced dental fricative. Professional linguists often assign this value to a non-roman letter, the rune [ð].

Following up the schematic algorithm sketched out above (see "Hybrid Units"), we could say that in this game, a "legal" move has the form of the mathematician's "Let x take the value y" where x is one of a known set of 26 tokens (the letters of the roman alphabet) and y is one of an unknown set of sounds (containing *more* than 26 members). Postulating a relationship between a letter and a sound constitutes a valid move in the game.

Using (or inventing) a non-roman symbol (such as ð) is "cheating." It's like putting a checkers piece on the board and calling it a chess piece.

Letting the value of ᴅ be the initial sound of *the law* was not regarded as "cheating" because in conventional Spanish spelling, *d* can already take that value. But in Spanish, that sound does not occur in initial position. In Spanish, you don't begin an utterance that way. The mathematical form of this move could therefore be articulated more precisely as: let this piece move here as it moves elsewhere; let ᴅ take, even in initial position, the value that it already takes in other positions.

Are Diacritics "Legal?" The Choice Between oʀ, oᴅ, oc, ó, and ooɴ for the Final Vowel of the law: ᴅOLOR, ᴅOLOD, ᴅOLOC, ᴅOLÓ, and тOLOON

In Spanish, words are normally stressed on the second-last syllable unless they end with a consonant other than [n] or [s]. Those who wrote ᴅOLOR, ᴅOLOD, ᴅOLOC added the letters ʀ, ᴅ, c after ᴅOLÓ merely to shift the accent onto the last syllable: *the láw*. (Compare *dolor*, *Usted*, and the many Nahuatl words ending in *c*, *Tepic*, *Anahuac*, *Tehuantepec*, etc.) When they saw the accent on ᴅOLÓ, they voted for that as a better "move" than their own solutions. In other words, ᴅOLOR, ᴅOLOD, ᴅOLOC were three ad hoc devices for representing stress. ʀ, ᴅ, c do not, in this instance, have the value of a speech-sound: they are (as in *Usted*) "silent consonants," not to be pronounced. They are not to be looked upon as

---

9. Harris (1988: 28).

representing mishearing, or mispronunciation. They are not evidence of Spanish accents due to "interference." They represent a strategy specifically designed to cope with and eliminate the "interference" of Spanish stress patterns.

One Letter, Two Sounds: The Use of ᴅ for the Initial Sounds of Both the and doesn't: ᴅᴏʟó ᴅᴀsɴ'ᴛ

We have seen ("Legal Moves," above) that in ᴅᴏʟó, ᴅ represents a fricative (*the law*). But in the next word, ᴅᴀsɴ'ᴛ, it doesn't. It represents a stop (*doesn't*). They did not (mis)pronounce these two ᴅs according to ordinary Spanish phonology. They did *not* say "De law thoesn't protect us." They let this one letter stand for two different sounds. In Spanish, these two sounds are perceived as having a "family resemblance"—in technical terms, as being allophones of one phoneme. But speakers of English do not perceive the family resemblance. To English ears, the two sounds belong to two different families—two different phonemes. That's because when it comes to family resemblances, English and Spanish have, as it were, different kinship structures.[10] Letting ᴅ take the value of both these sounds (although in ᴅᴏʟó ᴅᴀsɴ'ᴛ they are distributed back to front) thus represents a trade-off between linguistic values that allows one *alfabeto* to code two *abecedarios*. This trade-off creates what, for want of a better term,[11] I call a *hybrid phoneme*. It's something like bending the legal moves of a chess piece to let it "take" a square it could otherwise never reach—or maybe like letting a knight sometimes move like a bishop.

Strictly speaking, there can be no such thing as a hybrid phoneme because a phoneme, by definition, cannot contain alien sounds, foreign to the language in question. Alien principles of kinship peculiar to language *B* cannot be legitimately applied to sounds in language *A*. In Chapter 4, I discuss what it means to speak "strictly" about letters and sounds, and by what institutional authority hybrid families of sounds are denied the status of true phonemes. At this stage in my narrative, it's enough to say that a hybrid alphabet is structured, broadly speaking,

---

10. This metaphor is intended as a shorthand allusion to "Sapir's Theorem"—see Chapter 4 below, pp. 85–90.

11. As far as I know, Einar Haugen is the only professional linguist who proposed a serious study of what I call hybrid phonemes. He argued that calling some languages (and phonemes) "hybrid" was objectionable, because it "implies that there are other languages which are 'pure,' but these are scarcely any more observable than a 'pure race' in ethnology" (Haugen 1972b: 162). For this very reason, I prefer the term *hybrid* to Haugen's proposed term *diaphone*. "Diaphones could . . . be defined as *bilingual allophones* and would be (1) determined *analytically* by phonetic-distributional similarity and (2) checked *pragmatically* by the cases of interference resulting from the identifications. In these terms learning the sound system of another language could be described as a *phonemicizing of diaphones*" (Haugen 1956: 46, original emphasis). For more on Haugen, see p. 87 n. 12. On Haugen's ecological attitude to hybrid structures, see p. 120 below.

on the principle of one letter, one hybrid phoneme, where by *phoneme* I mean a "family of sounds."

The pun-like structure of DOLOR and DATSUN is relatively obvious; that of D is less so. DOLOR means both "the law" and "grief"; D "means" both a fricative and a stop. The strategy that produces hybrid phonemes can be laid out schematically in an algorithm analogous to the one laid out for larger units in "Hybrid Units" above (p. 37).

To create a hybrid phoneme: Given two sounds $[x_1]$ and $[x_2]$ in A, find two sounds $[y_1]$ and $[y_2]$ in B such that $[y_1]$ and $[y_2]$ are "close(st) to" $[x_1]$ and $[x_2]$, respectively. Given a letter Y that takes the values $[y_1]$ and $[y_2]$ in B, let Y take the values $[x_1]$ and $[x_2]$ in A. Look at Y and say either $[x_1]$ or $[x_2]$ as required by the context in A.

II

A Kind of Algebraic Notation

Considering texts such as these as records of strategic moves made in a game throws light on why the Mexicans in Cobden talked the way they did about what they were doing when they wrote English down the way it sounds: why they perceived themselves as making up and solving *rompecabezas* by hammering out and cracking a code. The puzzles interconnect. The texts, the moves, the strategies cohere into a collective discursive event.

The discourse that accompanied the game was conducted in a mixture of Spanish and English. Distinguishing between the discourse and the game helps resolve the paradox summed up in the riddle: In which language is JUELLULIB written? Is JUELLULIB written in no language? In two languages at once? In the "structural no man's land"[12] between languages? In an imagined universal language that contains all possible languages? These questions resemble the question "in which language does one play chess?"[13] It's like asking "in which language is $E = mc^2$ written?"

JUELLULIB records moves made in a game played in whatever "language" it is that one does mathematics, or plays chess. On August 6, the group in the basement used the letters of the common alphabet as a "kind of algebraic notation"[14] to work out 180 possible ways of analyzing *the law doesn't protect us*: all 180 were composed of "legal" moves in the game, all were *bueno*. But some were better than others. Only strategic reasoning can distinguish between a good move and a merely legal move, and only theorizing can tell why one strategy is better than

---

12. Weinreich (1953)—see below, Epilogue p. 120.
13. Harris (1988: 70).
14. This turn of phrase was coined by Henry Sweet (1888: x). See also Henderson (1971), Sweet (1884, 1994), Wrenn (1946, 1967: 159), and Wyld (1913).

another. DOLÓ DASN'T PROTECT AS was voted the best of the 180 possibilities by criteria which were variations on the meta-criterion of mathematical elegance. This text codifies a game played on the night of August 6, sustained and validated by a discourse that carried the game forward and outward, beyond that night, out of that dark basement.

III

New Contexts, New Texts, Same Moves

It's hard to imagine a social situation in which a Mexican would actually *say* to a local "the law doesn't protect us." Or even "everybody wants to learn." Compared to "where d'you live?" these are very "Freirean" sentences. They name the world at a deeper sociopolitical level.[15] But they are also very "academic" sentences. *Saying* them does not transform the world: saying "where d'you live?" to Martha did transform Panchito's world (p. 6, above). Panchito's humble text proved to be a "prophetic word" when he played his game all the way through to the end. An "organic" Key Word, in Sylvia Ashton-Warner's sense.[16]

Panchito wrote JUELLULIB for his own eyes only. "Let the value of this letter be that sound" was a move in his game. But he was playing solo. It looks the way it does because Panchito intended to say it to someone then and there. DOLÓ DASN'T PROTECT AS was written "by the people, for the people." The moves it records were made collectively in a game played by a team of players. It looks the way it does because it is intended to be *seen* by many people, not just one.

The texts displayed below record moves made in a series of related games played after the meeting in the basement on August 6 but before the meeting that produced the first glossary—the *diccionario mojado*—in the Village Hall on August 21. They can be interpreted as phases in the development of the collective strategy that produced that *diccionario*.

All text in UNIVERS is data (i.e., my transcription of handwritten letter-strings). For the benefit of monolingual readers, I have added glosses in conventional English spelling. These are in *italics*. Some texts record moves made by individuals playing solo (such as Panchito), some by teams who showed each other their moves and compared their strategies. Some texts are glossed in Spanish, some are "theoretical" studies of patterns. Readers uninterested in the details can skim or skip the commentary that follows the texts. Readers interested in the details will find much that I have not commented on.

---

15. On naming the world by "speaking a true word," see below, Chapter 3, p. 73, n. 49.
16. Ashton-Warner (1986).

1	a	*squash*		ESCUACHI	
	b	*this man needs another tree*		DISMEN NIS ANADA TRI	
2	a	*I.O.U.*		HAY OÚ YU	
	b			AI OU YUU	
	c			ALLG O LLU	
3	a	*I want to call*		AY GUANACON	
	b			AY WAN ACO	
	c			AY GUANA COÓ	
	d	*I want to call Mexico*		AI HUANA COF MEXICO	
4	a	*what number*		HUAT NOMBER	
	b			WANT NAMBER	
	c			WAT NOME	
	d			WUAN NANBER	
5	a	*half 'n' half*		JEFNJEF A MEDIAS	
	b			JAFIN JEF A MEDIAS	
6	a	*every day we go to work*		EBRI DAY WAY TW GWAC	
	b			EBRI DEY WY GO TU WERK	
	c			EBRI DEI WI GOU TO WORK	
	d			EVRI DEY WI GO TU WERK	
7	a	*every*	EVRI	CADA	
	b	*body/person*	BARI	PERSONA	
	c	*wants*	GUANTS	QUIERE	
	d	*to learn*		APRENDER	
	e	*nobody*	NOU BARI	NADIE	
	f	*somebody*	SAM BARI	ALGUIEN	
	g	*everybody*	EVRI BARI	TODO EL MUNDO	
	h	*nowhere*	NOU JUER		
	i	*somewhere*	SAM JUER		
	j	*everywhere*	EVRI JUER	DONDE QUIERA	
	k	*where*	JUER	DONDE	
	l	*no one*	NOU WAN	NINGUNO	
	m	*someone*	SAM WAN	ALGUNO	
	n	*everyone*	EVRI WAN		
	o	*one*	WAN	UNO	

	p	*some*	SAM	ALGO
	q	*some day*	SAMDEI	UN DIA
	r	*Sunday*	SAN DEI	DOMINGO
8	a	YOU KNOW I LOVE YOU GIRL	YUNO A LABIO GRO	TU SABES YO TE QUIERO NIÑA
	b	*and I want*	ENAI WAN	
	c	*want*	GUAN	
	d		HUAN	
	e		UAN	
	f	*and I want you to do right*	ENAI WAN YU TU DU RAIT	
9	a	*write*	RUAIT	ESCRIVIR
	b	*to rest*	TU RUEST	DESCANSAR
	c	*read*	RUIT	LEER
	d	*which*	JUICH	CUALES
	e	*anybody*	ENI VARI	ALGIEN
	f	*to give*	TU GIV	PERDONAR
	g	*any more*	ENI MOR	YA NO
	h	*what for*	WAT FOR	PAQUE ES ESO
10	a	WE CAN-TGO NOW	WI KEN-T GOU NAU	AHORA NO PODEMOS IR
	b	WHAT FOR		PARA QUE
	c	WILL YOU GO WITH ME	WI YOU GOU WED MI	QUIERE VENIR CONMIGO
	d	*when do you want to go*	WEN DU YOU WANT TU GOU	AONDE QUIERE IR
	e	*(I) believe not*	BOLIV NAT	CREO QUE NO
	f	*(I) believe so*	BOLIV SO	CREO QUE SI
	g	*I come to town*	AI CAM TU TAUN	YO VENGO AL PUEBLO

Notes

1a, 1b, and 2a were written by Tarascans.

1a: A First Word written in someone's kitchen by Francisco and Francisca, a Tarascan couple in their late thirties. Unglossed.

Tarascan words commonly end in a "silent" I or A. It is written but not (in the Cherán dialect) usually pronounced. I once saw Salvador, a Tarascan in his late forties with only one year of schooling, write *think* as TICI. He listened closely to how Anglos were saying it, as an isolated, decontextualized word, for his benefit. He said "k, k, k," thought for a couple of minutes, said "aha!" and then changed his transcription to TICA. It's my understanding that the choice between these two "silent" vowels represents two different "colors" of the final [k] (i.e., front [kⁱ] *versus* back [kᵃ]).[17] Since the final vowel in ESCUACHI is not due to "interference," perhaps the initial E is not either.

1b: A full unglossed sentence transcribed by Salvador (see 1a) in the field. Salvador was the foreman at one of the big growers.

2a, 2b, 2c: These three ways of writing the same phrase were written on three different occasions. The scribes did not see each other's solutions and did not compare and contrast strategies.

3–4: The scribes of these alternative transcriptions did look at each other's solutions, but did not compare them or vote for the best. They were written in the home of friendly Carbondale residents who made their phone available for long-distance calls. 4b: Note that "what number?" is what the caller *hears* the operator say.

5a, 5b: This phrase, with a Spanish gloss, was transcribed on two separate occasions by Tarascans: Francisco (see 1a, above) and Raúl (scribe of 2a, 3d, and 4a—and of the first lines of *Lucille*, see above, p. 5, left-hand column), respectively.

6a–d: Four young men worked on this sentence in the basement of the grocery store, with Martha as their teacher. Only one of them had been present on the night of August 6—a "veteran," who, in effect, inducted three new players into the game and its accompanying discourse on letters and sounds. The "academic" sentence was chosen by Martha and Rob, who dictated it to the scribes. The scribes compared their transcriptions but did not vote for the best. Note that the text is unglossed.

7: A page written by one of the men who wrote 6. He had not participated in the original collective transcription of EVRI BARI GUANTS TULEM (above, pp. 20–23). He took up where that left off. Note that 7q and 7r are a minimal pair: SAMDEI/SAN DEI.

8: A piece of a song.

9: A collection of eight glossed phrases; a "proto-glossary" compiled by Cipriano. His learned cousin Alfonso's influence is evident in the use of infinitives 9b TU RUEST, 9f TU GIV. Note that 9f PERDONAR means *to forgive*, not *to give*. Perhaps he heard "forgive" and thought he heard "to give." The initial RUA, RUE, RUI of 9a, 9b, 9c represent diphthongization common in the local dialect after initial [r] (cf. 8f RAIT). Incorrect Spanish spelling is evident in 9a ESCRIVIR (= *escribir*), 9e ALGIEN (= *alguién*), and 9h PAQUE (= *para qué*, cf. 10b). These represent transcriptions of Spanish the way it sounds, on the one letter, one sound principle: they are *bueno* but not *correcto* (pp. 18ff, above).

10a–c: A page of glossed phrases from a notebook kept jointly by Cipriano, Alfonso, and Renée. The glosses in standard English spelling 10a, 10b, 10c are the work of Alfonso and/or Renée (see above, p. 14). Note that 10d is a misunderstanding: AONDE (= *adonde*—the first *d* in *donde* is often not pronounced in Mexico) means *where*, not *when*.

IV

A Scene of Writing: The Village Hall

Viewed synoptically, these texts testify to the level of development reached by the communal discourse on letters and sounds in the two weeks following the

---

17. Warren Anderson, personal communication November 17, 1994.

August 6 meeting in the basement. In a series of very small steps, people were opening up a kind of dialogue new to Cobden, a scene of writing that entailed a momentary reversal in status, a new kind of relationship between local and picker, "legal" and "illegal," literate and illiterate, English and Spanish, citizen and alien. Specifically, there were now moments when an illegal alien felt free to ask a local citizen to repeat something over and over; free to carry a notebook and pen into new places—work, the bar, home; free to write in that notebook in the presence of Anglos; free to show what he had written to other illegal aliens and to look at what others had written; free to mimic the voice of a friend, a neighbor, a boss, an enemy.

To chart the sound patterns of spoken English, the authors of these texts were, in short, acting like fieldworkers jotting down initial impressionistic scratch notes of a hitherto unwritten language. Each English word or phrase in the above texts marks a moment, or a set of recurring moments, when a mojado in Cobden cast an Anglo in the role of a *native informant*. The texts decontextualize the informants' speech in order to study its formal structure.

The texts reproduced above are raw field notes. But they are not *my* field notes. They are field notes made by the subjects of my study. "The *institution* of field notes does exist, of course, widely understood to be a discrete textual corpus in some way produced by fieldwork and constituting a raw, or partly cooked, descriptive database for later generalization, synthesis, and theoretical elaboration."[18]

Clifford remarks that stories of ethnographic fieldwork often tell of a struggle to find and preserve "a separate place of writing, a place of reflection, analysis and interpretation . . . a tent with the flaps closed, a private room in a house, a typewriter set up in the corner of a room, or, minimally, a dry, relatively quiet spot in which to spread out of a few notebooks."[19] In Cobden in 1980, the authors of the above texts could claim no such separate place of writing to "write up" what they had "written down" in their scratch notes, to codify and systematize their strategies for writing English the way it sounds.[20] They had, collectively, no secure "room of one's own" in which they could freely assemble to engage in the "generalization, synthesis, and theoretical elaboration" of their database. They lacked, so to speak, a kitchen in which to cook their raw data.

Such a "kitchen" was unexpectedly provided by the Mayor of Cobden who, on Tuesday, August 19, spontaneously offered to open up the little Village Hall as a meeting place for mojados and Anglos to do whatever they wanted. His offer occurred as follows.

---

18. Clifford (1990: 52), original emphasis. For a more detailed analysis of field notes as a genre, see Chapter 4, pp. 90–95.
19. Clifford (1990: 52).
20. On "writing down" and "writing up," see Chapter 4, below.

In June, the Regional Advisory Council of the local Illinois Migrant Council had decided to move its monthly meetings from Carbondale to Cobden. On Tuesday, August 19, they parked their cars on the street and held their business meeting inside the grocery store. The Mexicans and Anglos who had intended to meet clandestinely in the basement of the store found themselves hanging around informally on the porch, looking down at the parked cars.

EL CORRIDO DE CARBONDALE

1. Cuando llegué a Carbondale
    todo pareció normal
   y cuando fuí con el Brad
    y los empleados también
   para ver si ellos podian
    nuestro caso resolver
2. El Brad nos contestaba
    el mismo que en el Ojala
   y el licenciado estudiante
    muchos papeles llenaba
   de preguntas y repuestas
    que el tendria que resolver
3. Mi esposa siempre decía
    nunca vamos a arreglar
   las leyes de migración
    ya cambiaron de a montón
   si nos agarra la migra
    nos tendremos que salir
4. Ya me voy ya me despido
    ya nos vamos a mover
   pa' nuestro Mexico lindo
    donde podemos vivir
   sin preocupación alguna
    que nos agarra la ley.

(1. When I got to Carbondale everything looked
fine/when I went to see Brad and the other
employees/to see if they could resolve our case.
2. Brad told us the same thing we heard in
Ojala/and the law student filled out many papers
/with questions and answers that he had to
resolve./ 3. My wife always said we'd never win
our case/the immigration laws have changed a lot
/if the migra catches us we will have to leave.
4. Now I'm going, farewell, we're moving/to our
beautiful Mexico where we can live/without any
worries about being trapped by the law.)

As sung by Juan. Transcribed and translated
by Tomás, October 5 1980.

Verse 1

For the first time since the death of Leonardo, Mexican music could again be heard in Cobden. Juan was singing us the *corrido* he had made up about his hassles with the Illinois Migrant Council in Carbondale. When Santiago accompanied it on the accordion, it sounded a lot like *Los mojados* (p. 3, above).

The song ended. The laughter died down. Eyes turned to a man walking up the hill toward us from the park. Everyone fell silent. The man reached the porch. He came up to me. He said, "I don't know what you folks are doing here, but the Village Hall is empty, and you may as well use that." He said he was the Mayor of Cobden. "Frankly," he said, "we're at a loss. We don't know what to do about the problem. The problem is, we don't know how to communicate."

The Village Hall was a small building on the other side of the park. The Mayor said it was available on Tuesdays and Thursdays. "I'm sure you'll be more comfortable there." Then he walked back down the hill.

El diccionario mojado

I attended the first meeting in the Village Hall, on Thursday, August 21. I walked into a well-lit, carpeted room. I saw about 15 migrant workers and half a dozen Anglos sitting in comfortable chairs around a handsome wooden table. The Mayor was not there. Someone was making coffee at the kitchen sink, and someone was commenting on the clean bathroom with hot and cold running water and soap. We had come a long way since the day Leonardo was buried.

Much was said that night. What concerns my narrative can be told in broad strokes. If anyone was in charge, it was Angie, the leader of the "clan" that included Constantino, Cipriano, and Alfonso.[21] Angie and her family had resided in Cobden for at least 10 years: they were considered the leading Mexican family in town. Angie held a key position at the Illinois Migrant Council.

Angie seemed to confine her role to facilitating a series of relatively formal introductions and then letting the meeting go wherever it wanted. The topic of traffic "fines" came up. More stories were told of surprising twists on the kinds of "fines" collected. Some conversations seemed to me to move toward, and then veer away from, serious political topics. One of the growers had just lowered his rate of pay from 60¢ to 55¢ a bushel (of peaches picked). I heard the word *huelga*— "strike." People talked about this in Spanish and the Anglos seemed uncomfortable. The topic of mastering English came up in this and similar circumstances, and the old-timers inducted the newcomers into what I have called the game of letters and sounds, and its accompanying discourse. For the benefit of the newcomers, the old-timers offered a rapid review of the decisions and developments narrated above.

People pulled out their notebooks and showed each other the bits of English they had written down. They tried "sight reading" each other's transcriptions aloud. Hitherto, I had heard people reading aloud transcriptions of phrases that they already knew how to say *líricamente*. Now, for the first time, I was hearing people reading aloud, at first sight, unknown sequences of sounds, one letter at a time, and the range of (mis)pronunciation was, of course, much wider. Sometimes, Anglos present could not catch the word: they thought it was Spanish even though it was meant to be English. "Sounds like Spanish to me." Then someone would recognize it and say it right.

This led to another round of discussion of the problem with dictionaries: they don't tell you how to pronounce the word.[22] Alfredo proposed that everyone present tonight contribute *una palabra* (a word) to a *diccionario* that they could then copy and share with other *compañeros* unable to attend that evening. They asked Angie if she could type it up and xerox it at her office. I volunteered to

---

21. See above, pp. 5, 10, 14, 16ff.
22. Compare above, pp. 19ff.

help with that task. I therefore felt free to spend the evening going around, listening to conversations and taking notes.

Rapidly, an agreement was reached: each person in turn pick a word, and everyone together work out the best way of writing it *como de veras se oye*, so that someone who doesn't know the word can read it aloud and be understood.

The words they picked, and the transcription voted best for each, were as follows.

1	*friend*	FREND	AMIGO
2	*discriminate*	DESCRIMINEIT	DESCRIMINAR
3	*ate*	EIT	COMI
			COMISTE
			COMIO
			COMIMOS
			COMIERON
4	*eight*	EIT	OCHO
5	*late*	LEIT	TARDE
6	*hate*	JEIT	ODIO
7	*dialogue*	DAELOG/DAYALOGG	DIALOGO
8	*for my self*	FOR MAI SEOF	PARA MI MISMO
9	*I'm sick*	AIM SIK	YO ESTOY ENFERMO
10	*pick*	PIK	PISCAR
11	*translator*	TRUENSLEIRO	INTERPRETE
			TRADUCTOR
12	*pleased to meet you*	PLIS TU MICHU	MUCHO GUSTO
13	*I don't care*	AI DON KER	NO ME IMPORTA
14	*I'm sleepy*	AIM SLIIPI	TENGO SUENO

Commentary

2 DESCRIMINEIT: DESCRIMINAR. Spanish *discriminar* and English *discriminate* are cognates. (Note that their spelling of the Spanish word is not quite correct. The Latin prefix *dis* does become *des* in Spanish words more often than not, but in this case it remains *dis*.)

Discussion focussed briefly on the differences in stress, which, in English, falls on the second syllable, in Spanish on the last; the consensus was that DESCRIMIN was "of equal value" (*vale igual*) in English and Spanish. Attention then concentrated on the isolated last syllable. People walked around saying it and listening to others say it. It came down to a choice between ET and EIT.

An Anglo asked, "How do you say *eight* in Spanish?" I thought he meant the past tense of *eat*, Angie thought he meant the number 8. In my pronunciation, they are homonyms, but in the local pronunciation there was a phonemic difference. Locals pronounced the past tense of *eat* as ᴇᴛ, the number as ᴇɪᴛ. The two people from Carbondale, however, pronounced both as ᴇɪᴛ, like me. Some discussion followed of regional variations between rural and urban speech in Mexico (*el campo y la capital*) and the United States. In the end, the vote was to write ᴇɪᴛ for all three (i.e., for the last syllabe of 2 ᴅᴇꜱᴄʀɪᴍɪɴᴇɪᴛ, and for the monosyllabic words 3 and 4.

5 ʟᴇɪᴛ: ᴛᴀʀᴅᴇ and 6 ᴊᴇɪᴛ: ᴏᴅɪᴏ were chosen (at least in part) because they sounded like 3 = 4 ᴇɪᴛ. The diphthong was no longer a problem. There was immediate agreement on the ʟ in ʟᴇɪᴛ. Some people practiced aspirating the *h* in *hate*; all agreed it did not sound like ᴊ in Spanish, but nevertheless preferred ᴊᴇɪᴛ to ʜᴇɪᴛ because *h* in written Spanish is always "silent."

7 ᴅᴇᴀʟᴏɢ/ᴅᴀʏᴀʟᴏɢɢ: ᴅɪᴀʟᴏɢᴏ. Spanish *dialogo* and English *dialogue* are cognates. It came down to counting syllables in the English pronunciation. ᴅᴀᴇʟᴏɢ was the local pronunciation—two syllables; ᴅᴀʏᴀʟᴏɢɢ recorded my pronunciation—three syllables. I urged them to ignore my pronunciation and stick to the local variety but they disagreed with me. Further discussion of regional variation: British English, Australian English, American English; Spanish Castilian (*castellano de españa*), Mexican Spanish, Caribbean Spanish. They voted to put both ᴅᴀᴇʟᴏɢ and ᴅᴀʏᴀʟᴏɢɢ in the *diccionario*.

8 ꜰᴏʀ ᴍᴀɪ ꜱᴇᴏꜰ. Note the diphthong ᴀɪ—compare ᴀᴇ in 7 ᴅᴀᴇʟᴏɢ and ᴀɪ in 9 ᴀɪᴍ ꜱɪᴋ. On the "quasi-diphthong" ᴇᴏ, compare ʟᴜꜱɪᴏ and ᴊɪᴏʟ in Alfredo's transcription of *Lucille* (p. 5, above) and ɢᴜɪᴏʟᴛʏ in Alfonso's *diccionario* below, pp. 52–53.

11 ᴛʀᴜᴇɴꜱʟᴇɪʀᴏ. This was called a tongue-twister (*trabalenguas*—cf. above, p. 18). Three other transcriptions were examined and rejected: ᴛʀᴇɴꜱʟᴇɪʀᴜ, ᴛʀᴏꜱ ʟᴇʏ ᴛᴏᴜ, and ᴛʀᴇɴꜱʟᴇɪᴅʀ. There was some discussion of the fact that English seemed not to distinguish between someone who translated orally (ɪɴᴛᴇʀᴘʀᴇᴛᴇ) and someone who translated in writing (ᴛʀᴀᴅᴜᴄᴛᴏʀ).

14 ᴀɪᴍ ꜱʟɪɪᴘɪ. For the long vowel in *sleepy*, they decided to double the ɪɪ, but for the long vowels of 12 ᴘʟɪꜱ ᴛᴜ ᴍɪᴄʜᴜ, they just used a single ɪ.

V

The Cobden Glossaries

Over the weekend, Angie and I typed up the text produced in the Village Hall, as requested. We photocopied it. Angie took about 100 copies to the next two meetings at the Village Hall (which I did not attend). From there, copies passed from hand to hand in and around Cobden. Meanwhile, I gave out about 50 copies, a half-dozen here, a dozen there. At first, the page of words was nicknamed *el diccionario mojado*—"the wetback glossary." After Constantino told people this name was too undignified, some jokingly referred to it as *el diccionario de oro*— "the golden glossary."

September was the peak of the picking season. All the migrant workers were working flat out. Meetings no longer took place in Cobden. But I heard on the grapevine that various individuals were collecting more words for the *diccionario*. In October, Jacinto, Cipriano, and Alfonso showed me the pages they had compiled, and asked me to copy—and publish—them. Jacinto and Cipriano had written a page each; Alfonso had a thick notebook with 30 pages filled in, including the correct English spelling for each word.[23]

---

23. On Alfonso's attitude to correct English spelling, see above, pp. 20–21.

By November, the season was over. Virtually all the Mexican migrant workers left the area, taking with them their hybrid alphabet, their strategies for coding two *abecedarios* with one *alfabeto*, their discourse on letters and sounds. The following glossaries compiled by Jacinto, Cipriano, and Alfonso in October can mark the end of the biliteracy event that began with Panchito jotting down JUELLULIB in the Village Park on July 7.

Jacinto's glossary

I'll be back	AVIVAC	AHORITA REGRESO
come back	CAMVAK	VOLVER
too much	TUMACH	DEMASIADO
much	MACH	MUCHO
lemme see	LIMISI	DEJAMEVER
I dunno	AIDONO	YO NO SE
waddayasay	GUARIYUSEI	QUE DICE USTE
broken	BROUKEN	ROTO
I have	AIJEF	TENGO
gimme	GIMI	DEME
not there (= no allí)	NODER	NO AY
li'l	LRERO	POQUITO
it	JIT	EL

Cipriano's glossary

ALEGRE	JAPI	*happy*
POBRE	POR	*poor*
ALGUNAS	SAM	*some*
VECES	TAIMS	*times*
ALGUNA COSA	ENI TENK	*anything*
FIESTA	PARI/PARTI	*party*
SIESTA	NEP	*nap*
CUANTO	JAMACH	*how much*
GANAS	DU YOU ORN	*do you earn*
NECESITO	AI NID	*I need*
AIRE	SAM ER	*some air*
COMPROMETIDO	ENGEICH(D)	*engaged*

YO FUI	AI GUENT	*I went*
AL PUEBLO	TU TAON	*to town*
PODEMOS IR	GUIQUEN GOU	*we can go*
AHORA	NAU	*now*
NO PODEMOS IR	GUIKENT GOU	*we can't go*

From Alfonso's three-column diccionario

TOWN	TAUN	PUEBLO
RIGHT	RUIT	DERECHA
LEFT	LEFX	IZQUIERDO
SOUTH	SAUTF	AL SUR
NORTH	NOURT	AL NORTE
EAST	IST	AL ESTE
WEST	UEST	AL OESTE
TO CALL	TO COU	LLAMAR
TO TELEPHONE	TU TELEFON	TELEFONEAR
TO LOOK UP	TU LUK UP	BUSCAR
SICK	SICK	EMFERMO
BROKEN	BROK	QUEBRADO
TO TRANSPORT	TU TRENSPORT	TRANSPORTAR
TO HURRY UP	TU URRILLAP	DARSEPRISA
GUILTY	GUIOLTY	CULPABLE
TRUTH	CHTRUD	VERDAD
LIE	LAI	MENTIRA
LANGUAGE	LENGUECH	IDIOMA
TRIP	TRUIP	VIAJE
TO BUY	TU BAI	COMPRAR
TO REACH	TU RUICH	ALCANZAR
TO COST	TO COST	COSTAR
TO DESIRE	TO DISIAR	DESEAR
RIGHT	RUAT	DERECHO, CORRECTO
RIGHT AWAY	RUAT AUEY	EN SEGUIDA
AWAY	AUEY	AUSENTE, FUERA

guare yu duen
que hace usted

town	taun	pueblo
right	ruit	derecho
left	LEFX	izquierdo
South	SAUTF	~~al~~ sur
north	nourt	al norte
East	ist	al este
west	uest	al oeste
to call	tu cou	llamar
to telephone	tu telefon	teleforear
to look up	tu luk up	buscar
sick	sick	Emfarmo
broken	broken	quebrado
to transport	tu trensport	transportar
to hurry up	tu urnllop	darse prisa
guilty	gviolty	culpable
truth	chtrued	verdad
lie	lai	mentira
language	lenguech	idioma
trip	trup	viaje
to buy	tu bai	Comprar
~~#~~	—	~~reach~~
to reach	tu frwich	alcanzar
to cost	tu cost	costar
to desire	tu disiar	desear
right	ruat	derecho,
right away	ruat auey	en seguida
away	Cuey	ausente, fuera

In Alfonso's own handwriting

3

SOME LAUGH, OTHERS FROWN

> The study of literacy ultimately requires us to study the social groups and institutions within which one is socialized to interpret certain types of words and certain sorts of worlds in certain ways.
>
> —Gee

In the preceding two chapters, I described how, in order to study the speech-sounds of English—*la pronunciación, el abecedario*—a group of Mexican migrant workers recorded a series of strategic moves in a game played with letters and sounds. A move in that game took the form *let this letter y in the roman alphabet take the value of this sound x in spoken English*. I described how what I called a discourse on letters and sounds accompanied that game. I argued that every time the game was played, "normal" relationships between illegal aliens and legal citizens were temporarily suspended to give place to what I called a scene of writing.

To suggest how game, discourse, and scene cohere, I invoked the analogy of an anthropologist jotting down initial scratch notes of an unknown and hitherto unwritten language in the field so as to begin communicating with "native informants" who speak only the language in question. In the next chapter, I argue that this is more than a mere metaphor; that the strategies fieldworkers use to produce their first glossaries of hitherto unanalyzed indigenous languages have the same formal structure as the strategies Mexicans used to record English the way it sounds in Cobden; and that the game played with letters and sounds by linguists in the field is the same game as that recorded in the Cobden glossaries. I show that in both cases, a hybrid writing system is improvised and then refined by letting letters of an alphabet take values on a sliding scale between speech-sounds in a known language and those in the unknown language.

But the analogy that casts the authors of the Cobden glossaries in the role of linguistic fieldworkers breaks down in one obvious particular: English is not, in fact, a hitherto unwritten language spoken by illiterate indigenous "natives." Under normal circumstances, the question of how to write English simply does not arise. Those of us who specialize in teaching literacy to adult speakers of minority languages rarely ask ourselves or "our" students when, if ever, writing English the way it sounds is better than writing it correctly.

In this chapter, I address the challenge of whether or not in our professional discourse and classroom practice adult educators can find a place for the perspective on English offered by the game played with letters and sounds in Cobden, the texts recording moves in that game in a hybrid alphabet, the discourse that accompanied the coding and decoding of those texts, and, above all, the contrast between the unfamiliar scene of writing situated in the institutional no man's land we call "the field" and the much more familiar scene of writing situated in the institution we call "the classroom."

As a first step toward addressing this challenge, I discuss and analyze the interpretive assumptions which educators invoke when they try to *read* one of the Cobden *diccionarios* without being told anything at all about who wrote it, why, when, where, or how. The data I draw on are of two kinds: (a) the discourse of professional educators who have participated in about two dozen workshops which I facilitated in New England between 1983 and 1994; and (b) the seven paragraphs on the Cobden glossaries that Nina Wallerstein wrote in her ground-breaking book *Language and Culture in Conflict: Problem-Posing in the ESL Classroom*, first published in 1983.

Despite the obvious limits of my approach, it does at least yield a clearer understanding of the range of attitudes educators can take toward the very idea of a hybrid alphabet, and suggests possible connections between such attitudes and the scope and limits of current professional discourse on "native language literacy" in learning English as a Second Language in the United States today.

I

"Is This Text a Joke, or What?"

After 1980, copies of Cobden *diccionarios* circulated, *samizdat* fashion, among Mexican migrant workers far from Cobden. I heard on the grapevine that new words were being added to the *diccionario* by Mexicans in Chicago and Florida. Meanwhile, I myself sent photocopies of some of the Cobden texts, along with copies of some of my own typewritten field notes,[1] to close friends and colleagues

---

1. Subsequently collected and published by the late Alfred Schenkman as *The Voice of Fulano* (Kalmar 1983). See p. 13 n. 5 above.

in the Illinois Migrant Council, who recopied them and passed them along to other colleagues (with or without the dubious benefit of my own decontextualized field notes). Some of these copies were then reprinted by the Latino Institute in Reston, Virginia in its newsletter *Educación Liberadora*, which circulated in a nationwide network of Freirean Hispanic grassroots adult literacy campaigns. It was in this manner that texts handwritten in 29¢ notebooks by illegal aliens in no man's land began crossing the border to be read in print by interpretive communities in legitimate educational institutions.[2]

In 1981, I was asked to report on my fieldwork at the annual conference of the Illinois Adult and Continuing Educators' Association in Springfield, Illinois. I began my presentation by handing out copies of Jacinto's *diccionario without* my annotations recording conventional English spellings of Jacinto's transcriptions.[3] I was motivated by curiosity: I wanted to see people's initial responses to the *diccionario* as patterned strings of letters, as pure text completely removed from its original context.

The first person who got a copy looked at it and protested, "*I* can't read this!"

"Why not?" I asked her, "Are you illiterate?"

In the basement on August 6, when Danon had first said she couldn't read JUELLULIB, this joke had triggered merry laughter.[4] In this professional context, the same joke was treated as being in poor taste.

"I can't read this," she explained, "because it's *Spanish!*"

"How do you know?" I asked.

"Well it sure as hell ain't English!"

This was no joke. No one laughed. The woman was denying that Jacinto's text was what, in fact, it claims to be: a codification of English. According to her (and to many others since then), it looks the way it does because it is obviously written by an illiterate who can't speak English and certainly doesn't know how to write it. She had a point. But so did Jacinto and his companions when they claimed that knowing how to code English speech accurately was of more use to them than trying to decode English spelling without being sure how it really sounds.

I choose to begin with this anecdote about a joke that is funny in one context and not at all funny in another because it reveals the need to take seriously the fact that when educators first look at the field glossaries compiled by Jacinto and his companions, some laugh while others frown. I propose to regard laughter and its opposite as helpful symptoms of the tensions within and between the discourses by which ESL teachers identify themselves *as* ESL teachers.[5] Naming

---

2. Including by Nina Wallerstein, see below pp. 75–76.

3. For the annotated version, see above, p. 51; for the plain version, see below, p. 61.

4. See p. 17, above.

5. "A Discourse is a sort of 'identity kit' which comes complete with the appropriate costume and instructions on how to act, talk, and often write, so as to take on a particular social role

these tensions may help suggest potential sites of struggle in the transfer of a hybrid writing system from the field to the classroom.

In choosing this point of departure, I am deeply influenced by Daniel Cottom's analysis of the joke as a genre or form of discourse in his study of the politics of interpretation, *Text and Culture*. His first chapter, "What is a joke?" begins by analyzing the discursive process of identification that is necessary if we are to enjoy a joke or even to recognize a text *as* a joke. He argues compellingly that even in the case of a trivial joke, this process of identification—"I get it" *versus* "I don't get it"—is always deeply entangled in the politics of identity and community, including problems of "mastery, deviancy, repression, violence, desire, reading and writing, teaching, and power."[6] He shows that what is true of the joke with which he begins his study[7] is just as true of any genre (including, I say, that of the Cobden texts) which can be (mis)read by various mixtures of interpretive communities in contradictory ways: namely, that complex political factors shape the ways in which people in different contexts and discourses do or do not "get it."

That "texts are given form and meaning by discourse and genre"[8] is a governing principle of what Gee calls "the new literacy studies."[9] Given that "discourses define, describe and delimit what it is possible to say and not possible to say (and by extension—what it is possible to do or not to do) with respect to the area of concern"[10] to the institutions that validate and are validated by the discourse in question, it follows that "certain discourses tend to have preferred relations with certain genres, and some genres are incompatible with certain discourses."[11]

> *Types* of texts and the various *ways of reading* them do not flow full-blown out of the individual soul (or biology); they are the social and historical inventions of various groups of people. One always and only learns to interpret texts of a certain type in certain ways through having access to,

---

Footnote 5 continued—

that others will recognize . . . Discourses . . . are always ways of displaying (through words, actions, values and beliefs) *membership* in a particular social group or social network (people who associate with each other around a common set of interests, goals and activities)." (Gee 1990: 142), original emphasis.

6. Cottom (1989: viii).

7. "A Texan is walking across Harvard Yard. He stops a guy and asks him, in his nasal drawl, 'Can you tell me where the library's at?' The guy looks him up and down, pauses, and says, 'At Harvard we do not end our sentences with prepositions.' The Texan apologizes, saying, 'Excuse me. Can you tell me where the library's at, asshole?'" (Cottom 1989: 3).

8. Halliday and Hasan (1989: 46).

9. Gee (1990, 1991, 1992).

10. Kress (1989: 7).

11. Kress (1989: 31).

and ample experience in, social settings where texts of that type are read in those ways. One is socialized or enculturated into a certain *social practice*.[12]

Supported by virtually all[13] the contemporary work on language and literacy development Gee formulates the empirical claim that:

> one does not learn to read texts of type X in way Y unless one has had experience in settings where texts of type X are read in way Y. One has to be socialized into a *practice* to learn to read texts of type X in way Y, a practice other people have already mastered.[14]

On first encountering a text X of the Cobden type, educators initially try different ways Y_1, Y_2, Y_3 of reading them. Answering the question of what these ways are comes before any question of how educators might benefit from learning to read them "the Cobden way." Suggesting that professional educators could be "socialized into a practice" of illegal aliens is, again, no joke.

Why Some Laugh and Others Frown

Since 1983, as part of my professional activities in New England, I have facilitated about 50 staff development workshops designed to help adult educators talk to one another about the transfer of literacy from language to language, and from classroom to community.[15] I usually begin my workshops with an icebreaker or two—a simple activity intended to open up, in a manageable way, the Pandora's box of complex pedagogical, social, cultural, and political controversies that must be part of any serious dialogue on linguistic diversity in the United States. In about two dozen of the workshops, I have used Jacinto's *diccionario* (as in Figure B, p. 61) to break the ice: I ask participants to note the steps they go through to make sense of the text "cold turkey"—with no contextual information at all.

Sometimes, before doing this exercise with Jacinto's *diccionario*, I ask them to do it with a sample of the Kassel glossary (Figure A, p. 61). I experimented with this text as an icebreaker because it represents the same genre as the Cobden

---

12. Gee (1990: 45).
13. Gee cites as examples Heath (1983), Smith (1988), and Garton and Pratt (1989).
14. Gee (1991: 43).
15. A short early version of the following pages was included in Kalmar (1994: 130–135). Many of the professionals who participated in my workshops were connected with the Boston Adult Literacy Initiative and the Lawrence Literacy Coalition. They were not, I should think, representative of professional adult educators in general: they had higher than average academic credentials, included more bilingual and immigrant professionals, were more likely to work in community-based organizations, and tended to be more familiar with Freirean discourse (Kalmar 1988a, 1988b, 1988c, 1992).

glossaries. In both cases, letters of the roman alphabet are used to code the speech-sounds of two different languages, but in the case of the Kassel glossaries no one knows the languages. (They are rural dialects spoken for a brief period of time by a very small number of people in Europe 1,000 years ago—see below, pp. 62–63.) Refraining from telling participants in my workshops anything about the game, the discourse, the scene that produced Jacinto's *diccionario*, is a voluntary decision on my part. In the case of the Kassel glossary, one has no choice: apart from the fact that it was written in Europe in the ninth century, nothing at all is known about who wrote this text, when, where, why, or how. Scholars must reconstruct from internal evidence alone whatever scene of writing makes sense out of their preferred interpretation of the text.

There is an interesting difference between what happens when people have discoursed on the Kassel glossary before setting eyes on Jacinto's *diccionario* and what happens when they interpret Jacinto's *diccionario* without having first "cracked the code" of the Kassel glossary. Experience has taught me to expect an interesting recurrent pattern, a difference in the group dynamics set in motion by these alternative opening moves in my workshops, a difference in how the ice breaks, what people do to make sense out of the text, what discourses they bring to the task of "cracking the code," what scenes of writing they imagine, what values and beliefs they defend and attack, and, above all, in the range of negative and positive *feelings* people express towards the use of a hybrid alphabet to code speech the way it sounds in the classroom and in the community.

II

Cracking the Ninth-Century Code: Three Scenes of Reading

When I begin by inviting participants to see what sense they can make out of the Kassel glossary, and to note the strategies they come up with in the process, the first phase usually lasts a couple of minutes. During this phase, individuals tend to stare at the document, silent and alone. (This phase reproduces the "scene of reading" of individual students reading decontextualized texts in a generic classroom, a scene that situates literacy skills in the "decontextualized heads" of individuals, not in the social interaction between them.)[16]

After a couple of minutes of silence, people start declaring that the text makes no sense whatsoever. They want to know who wrote it, what use it is, what

16. On "scenes of reading," as distinct from "scenes of writing," see the collection of studies edited by Jonathan Boyarin (1993). On treating "generalized skills isolable from specific contents and contexts" as "private psychic possessions of decontextualized heads," see Gee (1992: 32–33).

language it's in, *where it comes from.* I decline to suggest any answers to these questions. Tensions build up. Small groups spontaneously start forming to share their frustrations, pool their partial insights, and help each other make sense out of the text collaboratively. (This second phase reproduces in microcosm the "scene of reading" of a community of scholars, especially nineteenth-century philologists collaborating on the joint interpretation of a newly discovered text in an unidentified language.)

PEDES	FOOZI
FIGIDO	LEPARA
PULLI	HONIR
PULCINS	HONCHLI
CALLUS	HANO
GALINA	HANIN
PRIDIAS	UUANTI
MUFFLAS	HANTSCOH
IMPLENUS EST	FOL IST
MANNEIRAS	PARTA
MARTEL	HAMAR
PUTICLA	FLASCA
FIDELLI	CHALPIR
FOMERAS	UUAGANSO
RADI MEO PARBA	SKIR MINAN PART

FIGURE A Sample of Kassel glossary

AVIVAC	AHORITA
	REGRESO
CAMVAK	VOLVER
TUMACH	DEMASIADO
MACH	MUCHO
LIMISI	DEJAMEVER
AIDONO	YO NO SE
GUARIYUSEI	QUE DICE USTE
BROUKEN	ROTO
AIJEF	TENGO
GIMI	DEME
NODER	NO AY
LRERO	POQUITO
JIT	EL

FIGURE B Jacinto's *diccionario*[17]

It has never taken the small groups more than about 15 or 20 minutes to convince one another (with no help from me) that:

- the Kassel glossary is "some sort of dictionary";
- the left-hand column records some sort of Romance language;
- the right-hand column records some sort of Germanic language; and
- the "same" word appears simultaneously in Romance and Germanic.

---

17. Cf. above, p. 51.

Many groups guess (correctly) the meaning of at least some words in the list (e.g., MARTEL = HAMAR = *hammer*) and quite a few guess (again correctly) that the document is not a made-up puzzle, but an authentic early medieval European text.

When I then ask them to describe the strategies they used to make sense of the text, they always identify a critical turning point in the small-group dynamics: the moment when people start listening to one another *trying to read aloud* various strings of letters in the text. "That's how we cracked the code."

In order to talk to one another about what they're experiencing, they improvise what could fairly be called a discourse on letters and sounds. (This reproduces in microcosm the scene of reading in which philologists give voice to hitherto dead languages by fixing the values of the alphabet they are written in.) For it is only after people *hear* the speech-sounds coded as, say, CALLUS and GALINA, HANO and HANIN, that they make the connection with what they already know and exclaim; for example, "Aha! GALINA is the feminine of CALLUS. It's gotta be *hen*." And then someone else will exclaim, "Aha! So HANIN is the feminine of HANO . . ." and someone will butt in, "I get it! They're the same thing, they're both *hen*."

The interesting point, for present purposes, is that my workshop participants by no means claim to be pronouncing each letter in a given word "correctly." They let each letter take a range of values on a sliding scale. There's a lot of room for play. The precise sounds or allophones that would have been used in the ninth century by native speakers of the languages in question remain unknown. But this doesn't matter. The generic phonemes of what Whorf called Standard Average European speech turn out to be good enough. Which goes to show that a knowledge of a generic hybrid alphabet as a kind of algebraic notation system is, in some nontrivial sense, part of our common culture today—at least among the kind of people who attend my kind of workshops.

Only through speculation can we replay the actual game of letters and sounds recorded in the Kassel glossary, reconstruct the discourse which validated that game, or imagine the ninth-century European scene of writing in which it was originally played out.[18] The strategies used by small groups to decode the Kassel text in my workshops resemble those used by nineteenth-century philologists who imagined the manuscript's original scene of writing situated in a small community at the margins of the former Roman Empire, where barely literate "Barbarians" and "Romans" speaking two different languages joined in some sort of give and take: a situation, in short, like that of Cobden in 1980. The ninth-century "Barbarians" spoke a vernacular dialect of what is now labeled Old Bavarian. The "Romans" spoke something in between what are now labeled

---

18. See Elcock (1960: 317–322). See also Marchot (1895) and Titz (1923). Illich and Sanders (1988: 52–65) provide an engaging and illuminating account of the ninth-century European discourse on letters and sounds, especially on the interplay between Germanic and Romance languages and literacies.

Late Vulgar Latin and Early Proto-Romance (comparable in cultural status and prestige, perhaps, to Cobden English)!

Philologists have argued that the glossaries were written not by the "Romans," but by the "Barbarians," who (like the authors of the Cobden glossaries) decided to ignore the conservative conventions of correct (in this case, Latin) spelling. By taking off from the Late Latin values of the alphabet as they knew it, they coded Romance and Germanic speech the way both really sounded. Like the Mexicans in Cobden, they thus hybridized the Roman alphabet. For example, CALLUS and PARBA represent how the "Barbarians" coded what the "Romans" said. If c and P are given the Germanic values of unvoiced initial consonants, CALLUS and PARBA sound like Romance GALLUS and BARBA spoken with a "thick German accent" (just as, if each letter is given its Spanish value, DOLÓ DASN'T PROTECT AS can sound like English spoken with a thick Spanish accent).[19]

The Kassel glossary is therefore, like the Cobden glossaries, coded in a homemade hybrid alphabet, and if we can decode it today, it is thanks to a folk tradition of using the Roman alphabet as a sort of generic International Phonetic Alphabet from the ninth century to the present.

From Ninth-Century Europe to Twentieth-Century America

Small groups that have cut their teeth on the Kassel glossary and are then shown Jacinto's *diccionario* usually burst out laughing. There is often a double take. Since this text is obviously the same genre as the one they've just looked at—and uses a similar code—many people laugh as soon as they realize that, in this case, at least one of the languages is contemporary Spanish. Meanwhile, bilingual Latinos are laughing because they recognize the English as English. But not everyone gets the joke. By and large, bilingual Latinos who laugh at an in-joke in the company of monolingual Anglos are under some social pressure to at least explain in plain English what's so funny. This further develops the incipient discourse on letters and sounds.

As the shock of recognition spreads, the small groups rapidly decide, collectively, that A and B are indeed variations on a common genre, and that B, like A, is some sort of dictionary in which:

- the left-hand column records a Romance language (namely, Spanish);
- the right-hand column records a Germanic language (namely, English); and
- the "same word" appears in both languages.

There are usually some people, however, who argue seriously, sometimes indignantly, that this is no laughing matter. What was good enough in medieval

---

19. See above, p. 40.

Europe is not good enough in twentieth-century America. The sight of English speech-sounds coded in a homemade hybrid alphabet seems to be particularly disturbing to teachers who regard themselves as professional gatekeepers charged with maintaining the standards of traditional English literacy. So while some laugh, others frown.

III

Three Ways of Reading a Cobden Glossary

Beginning with Jacinto

When I begin a workshop by inviting participants to see what sense they can make out of Jacinto's *diccionario* (without having the Kassel glossary to compare it to), the results are far more dramatic. Often, people assume they know who wrote it, what use it is, what language it's in, *where it comes from*.[20] They assume it was written by a low-level ESL student in a classroom of the sort with which they are familiar. They frown, and some groan with dismay.

Meanwhile, the bilingual Latinos are exclaiming things such as "This is beautiful! This is neat! This is really clever!" They smile, and some chuckle with delight.

Those who frown with dismay often take offense at those who laugh with delight—and vice versa. Tempers flare, people interrupt one another, angry voices are heard. The small groups that form spontaneously tend to be "Anglos *versus* Latinos" rather than "collaborative learning groups." Since the frowners tend to be monolingual English speakers while the laughers tend to be biliterate Latinos, the dialectic that cracks Jacinto's code is usually mediated by broad-minded English-speakers who are pro-Spanish. This results in an intense dialectic, a ritual drama[21] of strong and contradictory feelings, aggressive and defensive attitudes toward imagined situations, conflicting ideologies and discourses on purity and pollution, definitions and redefinitions of linguistic, pedagogic, social, political and economic positions and values.

It is as if opening the workshop with an innocuous hybrid alphabet that codes two *unknown* languages offers a sort of antidote to controversy over the privileged status of English. Without this antidote, Jacinto's hybrid alphabet seems to strike some ESL teachers as a poisonous threat polluting English literacy.

Every document bequeathed us by history (said Kenneth Burke)[22] must be treated as a *strategy for encompassing a situation*. Whether Jacinto's strategy for

---

20. Cf above, pp. 60–61.
21. In Kenneth Burke's sense. His work, especially his *Grammar of Motives* (Burke 1962), has influenced my understanding of the group dynamics reported here.
22. Burke (1973[1941]: 109).

encompassing his situation is judged good or bad depends, of course, on who gets to define the situation in question. The authors of the Cobden glossaries defined their own situation and called their strategy for encompassing it good— better than the institutionally legitimized strategy of "correct spelling."

A Positive Attitude: "This is Beautiful!"

Biliterate Latinos also tend to call it good. They say things such as "My brother wrote like this when he first came here." "My grandmother still does." The situation they imagine (and try to recreate in my workshops) is not the ESL classroom: it is a diglossic community on the margins of literacy (much like the medieval community imagined by philologists as the natural habitat of the Kassel glossary), a community in which people who speak different ways are engaged in the give and take of every day life and are trying to make speech-sounds intelligible to one another. They defend the empirical or *descriptive* validity[23] of Jacinto's text: they explain to their monolingual colleagues that this text records—with wit, logic, and panache—what gringos *really sound like* to monolingual Spanish speakers.

LRERO, for example, often becomes a "site of struggle" in my workshops. Monolingual English speakers who, like the teacher in Illinois, feel strongly that "it sure as hell ain't English" need considerable persuasion before they can accept, more or less reluctantly, the notion that "anyone in her right mind" could classify LRERO as English. To them, it is "obviously Spanish." Some back this up by pointing out that ERO is a Spanish, not an English, ending—"as in sombrero."[24] And no English word could possibly begin with that strange-looking LR. (Actually, neither can any Spanish word. But this they don't realize—not knowing Spanish.) The poetry that biliterates see and hear in words such as LRERO is inaudible to monoliterates. *Little* is a poor guide to saying the English word with a "Southern twang." The traditional "dialect" spelling *li'l* is not much better, since the one letter *l* takes two quite different values (i.e., allophones). On occasion, a bilingual Latino will argue that coupling the Roman letters L and R (with values "close to" their values in Spanish) reproduces the way the tongue moves in pronouncing the initial *l* of *li'l*. Or that ERO captures the vowels, the intonation, or the rhythm of the word *li'l* as actually spoken by Southerners.[25]

A Negative Attitude: "This is Worse than Nothing!"

The frowners and groaners are ESL teachers who assume that Jacinto wrote his glossary in a conventional ESL classroom, under the authority of a legitimate ESL

---

23. In Maxwell's sense (Maxwell 1992).
24. ERO has a "pun-like" structure, on which, see above, pp. 37 and 40.
25. Cf. my comments (pp. 50 #8, above) on the "pseudo-diphthongs" EO and IO in SEOF, JIOL, LUSIO, GUIOLTY.

teacher like themselves. They imagine (and try to reproduce in my workshops) a situation in which inventing a new code by playing with letters and sounds is, at best, a dubious strategy, and, at worst, no strategy at all. "I'd never be allowed to let my students get away with this sort of thing," is a typical response. "This isn't English, it isn't Spanish, it's nothing, it's worse than nothing, it's not bilingual, it's zero-lingual," is another. One person was applauded when he said, "This is like letting them mint their own coins! This is *counterfeit!*" The most negative feelings are those directed at me personally: "You are condemning these people to second-class citizenship."

"These people" are all too familiar to ESL teachers in publicly funded programs. They are the adult speakers of minority languages, especially Spanish, who "can't even write their own language."[26] They are the target population referred to in some adult literacy circles as "zero-zero people"—zero English, zero literacy.[27] Meeting their needs has always been a nagging headache to overworked, underpaid part-time ESL and ABE teachers throughout the United States. The headache won't go away: it's getting worse. Thanks to Amnesty, formerly illegal aliens are raising the percentage of "zero-zero people" enrolling in publicly funded programs. In this context, Jacinto's hybrid alphabet looks like the cause of the headache, not the cure for it.

A Freirean Attitude: "Stop Blaming the Victim"

Caught in the middle are the progressive ESL teachers who want to empower their students by "problem-posing in the ESL classroom," especially those who call themselves Freirean educators. The situation they imagine (and try to recreate in my workshops) is a community-based learning environment that simulates the conflicts of oppressive and oppressed languages and cultures in the real world. In the classroom, Freirean ESL teachers simulate a site of struggle by creating "codifications"—role-plays, fictional dialogues, pictures—portraying problematic situations familiar to the oppressed. In my workshops, they interpret Jacinto's hybrid alphabet as a symptom of oppression.

To defend Jacinto's hybrid alphabet against attacks from their less liberal colleagues, they rely on contradictory interpretive assumptions that land them in a dilemma. They assume that Jacinto was my student, that he wrote his *diccionario* in my classroom, that, as his teacher, I knew what I was doing, and that what I was doing was teaching ESL according to the "dialogue model" as opposed to the "banking model" of education: in short, that I was trying to "empower" Jacinto (and his fellow students) by the problems which *I* posed for him to solve. But they find it hard to imagine a problem to which Jacinto's hybrid alphabet

---

26. de Tal (1988).
27. Kalmar (1988a, 1992).

could count as a valid solution. In particular, they cannot imagine themselves learning from their students "how English really sounds."

It may be worth speculating on what it is that prevents them from attempting a fully Freirean interpretation of Jacinto's codification. In the rest of this chapter, I consider three contradictions in their discourse and praxis that may contribute to their dilemma. First, I consider some effects of mixing Freirean with non- (or anti-)Freirean ways of talking about the roles of teachers and students in the ESL classroom. Then I suggest that Freire's own discourse on letters and sounds is "lost in translation" when Freirean discourse is conducted entirely *in English*. Finally, an analysis of Nina Wallerstein's response to the Cobden glossaries suggests that the Cobden texts challenge one of Freire's guiding principles: that the educator is the one who codes and the educatees the ones who decode.

IV

Freirean Dilemmas

Teacher versus *Student*

First, in talking about issues raised by Jacinto's *diccionario*, members of this group "code-switch" between two incompatible discourses: the "unconverted" discourse of mainstream teachers, and the "converted" discourse of Freirean educators. For example, many of them say something like, "I swear I learn more from my students than they ever learn from me . . ." Nevertheless, they continue to refer to themselves as teachers, not as students, and they continue to refer to those from whom they learn so much as "my students," not as "my teachers"—even though, as Freire puts it, educators "cannot treat the oppressed as their possession."[28]

In the authentic give and take that characterizes genuine conscientization, according to Freire, you can no longer tell the educator from the educatee: everyone engaged in existential dialogue[29] is simultaneously educator and educatee. This is in contrast to the "banking model," in which, to quote Freire's oft-cited list, there are at least 10 ways of telling the educator from the educatee:

1. The educator is always the one doing the educating: the educatee is the one being educated.
2. The educator is the one who knows: the educatees are the ones who don't know.
3. The educator is the subject of the process, the one who does the thinking: the educatees are the objects, the ones being thought about.

---

28. Freire (tr. Ramos) (1971: 120).
29. On the existential dimensions of Freirean dialogue, see below, pp. 72–73.

4. The educator is the one who talks: the educatees are the ones who listen, docile.[30]

5. The educator is the one who trains: the educatees are the ones being trained.

6. The educator is the one who makes and prescribes choices: the educatees are the ones who follow the prescription.

7. The educator is the one who acts: the educatees are the ones who are under the illusion that they are acting through the educator's actions.

8. The educator picks the scheduled subject matter: the educatees, never consulted, adjust themselves to it.

9. The educator [is the one who] equates his/her official authority, which contradicts the freedom of the educatees, with cognitive authority: the educatees have to abide by the educator's rulings.

10. In short, the educator is the subject of the process: the educatees, merely its objects.[31]

This is my translation. Where I say *educator* and *educatee*,[32] the standard English translation (by Myra Bergman Ramos) says *teacher* and *student* (or, in one instance, *pupil*).[33] To preserve the sense of Freire's wordplay with the suffixes that modulate the root idea of *education*, my literal translation of these fundamental terms creates

---

30. Note that etymologically, docile means teachable.

31. Freire (1975: 74) (my translation).

32. As do Bigwood and Marshall in their 1983 English translation of Freire's 1968 Chilean essay, *Extensión y Comunicación* (e.g., p. 121) and Goulet in his Preface to Freire (1983) (e.g., p. viii).

33. Here, for comparison's sake, is the standard English translation by Myra Bergman Ramos of Freire's list of contradictions (Freire 1971: 59):

(a) the teacher teaches and the students are taught;

(b) the teacher knows everything and the students know nothing;

(c) the teacher thinks and the students are thought about;

(d) the teacher talks and the students listen—meekly;

(e) the teacher disciplines and the students are disciplined;

(f) the teacher chooses and enforces his choice, and the students comply;

(g) the teacher acts and the students have the illusion of acting through the action of the teacher;

(h) the teacher chooses the program content, and the students (who were not consulted) adapt to it;

(i) the teacher confuses the authority of knowledge with his own professional authority, which he sets in opposition to the freedom of the students;

(j) the teacher is the Subject of the learning process, while the pupils are mere objects.

And here, for the sake of completeness, is Freire's original Portuguese version (Freire 1975: 84–85):

(a) O educador é o que educa; os educandos, os que são educados.

(b) O educador é o que sabe; os educandos, os que não sabem.

(c) O educador é o que pensa; os educandos, os pensados.

(d) O educador é o que diz a palavra; os educandos, os que a escutam dòcilmente.

jargon as alien to idiomatic English as the word *conscientization*. In most contexts, the more idiomatic terms *teacher* and *student* are obviously better than *educator* and *educatee*. But in Freirean discourse, the terms *teacher* and *student* must be used in their "converted" or Freirean sense, in which possessive pronouns *my* and *our* in phrases such as "*my* students" or "*our* teacher" are, as it were, ungrammatical, politically incorrect.

In some contexts, we pay a price for using the idiomatic "unconverted" terms *teacher* and *student* instead of the jargon "converted" terms *educator* and *educatee*. When, for example, Cipriano, Alfonso, and Renee kept their joint notebook,[34] it makes sense to say that "it was hard to tell the educators from the educatees." All three were both educators and educatees of one another.

But in an ESL classroom, you can always tell the teacher from the students. There's usually one person speaking English freely and fluently: that's the teacher, who speaks with authority. There are many adults who speak English poorly, incorrectly: they're the students, whose speech lacks legitimacy.

This contradiction may help explain, perhaps, why even the most progressive ESL teachers find it hard to imagine a scene of writing in which Jacinto is the *educator* and they themselves are the *educatees*, hard to imagine what lesson, if any, they can learn from his hybrid alphabet.

Lost in Translation: Freire's Discourse on Letters and Sounds

Second, like their less liberal colleagues, the Freirean groups seem to lack a terminology with which to articulate anything approaching Constantino's distinction between an *abecedario* and an *alfabeto*, or between the *escritura* of English and its *pronunciación*.[35] They do not interpret the *linguistic* details of Jacinto's hybrid alphabet.

A common response, for example, to a biliterate Latino who argues that Jacinto's *diccionario* is English, "the way it sounds," is to say, "The problem is that Spanish is a phonetic language and English is not." Those who point this out tend to

Footnote 33 continued—

(e) O educador é o que disciplina; os educandos, os disciplinados.

(f) O educador é o que opta e prescreve sua opção; os educandos os que seguem a prescrição.

(g) O educador é o que actua; os educandos, os que têm a ilusão de que actuam, na actuação do educador.

(h) O educador escolhe o conteúdo programático; os educandos, jamais ouvidos nesta escolha, se acomodam a ele.

(i) O educador identifica a autoridade do saber com sua autoridade funcional, que opõe antagònicamente à liberdade dos educandos; estes devem adaptar-se às determinações daquele.

(j) O educador, finalmente, é o sujeito do processo; os educandos, meros objectos.

34. See above, pp. 14, 45 #10.
35. See above, pp. 20–23.

argue that Jacinto's text isn't really in English, because it's in "Spanish phonetics." This loose way of speaking is too imprecise to engage theoretical constructs that might capture the technical details. Put in more technical terms, what they have in mind is that (for historical reasons) the traditional writing system of English, unlike that of Spanish, is not systematically structured on the principle of one phoneme, one letter, and that this poses a problem.

From a linguistic point of view, there is no such thing as a non-phonetic language. All languages, including English, are "phonetic" in the sense that they can all be analyzed and adequately transcribed in a phonetic (or phonemic) notation system. This basic linguistic principle seems occult to many ESL teachers. Even the Freireans seem to lack a discourse on letters and sounds precise enough to decode Jacinto's codification.

Less blatantly than those who say "it sure as hell ain't English," even the Freirean ESL teachers in my workshops end up convincing themselves that Jacinto's text is not really what it claims to be: a codification of English. It is as if they accept a syllogism that goes like this:

1.   Unlike Spanish, English *cannot* be written the way it sounds.
2.   This *is* written the way it sounds.
3.   Therefore, this *cannot* really be English.

The paradox is that a full-fledged Freirean literacy campaign is unthinkable without an adequate discourse on letters and sounds. It is only in the United States that Freireans dispense with such a discourse: in the Third World (Brazil, Chile, Cuba, Nicaragua), a "canonical" Freirean literacy campaign has always been inaugurated with a discourse on letters and sounds "in order to challenge critical consciousness from the beginning."[36]

In his early writings, Freire himself was quite explicit on this point. The initial step in a Freirean literacy campaign is to codify a set of generative words. The teams of revolutionary educators who undertake the codification choose words that are "generative" according to two quite different criteria. (1) A generative word "names the world." Unlike *the cat sat on the mat* or *see Dick run*, the first words studied by illiterates in Freirean campaigns are charged with so much meaning that they "generate" serious collective reflection on existential problems, reflection that in turn generates effective collective action to solve the problems.[37] (2) A generative word is composed of a finite set of elements. Decoding a generative word includes playing around with permutations and combinations of these elements to "generate phonemic families."[38] This demystifies the structure of literacy as a reduction of speech to script.

---

36. Freire, in Davis (1970), reprinted in Mackie (1981: 61).
37. See, for example, Freire (1965, 1983: 49).
38. Freire (1965, 1983) (e.g., pp. 52–54, tr. Myra Bergman Ramos).

Freire used *phonemic* in the broadest possible sense.[39] Syllables, for example, can count as phonemes in his sense since by permuting and recombining the *syllables* of a generative word in Spanish or Portuguese, one can generate other words.[40] But the precision with which he uses his term *phonemic* is evident in his calculation that 17 generative words are enough to capture the "phonetic richness" of all the "phonemic families" in Portuguese[41] or Spanish.[42]

How many "generative words" are needed to do the same for English?

This is an interesting question. Studying the Cobden glossaries might help anyone looking for an answer. But the surprising thing is that Freireans in the United States are not looking for an answer to this question: it has not been asked by those proposing to inaugurate Freirean English literacy campaigns for adult speakers of minority languages. A definitive answer would require (at the very least) considerable theoretical linguistic analysis, but the first step in any such analysis must be to bypass traditional English spelling in favor of a more rational notation system, just as Constantino and his companions did in Cobden.

In the literature written in English on Freirean pedagogy, there has been much discussion of how to "translate" Freirean principles from revolutionary situations in the Third World to non-revolutionary situations in the United States.[43] But there has been no discussion (that I have seen) of how to adapt Freire's "phonemic" criterion for generativity from monolingual to bilingual situations, or from Spanish to English. Freire's discourse on letters and sounds, on phonetic richness and phonemic families, has been simply "lost in translation." Perhaps this is one reason why an interpretation of Jacinto's *diccionario* as a Freirean codification of 13 generative words has never been suggested by anyone in my workshops.

Illegal Aliens versus Revolutionary Educators

If the Cobden glossaries do belong to a genre with which Freirean discourse has a "preferred relationship,"[44] it does not necessarily follow that they are best interpreted as Freirean codifications. For I find that in addition to the terminological contradictions in the discourse of Freirean ESL teachers, which make it difficult to regard Jacinto as potentially their educator, and in addition to their lack of a discourse on letters and sounds, which makes it difficult to interpret Jacinto's hybrid alphabet as a code that captures some of the phonetic richness of the phonemic families of English, there is a third obstacle to interpreting Jacinto's *diccionario* as a genuinely Freirean "codification," namely the principle,

---

39. Cf. my remarks above on hybrid phonemes.
40. For an example of this from Cobden, see QUITELATEQUI in Kalmar (1983: 21–23).
41. Freire (1965, 1983: 82).
42. Freire in Davis (1970), reprinted in Mackie (1981: 64).
43. For example, Kozol (1981), and his preface to Mackie (1981).
44. See above, p. 58.

fundamental to Freirean praxis, that valid "codifications" are created not by the oppressed themselves, but by their "revolutionary educators."

In Freirean discourse, "codification" is a technical term. It means "intelligently conceived and executed anthropological research on the objective situation and the phenomenal world of the illiterate group being worked with."[45] The question is: Who conceives and executes the research—the educators or the educatees?

To illustrate this third contradiction, and the way it interacts with the first two, I conclude this chapter by looking closely at the place that Nina Wallerstein found in 1983 for her interpretation of the Cobden glossaries in her ground-breaking book, *Language and Culture in Conflict: Problem-Posing in the ESL Classroom.* Three considerations motivate my choice of this approach. First, Wallerstein's book broke new ground by offering a practical resource guide, written in plain English free of Freirean jargon, to ESL teachers seeking to convert from the "banking" model of education to the "dialogue" model. Second, hers is the only published interpretation of the case of the Cobden glossaries. Third, the question of "whether students should be allowed to speak their native language in the classroom"[46] occupies less than two pages in her book: the case of the Cobden glossaries is the only example she gives to illustrate this "controversial subject."

V

Wallerstein on the Case of the Cobden Glossaries

Wallerstein's book is in two parts. The first part introduces basic principles and techniques of Freirean pedagogy as a problem-posing method that can be used in the ESL classroom. The second part, the bulk of the book, "translates the problem-posing method and teaching techniques into eight curriculum units which may serve as examples for teachers interested in this approach."[47] Each unit is made up of eight "codes"—Wallerstein's shorthand term for Freirean "codifications."

In a Freirean ESL classroom, the task of the students is to decode what the teacher has coded: their own cultural conflicts, social needs, fears, and hopes. Students dialogue with one another and with the teacher *in English* about what they see and recognize in stories, fictional dialogues, and pictures that portray their own problematic situations. In a "banking" model, ESL students memorize and recite formulaic speech. In a "dialogue" model, ESL students are not drilled

---

45. Stanley (1972: 64), quoted in Connolly (1981: 76).
46. Wallerstein (1983: 37).
47. Wallerstein (1983: 45). The eight units are on the themes of Autobiography, The Family, Culture and Conflict, Neighborhoods, Immigration, Health, Work, and Money.

by the teacher. They speak up in their own voice. Their dialogue and their speech, although in a tongue alien to them, is authentic in the existential sense of the term. And dialogue, says Freire, is an existential necessity.[48] "Speaking a true word" is more important than saying it correctly.[49]

In the first part of her book, Wallerstein explains how teachers can make and use codes. The problem-posing teacher puts conflicts—"the difficulties students have in living in the U.S., their feelings of vulnerability, and their desire to learn English while maintaining their own culture"—at the center of the ESL curriculum.[50]

> Problem-posing . . . begins by listening for students' issues. Based on the listening, teachers then select and present the familiar situations back to the students in a codified form: a photograph, a written dialogue, a story, or a drawing. Each situation contains personal and social conflicts which are emotionally charged for students. Teachers ask a series of inductive questions which move the discussion of the situation from the concrete to a more analytical level. The problem-posing process directs students to name the problem [in English], understand how it applies to them, determine the causes of the problem, generalize to others, and finally, suggest alternatives or solutions to the problem.[51]

Here is how Wallerstein introduces the idea and value of "codes":

> After teachers listen to the concerns of their students and select a theme or a series of problems, they draw up lessons in the form of codes to stimulate problem-posing. Codes (or "codifications" in Freire's terms) are concrete physical expressions that combine all the elements of the theme into one representation. They can take many forms: photographs, drawings, collages, stories, written dialogues, movies, songs. Codes are more than visual aids for teaching. They are at the heart of the educational process because they initiate critical thinking.
>
> No matter what the form, a code is a projective device that is emotionally laden and identifiable to students. Discussion of the problem will liberate energy that can stimulate creativity and raise motivation for using English . . .[52]

---

48. Freire (1971: 77).
49. "To speak a true word is to transform the world" (Freire 1971: 75). Freire here draws on Christian existentialism, especially as developed by Gabriel Marcel—see Mackie (1981: 115).
50. Wallerstein (1983: 10).
51. Wallerstein (1983: 17).
52. Wallerstein (1983: 20).

Note that Wallerstein does not include a *list of generative words* as a genre or form that a "code" can take. This is surely due to her assumption, widely shared by other English-speaking Freireans, that "Freire's phonetic literacy method is not directly applicable to the United States."[53]

Of particular relevance to the case of the Cobden glossaries is Wallerstein's choice of an example of the sort of problematic situation that can and should be coded:

> For example, students often have difficulty not being understood and not understanding English-speakers. This problem can be codified [by the teacher] into many situations . . . After codifying the problem, teachers present the code and use the inductive questioning process to "decode" the problem.[54]

Like the progressive ESL teachers in my workshops, Wallerstein feels that "unfortunately, much of traditional ESL instruction ignores students' bilingual/bicultural identities."[55] Throughout her book, she pays close attention to the *bicultural* dimensions of the problematic situations in which ESL students find themselves. But she gives only marginal attention to the *bilingual* dimensions of these problematic situations. Like her less liberal ESL colleagues, she seems to take it for granted that teachers are responsible for helping students keep their languages apart. She overlooks the possibility of coding ordinary hybrid situations in which people are themselves coding and decoding two different languages at the same time.

This may be why, in her otherwise excellent chapter on teaching techniques, she gives only three paragraphs to the topic of "Foreign language in the classroom." The first paragraph begins, "Whether students should be allowed to speak their native language in the classroom is the subject of much controversy . . ."[56] Wallerstein expresses sympathy for teachers who "create a supportive, non-stressful atmosphere" by "*allowing* students to translate and explain meanings to each other."[57] But she does not identify the controversy as part of a larger problem confronting immigrants in the United States, where teachers are by no means the only people who claim the authority to decide when and where immigrants can or cannot speak what languages. This politically and ideologically charged problem certainly "contains personal and social conflicts which are emotionally charged for students."

---

53. Wallerstein (1983: 12). Cf. above, pp. 70–71.
54. Wallerstein (1983: 20).
55. Wallerstein (1983: 9).
56. Wallerstein (1983: 37).
57. Wallerstein (1983: 37), my emphasis.

The situation in Cobden was the inverse of that in the ESL classroom. In Cobden, the subject of controversy was not whether Mexicans should be "allowed" to speak to one another in Spanish: it was whether they should be "allowed" to speak to the locals in English.[58]

Wallerstein ends her brief section on this controversial subject by remarking that "teachers with bilingual abilities also affirm the validity of bicultural/bilingual communities in the United States."[59] And it is to illustrate this point that she chooses to insert her version of the case of the Cobden glossaries, which I reproduce here in its entirety:

Bilingual Literacy

One bilingual literacy method enables students to begin writing "English" without knowing how to spell. Speakers of Spanish (and other phonetic languages) often have difficulty writing, spelling, and even pronouncing English. Teachers therefore may often wonder what students are trying to say or write. Many times students want to know the meaning of an English expression, but teachers can't understand them enough to respond.

One Illinois teacher, Tomás Kalmar, began to solve this problem by asking his Spanish-speaking students to write down the expressions they heard—as they heard them. Students responded, writing in Spanish phonetics: "Urrillap," and "Juaruyusei?" [sic] Another student wanted to know: "Limisi." And another "Jamach?" These expressions translated into the English: (1) "Hurry up." (2) "How do you say?" (3) "Let me see." and (4) "How much?" Though the correct English spelling was very different, spelling the words in "eye dialect" made them accessible. This technique excited students to learn as they eagerly compiled a daily dictionary of phrases they wanted to know.

Although the underlying linguistic assumptions for this new method are not clear yet, teachers can experiment with its effectiveness in their own classrooms. This method works from two different angles.

In the first approach, students write down the English expressions they have heard (as they've heard them) in a column in the middle of the board. Then the teacher determines the meaning of the eye dialect (or phonetic spelling) and writes the correct English words in a left-hand column and the Spanish translations on the right. The second angle is for students to start from the Spanish words they want to learn. After they write the Spanish, the teacher tells them the English and asks them to write the words as they phonetically hear the sounds. The teacher will then transpose the words into correct English spelling.

---

58. And I was perceived—for example, by the Chief of Police, p. 8, above—as "allowing" them to do so, because I didn't exercise my authority *as a teacher* to forbid them.

59. Wallerstein (1983: 37).

If this technique is incorporated into every class period for a short time, different students can record the three-column list for the whole class. The teacher can xerox and hand back the list to all students for a class dictionary.

One class wrote these phrases: (Read the middle column first.)

I need	ai nid	necesito
truth	chrud	la verdad
where's he from?	uers ji from?	de donde viene el
how old are you?	ja oldayu?	cuantos años tienes
I'll be back	avivac	ahorita regreso

With this method, the words that students learn are not memorized nonsensical sounds from a text or a teacher. Instead, the learning begins and ends with students' naming the words they want to know and the reality they want to understand.[60]

The following commentary on the contrast between Wallerstein's imagined situation and the actual situation in Cobden is in no way meant to imply a negative judgment on any other part of her excellent and rightly respected book. On the contrary, it is precisely the virtues of her book in other respects that make her (mis)reading of the Cobden glossaries so interesting. The *only* example of a "bilingual literacy method" provided even by Nina Wallerstein is—as my commentary shows—incompatible with the discourse and practice of the ESL classroom: this contradiction can itself be interpreted as one illustration of the marginal status assigned to adult biliteracy by educators in the United States today.

1. Actual versus Imagined Context

Wallerstein imagines a context in which the Cobden texts can make sense to ESL teachers. She imagines a situation—a game, a discourse, a scene of writing—that contrasts with the actual situation in Cobden described in my first two chapters. This contrast between the imagined and the actual situation is worth considering in detail for the light it throws on issues raised in this chapter.

Like the ESL teachers in my workshops, Wallerstein envisions a *generic* ESL classroom as the scene of writing for the Cobden texts. By *generic*, I mean replicable, hence fundable. "The" ESL classroom is a classroom acceptable to local, state and national agencies that fund adult education. (Wallerstein's own Freirean classroom closed down when the public funds ran out; proposals to refund it

---

60. Wallerstein (1983: 37–38).

were rejected.)[61] In such classrooms, the question is not whether to "allow" illegal aliens to speak in their own tongue rather than in English: the controversial question is whether to let them speak at all, whether to even let them walk into the classroom. If they are present, then the classroom is itself "illegal" and everyone connected with it is in, at best, a dubious relation with the law.[62] The law itself poses a major part of the problem to be solved. From the viewpoint of people like the authors of the Cobden glossaries, the problem with *the* ESL classroom is precisely the legitimacy implied by the definite article.

The hybrid writing system developed in Cobden looks the way it does precisely because it constitutes a solution to a problem posed by adults reasoning with one another in the institutional no man's land between two legal systems, two economies, two sovereign states, two languages, and, ultimately, between two institutionalized forms of alphabetic literacy. As I discuss in my next chapter, such a situation is naturally open to various ways of writing a language. Back in *the* ESL classroom, however, "How shall I write this language?" is not a true question: the answer is always already given.

2. Teacher versus Student

Like the ESL teachers in my workshops, Wallerstein casts the authors of the Cobden glossaries in the role of ESL students, and me in the role of their ESL teacher. She characterizes their game of letters and sounds as a "bilingual literacy method" and attributes its invention not to them in their imagined role as "students," but to me in my imagined role as "teacher." This "new method" is described as solving a problem often encountered by ESL teachers. The problem is that "*teachers* . . . may often wonder what *students* are trying to say or write." (As the Mayor of Cobden put it, "The problem is, we don't know how to communicate.")[63] This is the inverse of the problem *immigrants* have understanding *native English speakers* (including, presumably, their monolingual teachers), which earlier in her book she chose as an example of the sort of situation that can and should be codified by a Freirean teacher (see above, p. 73). But now Wallerstein describes the *students* as posing the problem and the *teacher* as coming up with a solution: "One teacher began to solve this problem . . ."

The solution proposed by the teacher is to play a kind of game in which students pose puzzles for the teacher to solve. Wallerstein describes two ways of playing this game. One way begins with a student offering the teacher an English phrase coded in what Wallerstein calls "eye dialect" or "Spanish phonetics": the teacher decodes the phrase by: (a) rewriting it in correct English spelling; and (b) writing a Spanish gloss. The other way begins with the student coding Spanish:

---

61. See Wallerstein's Preface, last paragraph.
62. Cf. above, pp. 12–14.
63. See p. 47, above.

the (bilingual) teacher translates from *written* Spanish into *spoken* English: the students code the English speech-sounds: the teacher recodes correctly what the students have coded incorrectly.

The exercise of power that Wallerstein distributes between the roles of teacher and student was not hierarchically divided in Cobden. The authors of the Cobden glossaries coded English and glossed it in Spanish themselves, sometimes collectively, sometimes as individuals "playing solo."[64] Only one of them, Alfonso, added glosses in correct English spelling, and he is the exception[65] that proves the rule: the whole point of the exercise, as conceived and executed by the Mexicans in Cobden, was precisely to ignore la escritura de inglés, the correct spelling with which, in Wallerstein's version, the teacher completes—and justifies—the "method."

3. Lost in Translation: A Discourse on Letters and Sounds

Consequently, in Wallerstein's classroom game, the values that letters can take are not negotiable. Teachers and students in a classroom are confined to a scene of writing that does not permit the hybridization of an alphabet. Even Freirean teachers committed to changing the oppressive structures of society tend to draw the line at changing the structures of the alphabet. Thus, the *abecedario* of English does not, in Wallerstein's classroom, become a topic in a discourse on letters and sounds. There is no room for strategic play. Since no one evaluates the accuracy of the codifications, no one discusses which of various strategic moves in the game is best and why. No one *votes*. Crucial to the development of the game as played in Cobden was the cumulative choice by majority vote of the "best" way of coding English, word by word, sound by sound, letter by letter.[66] Paradoxically, this democratic dimension is missing from Wallerstein's "Freirean" version of the game.

Wallerstein's way of talking about the linguistic details of the Cobden "method" is good enough for her purposes. Like the ESL teachers in my workshops, she refers loosely to Spanish as a "phonetic language." What I call a "hybrid alphabet" she calls "Spanish phonetics" and "eye dialect." From her point of view, what students write this way is not really English. The four examples[67] she gives in her second paragraph still need to be "translated," by the teacher, "into English."

---

64. See p. 43, above.
65. On Alfonso, see above, pp. 20, 53–54.
66. See above, pp. 20–23.
67. The sources of her four examples are as follows:

URRILLAP   This was written by Alfonso (p. 52 #14).
JUARUYUSEI   If Wallerstein's "translation" is right ("How do you say?"), this looks like a misprint for JAURUYUSEI. But maybe Wallerstein misread or miscopied Jacinto's (unaspirated) GUARIYUSEI (= *waddayasay*) (p. 51 #7).

Her linguistic terminology (like that of the ESL teachers in my workshops) is too loose to capture the precise details that so engaged the attention of the men who wrote the *diccionarios*. In her classroom game, there is no need to work out collective answers to the kinds of questions I listed at the beginning of Chapter 2:

> Is this one sound or two? Are these two sounds the same or different? If I let this letter stand for this sound here, can I let it stand for a different sound there? Must the value of a letter be fixed, or can it vary on a "sliding scale"? What if my answers to these questions differ from yours? Can we read each other's transcriptions? If I let this letter stand for this sound, can you let it stand for a different sound? How do these puzzles interconnect? Are we making moves in the same game? Or are we playing different games?

Overlooking the details that could be supplied only by an adequate discourse on letters and sounds, Wallerstein remarks that the underlying linguistic assumptions for this "new method" are not clear yet. This remark can be taken with a grain of salt. Although the game played with letters and sounds in Cobden seems new to ESL teachers in the United States, we have seen above that it is, in reality, at least as old as the ninth-century Kassel glossaries. In my next chapter, I argue that outside the United States, its underlying linguistic assumptions have been spelled out in detail in the discourse and practice of professional linguists, Christian missionaries, and revolutionary educators. And in the Epilogue, I wonder whether the game is as old as the alphabet itself.

Footnote 67 continued—

LIMISI	By Jacinto (p. 51 #5), first written on the palm of his hand while picking peaches (see p. 35).
JAMACH	By Cipriano (p. 51 #8). The first half of JAMACH DU YOU ORN (= *how much do you earn?*).

For the sake of completeness, I offer the following comments on the sources of the items, which she says (in her second-last paragraph) were written by "one class":

AI NID	By Cipriano (p. 53 #10). The first half of AI NID SAM ER (= *I need some air*).
CHRUD	By Alfonso, who actually wrote CHT RUD (p. 52, #16, see p. 53). Alfonso also wrote TRUTH and VERDAD (not LA VERDAD).
UERS JI FROM? and JA OLDAYU?	Not (as far as I know) from Cobden. Perhaps from one of Wallerstein's actual classes.
AVIVAC	By Jacinto (p. 51 #1). This is actually a double pun comparable to DOLOR and DATSUN (see above, p. 37). It is a portmanteau word made up of the two Spanish words, AVIVA "quicken" and VIVAC, "bivouac." (Calling it "eye dialect" certainly misses the witty pun.)

Who Codifies: The Educator or the Educatee?

As understood by Wallerstein, the Freirean educator creates appropriate codifications by leaving the classroom and entering the community to do fieldwork, until he/she understands the problems the community is facing. This phase casts the teacher in the role of anthropological fieldworker and the students in the role of native informants. Back in the classroom, the teacher translates these problems into English. Translation into English is central to Wallerstein's version of Freire's "codification" stage. For the ESL classroom, to translate into English *is* to codify. Back in the classroom, the "native informants," who posed the problem for themselves in the community by speaking freely in whatever language *or mixture of languages* they preferred, are cast into the role of students dialoguing with the teacher about their own problems—*in English.*

In Cobden, however, the "intelligently conceived and executed"[68] linguistic fieldwork was carried out by those whom Wallerstein perceives as "students," while the role of "native informants" was played by monolingual English-speaking locals (who would never enroll in an ESL class). The hierarchical relationship between fieldworker and informant in Wallerstein's imagined situation *inverts* that of the actual situation in Cobden. In my next chapter, I argue that the Cobden glossaries are best interpreted as field notes made by Mexicans-as-fieldworkers recording the speech of US-citizens-as-native-informants.

The Price of Legitimacy

At best, Wallerstein's imagined classroom exercise merely *simulates* the process that actually produced the Cobden glossaries in the first place. In order to legitimize this process, she imagines an institutional, that is to say legal, context. As Halliday and Hasan put it:

> For any "text" in school—teacher talk in the classroom, pupil's notes or essay, passages from a textbook—there is always a context of situation: the lesson, with its concept of what is to be achieved; the relationship of teacher to pupil, or textbook writer to reader; the "mode" of question-and-answer, expository writing, and so on. But these in turn are instances of, and derive their meaning from, the school as an institution in the culture: the concept of education, and of educational knowledge as distinct from commonsense knowledge; the notion of the curriculum and of school "subjects" [including ESL], the complex role structures of teaching staff, school principals, consultants, inspectorate, departments of education, and the like; and the unspoken assumptions about learning and the place of language within it.[69]

---

68. Cf. Stanley quote above, p. 72, n. 45.
69. Halliday and Hasan (1989: 46).

This contrasts with the actual situation in Cobden, which had no public funding, no teachers, no students, no classroom, no schedule, no curriculum, no books, no equipment, no material resources, and, above all, no legitimacy.

Misrepresenting the social situation, Wallerstein misrepresents the genre of the Cobden glossaries as student exercises subject to teacherly correction. So she misunderstands the texts produced by Jacinto, Cipriano, Alfonso, and their companions. Hence, she misunderstands the isolated words and sentences. Consequently, she misreads the isolated letters and sounds. She gives the letters the values of Spanish phonemes (which she calls "Spanish phonetics"). But, as I have shown above, those who chose these letters gave them the values of English speech-sounds, thereby creating what I called a hybrid alphabet. To be misread as "merely" a Spanish alphabet may be the price this hybrid alphabet must pay for legitimate entry into the ESL classroom. The game as actually played in Cobden seems to be incompatible with the discourse and classroom practice of even Freirean ESL teachers, let alone "mainstream" monolingual educators.

VI

Conclusion

The Cobden glossaries record moves made in a game that is unfamiliar to many monolingual North Americans. Like participants in my workshops, Wallerstein interprets the use of a hybrid alphabet to code two languages as "a new method." But we have seen above that in the real world, outside the classroom, it is at least 1,000 years old. In the next chapter, I argue that although the Cobden "method"—the game, the discourse, the scene of writing—is unknown to educational discourse in the United States, it nevertheless has a long and sometimes illustrious history outside the United States, especially in Mexico. The case of the Cobden glossaries is best interpreted, I claim, as one more chapter in that forgotten history.

4

MAKING IT LEGAL

The Social Construction of Hybrid Alphabets

> One must have a "sliding scale," a small flexible alphabet
> whose letters in one language represent sounds of one
> shade, but in another a different, though similar sound.
> —Pike[1]

The Mexicans in Cobden who made up their own hybrid alphabet did so as a means to an end: to produce records of bits of English the way it really sounds. These records were in turn a means to a further end: to improve communication with the local residents by mastering the (local) pronunciation of spoken English in general, or, as they put it, by learning the *abecedario* of English, the (finite) set of English speech-sounds. At first, the Mexicans recorded phrases that they had already learned by ear, by heart, or, as they put it, *líricamente*. At the meeting in the Village Hall, they took a further step: creating glossaries which absent companions, unable to attend the meetings in Cobden, could read aloud "at sight" and be understood by local monolingual Anglos.

I claim that, in this regard, they were behaving like fieldworkers jotting down initial scratch notes of a hitherto unwritten language the way it sounds, and that the Cobden *diccionarios* are best interpreted as belonging to a genre of *field notes* (as distinct from, say, a genre of student exercises—see Chapter 3). In this chapter, I offer support for this claim and speculate on the crucial role played by hybrid "field alphabets" in the initial creation of alphabetic writing systems for unwritten languages, not only today, but whenever any alphabet crossed a border between one language and another, throughout the long history of alphabetic literacy.

---

1. Pike (1938: 86).

My aim here is to suggest why hybrid alphabets and bilingual glossaries of the sort produced in Cobden merit serious theoretical and socio-historical study. Hybrid alphabets have been produced in many situations other than the one described in Chapters 1 and 2. Often, they were merely means to an immediate end, comparable to that of the Mexicans in Cobden: to begin communicating with natives in a local lingo. Sometimes, the goal was more long-range: to produce "a discrete textual corpus constituting a raw, or partly cooked, descriptive database for later generalization, synthesis and theoretical elaboration."[2] Linguistic fieldworkers primarily interested in "writing up" the phonological structure of a hitherto unstudied language rewrite their initial field glossaries over and over, as they figure out the unique structure of the language in question, including, of course, its phonemic system, its *abecedario*. What they write down in the field, they write up in the study. "The image of transcription (of writing over) interrupts the smooth passage from writing down to writing up."[3] But when they first write a language down, the values they give to letters in their field notes make up a hybrid code that is inevitably, as I will argue below, impressionistic, ad hoc, or just plain messy. Writing up a bilingual glossary entails "purifying" a hybrid field-alphabet.

Christian missionaries now do the same: they too phonemicize their hybrid field-alphabets. But their final goal is to produce a practical (rather than a "merely" scientific) writing system: a standardized *orthography* which, they hope, will actually be used by the natives themselves, to read the scriptures translated into that language and written in that orthography. Since 1934, for example, missionaries trained by the Summer Institute of Linguistics have designed over 1,200 orthographies for hitherto unwritten indigenous languages[4] (of which one of the first, incidentally, was Tarascan); all of these, as I argue below, began as impressionistic hybrid field-alphabets, were then "scientifically" purified, and were finally *rehybridized* so as to maximize their chance of being adopted by natives with a strong interest in becoming *biliterate*—literate not just in their native tongue, but also in the standard orthography of the high-prestige national, trade, or colonial language of their region.

We've seen in Chapter 3 that there are contexts, especially the classroom, in which a biliterate glossary written in a hybrid alphabet doesn't make sense and lacks legitimacy. But there have been many other contexts in which this genre does make sense and does gain recognition and legitimacy from professional discourses, social practices, and "scenes of writing" institutionalized by the State, the Church, and the Academy. In this chapter, I compare and contrast some of these cases to explore perspectives offered by socio-historical study of variations

---

2. Clifford (1990: 52), see above, p. 46.
3. Clifford (1990: 57–58).
4. Robbin (1992: xii).

on the theme represented by the case of the Cobden glossaries. This exploration of the social construction of bilingual glossaries and hybrid alphabets in theory and practice, out in the field and back in the study, suggests ways of looking at the Cobden glossaries in particular as a *case*, as something more than a mere curiosity of trivial value.

I

Strictly Speaking: Emic *versus* Etic

Crucial to the logic of my argument is the claim that the formal structure of the game played with letters and sounds by (amateur or professional) linguists compiling their first glossaries in a "field-language" is the same as that of the game recorded in the Cobden glossaries. At the heart of the game recorded in the Cobden glossaries was the decision to let a single letter of the alphabet take the value of two sounds, one in Spanish and the other in English. In my schematic algorithm, I represented this as the second and third steps of a "move":

2. Given a unit [x] in language A, find a unit [y] in language B that "sounds like" [x].
3. Given a letter ʏ that takes the value [y] in B, let ʏ take the value [x] in A. Look at ʏ and say [x].[5]

Each such move recorded a decision to trade linguistic values between two speech communities, so as to let one alphabet code the speech of both communities: each such trade-off creates what I called[6] a *hybrid phoneme*, a family of sounds some of whose members belong to one "kinship structure," some another.

However, as I mentioned when I introduced the term *hybrid alphabet*,[7] "strictly speaking, the sound patterns of two different languages are structurally incommensurate" and therefore "what is impossible in pure theory becomes possible in practice only by 'fudging' the application of the code's basic ground rule: one letter, one sound." To explain precisely what I mean by the formal structure of the game that creates hybrid alphabets and hybrid phonemes, I must clarify this paradox, this contradiction between what is impossible in theory and what, as we shall see below, people nevertheless do whenever they use the letters of one alphabet to simultaneously code the sound patterns of two different languages the way both "really sound."

The crux of the matter is that strictly speaking, that is to say within the theoretical discourse of professional twentieth-century linguistics, step 2 of the

---

5. See pp. 37, 41, above.
6. See p. 41, above.
7. See p. 36, above.

algorithm is inadmissible, not a "legal" move. Given a single sound [x] in one language A, there is, as a rule, *no* [y] in another language B which is *really* the same as [x] in A. Sometimes, one can find a [y] in B that is the same as [x] from an etic point of view, but then it is not the same from an emic point of view. And vice versa. Strictly speaking, anyone who looks at ʏ and says [x] is "cheating."

This important principle can fairly be regarded as a fundamental theorem of twentieth-century structural linguistics. It is not usually regarded as a "self-evident truth" or axiom. Since the 1930s, an understanding of this theorem and its implications has distinguished linguists from non-linguists, and scientific from non-scientific linguists. The theorem was first proved with mathematical rigor by Sapir in his classic paper "Sound patterns in language," published in 1925 in the inaugural issue of *Language*, the house organ of the newly founded professional association, the Linguistic Society of America.[8] To facilitate comparison with my algorithm, I present Sapir's proof in schematic form.

Pick two languages "at random." Call them X and Y. Let /x/ be "one sound" in X; that is to say let /x/ be a family of sounds, perceived by monoglot native speakers of X as sharing a family resemblance and functioning as a psychological (emic) unit.

To prove that, as a rule, monoglot native speakers of Y may not perceive /x/ as being a single family, according to the "kinship rules" recognized by speakers of Y, and that therefore they can *not* find "one sound" /y/ in Y that is the same as /x/ in X, Sapir constructs two extreme cases or "ideal types." First, he lays out in detail the sound patterns of two imagined languages A and B which use exactly the same sounds (i.e., allophones) but group them in families according to totally incompatible "kinship" rules. A and B are phonetically isomorphic: given any sound [x] in A, there is (always) a sound [y] in B such that [x] = [y]. But they are phonemically incommensurate. Given any /x/ in A and any /y/ in B, /x/ $\neq$ /y/. That is to say, A and B have no "family of sounds" in common: given *any* phoneme /x/ in A there is (thanks to Sapir's ingenious construction) *no* phoneme /y/ in B such that /x/ = /y/. Then he imagines two languages C and D that are at the other extreme. From an emic point of view, they are isomorphic. Given any /x/ in C, there is always a /y/ in D such that /x/ = /y/. The "kinship rules" by which C and D group sounds into families are identical.[9] But from an etic point of view, they have not a single sound (allophone) in

---

8. And often reprinted (e.g., in Sapir 1949 and in Joos 1958). "After the founding of the Linguistic Society of America in 1925, anthropological linguistics took its place within a broader community of scholars committed to the 'science of language' as the connecting link between the natural and the human sciences" (Stocking 1976: 27).

9. "If we allowed ourselves to speculate generally, we might suspect, on general principles, that the phonetic similarities between A and B, which we will suppose to be contiguous languages, are due to historical contact, but that the deeper pattern of resemblance between C and D is an index of genetic relationship" (Sapir 1925, cited in Joos 1958: 23).

common. *No* individual member [x] of a family of sounds /x/ in *C* is identical to *any* individual member [y] of a family of sounds /y/ in *D*. Since any two *actual* languages *X* and *Y* chosen at random will fall somewhere between these two *imagined* extremes, the theorem follows.

The implications of this theorem for the explorations I pursue in this chapter are as follows. Anyone claiming to have written a language the way it sounds must choose between an emic and an etic version of the claim.[10] A transcription system may claim to represent the way the language sounds to an insider (i.e., to a native speaker). Or it may claim to represent the way the language sounds to an outsider (e.g., to a scientifically trained phonetician who deliberately ignores the "family resemblances" that make speakers of the language perceive two objectively different sounds as being subjectively "the same sound"). But if a single notation system claims both emic and etic validity at the same time, it becomes, from a scientific point of view, impure (i.e., theoretically invalid). A scientifically accurate writing system must be *either* consistently phonetic *or* consistently phonemic: it cannot inadvertently mix both levels without damaging its claims to interpretive and theoretical validity.

It follows that whenever one *alfabeto* is used to code two *abecedarios* simultaneously, in other words whenever one transcription system is used for two languages at the same time, symbols in that system must be used as "a kind of algebraic notation"[11] taking *variable* values that cannot be restricted to pure phonemes as *constants*. This inevitably results in a hybrid code that fails to chart the (theoretically) true structures of both languages. Letting a hybrid phoneme count as one eligible sound, fit to be "taken" by a single symbol (e.g., a letter of an alphabet) inevitably means mixing etic and emic levels of analysis. Hence, hybrid alphabets that mix sounds from two different languages must also mix etic and emic representations of the sounds in question.[12]

---

10. Headland, Pike, and Harris (1990). When Kenneth Pike (1982: 27) "extended the terms *phonemic* and *phonetic* to behavior as a whole by dropping the *phon-* (implying pronunciation) and using only their endings *emic* and *etic*," he claimed—rightly, I believe—to be a faithful disciple of Sapir's teachings. Pike regarded Sapir's 1925 proof that "two languages might have identical etic systems but different emic ones" as "the source of the basic understanding in the linguistic field of the systematic relations of emic units, and of the nature of emic systems as such" (Pike 1967: 53). Early in his *magnum opus* on Tagmemics, *Language in Relation to a Unified Theory of the Structure of Human Behavior*, Pike presents and discusses in etic and emic terminology the phonology of (an improved version of) Sapir's imagined languages *A* and *B* (pp. 49–50). On the importance of Pike's initiatory experiences as a fieldworker in Mexico in 1936 transcribing Mixtec from scratch by the seat of his pants, see Pike (1967: 34; 1981: 181–182), and p. 109, below.

11. See above, p. 41, n. 14.

12. This was made clear by Einar Haugen in his review of Weinreich's *Languages in Contact*. Weinreich maintained that, for example, "Russian /p/ cannot be regarded in principle as being the 'same' as English /p/, since they are parts of different structures. As structural units they are incommensurable, but in spite of this the bilingual [including the theoretician and the

The linguistic assumptions implicit in the construction of any hybrid alphabet (including the one developed in Cobden) are therefore more complicated than might appear at first sight. To spell them out in detail seems a fruitful area for serious theoretical work. The above observations may be enough to make clear what I mean by saying that whenever a person or group of people modify a pre-existing alphabetic writing system to code the sound patterns of a hitherto uncoded language by "fudging" Sapir's theorem (i.e., by taking the "illegal" steps numbered 2 and 3 in my algorithm), they are "playing the same game" as that recorded in the Cobden glossaries.

The irony is that even professional linguists play the same game. They, too, "fudge." They don't practice what they preach. They don't, that is to say, find it "necessary to have different symbols for *each new language*."[13] In theory, each phoneme *in each language* should have its own unique symbol: for example, "the English voiceless labial stop [should] be written differently from that of French."[14] In practice, of course, it is not. This creates no contradiction as long as the "universe of discourse is limited to one dialect or one language"[15] at a time, which it usually is. But when the universe of discourse is extended to more than one language at a time, linguists resort, willy-nilly, to letting letters of an alphabet take the values of historically determined "generic phonemes," most of which are, in the final analysis, hybrid phonemes of what Whorf called Standard Average European.[16] This contradiction between theory and practice was candidly explicated by Chao in his classic 1934 paper on the non-uniqueness of phonemic solutions to phonetic systems:

> All this points to a conception which seems to be assumed by many, that there are such things as phonemes in general, apart from reference to any

---

Footnote 12 continued—

fieldworker] identifies them 'astride the limits of the languages' because they have a 'physical resemblance.' In Copenhagen [Hjelmslev] terms, it is their [etic] substance that is identified, and only indirectly their 'real' or structural [emic] selves. But if this be true," wrote Haugen, "it is the [etic] substance and not the [emic] structure that should be compared" (Haugen 1954: 243ff.).

Throughout his distinguished career, Haugen was a phonetic realist who objected to trimming phonetic facts to suit phonemic patterns (Haugen 1942: 97). In a series of papers read and published between 1950 and 1957, he urged his professional colleagues to make room for a discourse (which he called *dialinguistics*) on the topic of hybrid phonemes, which he called *diaphones* (see p. 40, n. 11, above). Haugen chose the term *diaphone*, rather than *diaphoneme*, precisely to draw attention to the need to include what he called this "third dimension" (Haugen 1972b: 331ff) in the transcription, description, and analysis of bilingual speech. See also Haugen (1950, 1951, 1954b, 1955, 1956, 1972b), and cf. p. 120, below.

13. Swadesh (1934), cited in Joos (1958: 36), my emphases.

14. Swadesh (1934), cited in Joos (1958: 36), my emphases.

15. Chao (1934), cited in Joos (1958: 42). The arguments laid out in Chao's classic, and oft-reprinted, paper are central to the issues I touch on in this chapter.

16. IPA's Eurocentric values were astutely analyzed in Entwistle (1953: 118–121).

particular language, and that all we need to do either for the study of one language or for comparative work is to use one consistent phonemic transcription for all languages. This would of course be recognized by anyone as an impossible illusion as soon as the situation is thus made explicit, as we may be called upon at any time to make phonemic distinctions between shades of sounds whose differentiation we never anticipated in either our narrow or broad system of phonetic symbols [i.e., in either our etic or emic alphabetic writing system]. The idea of general phonemes, which we have just proposed and condemned in the same breath, is therefore not entirely baseless. Without entertaining the idea of general phonemes as such, the writer [*viz.* Chao] wishes to propose the term *typical phoneme*, to be defined as those groups of sounds which very often go together to form phonemes in many of the major languages studied by phoneticians.[17] This definition of course makes the idea of a typical phoneme depend again on historical accident, the fact that most contemporary phoneticians are speakers of the Germanic and Romance languages. The troublesome part of the transcription problem comes from the inconsistency in using the same symbol sometimes in a general and sometimes in a particular sense.[18]

This interesting contradiction between the way it is and the way it's supposed to be, between the game linguists actually play with letters and sounds and the ideal types of notation systems represented in their theoretical discourse, suggests the need for socio-historical study of "in-house" controversies over the legitimacy of "technographies"[19] (i.e., of the social construction of professional transcription-systems used by linguists from Sweet and the International Phonetic Association, *via* Boas, Sapir, Swadesh, to the present).[20] For example, disagreements over the values that individual letter shapes may or may not be allowed to take can be interpreted as sites of struggle in the politics of professional identity.[21]

Such a study could take as its point of departure the work of Roy Harris, especially his analysis of contradictions in twentieth-century attitudes to nineteenth-century "scriptism."[22] The similarity between the game played naïvely

17. Note that Chao's data come primarily from "major" (i.e., *not* hitherto unwritten) languages.
18. Chao (1934), cited in Joos (1958: 53).
19. I follow Mountford (1990) on the distinction between technographies and orthographies.
20. See, for example, Boas et al. (1916), Herzog et al. (1934), Swadesh (1934), Haas (1975).
21. For an example, see Entwistle (1953) and Joos (1958) on phonemic discourse as establishing an American *versus* a British professional identity. For a "historical and comparative perspective on the business of phonetic transcriptions," see Pullum and Ladusaw (1986). Their descriptive dictionary of actual usage offers a valuable road-map of some sites of struggle in the history of phonetic symbols "encountered in linguistic writings of all sorts" (xv): they include valuable bibliographic references to professional disagreements over values that a given symbol may or may not take.
22. Harris (1980, 1981, 1986, 1987a, 1987b, 1988), Davis and Taylor (1990).

by the Mexicans in Cobden and that played rigorously by professional linguists is evident in his trenchant critique of the rule of thumb linguists adopt to map the topography of speech:

> The pretence that one is being presented with a description strictly of spoken language begins to wear thin as soon as it occurs to the reader that the real "discovery procedure" being employed is invariably: "*Assume that standard orthography identifies all the relevant distinctions, until you are forced to assume otherwise.*" It is as if the two basic principles of geographical surveying were taken to be (i) that an existing map is always accurate until it is proved inaccurate, and (ii) that no existing map can be totally inaccurate. The consequence of these two principles would be that the surveyor should never start from scratch making a new map of an area already charted, but make only the minimum adjustments to the existing map. This corresponds roughly to *the rule of thumb modern linguistics has adopted, whereby an existing orthographic map is made wherever possible to serve as a guide to the topography of speech.*[23]

II

Writing in the No Man's Land Between Languages

Roy Harris's apt metaphor illuminates every hybrid cross-fertilization in the genealogy of all "actually existing" alphabets, including the field–alphabets created by amateurs and professionals to describe native and exotic languages. The fieldworker brings into the "structural no man's land"[24] between one language and the next a code, a paradigmatic writing system, a *mental chart* of relations between letters and sounds in one or more known languages, and hopes to *transform* this into a *real chart* of the new language. By *collecting, manipulating, and fixing* new data, new sound patterns, a new *abecedario*, the fieldworker *materializes the chart into a diagram, a plan, an exhaustive, synoptic table of cases* in the form of a glossary.[25]

---

23. Harris (1980: 9), my emphasis.
24. Weinreich (1953).
25. The phrases in italics in this paragraph are taken from Malinowski's introduction to his classic 1922 text, *Argonauts of the Western Pacific* (reprinted in 1961, see pp. 6–14). In that introduction, he claimed that it was by living "without other white men, right among the natives" that he was able to find out "where lay the secret of effective field-work ... the ethnographer's magic, by which he is able to evoke the real spirit of the natives, the true picture of tribal life." The passages from which I have borrowed Malinowski's key phrases are as follows: "The collecting of concrete data over a wide range of facts is thus one of the main points of field method. The obligation is not to enumerate a few examples only, but to exhaust as far as possible all the cases within reach; and, on this search for cases, the investigator will score most whose *mental chart* is clearest. But, whenever the material of the search allows it, this *mental*

In the course of preparing this book, I kept imagining in my mind's eye a sort of holy relic: the very first bilingual glossary jotted down by Boas or Sapir or Pike or Malinowski himself on their very first day in the field. What I saw in my imagination looked surprisingly like what I actually saw in the first handwritten glossaries jotted down by Jacinto, Alfonso, Cipriano, and the others in Cobden. It seemed to me that if I could just find in reality what I saw in my imagination, if I could find just one such authentic "first field glossary," I could, at this point in my argument, exhibit a facsimile of it and so clinch my point that even the greatest American linguists initiated their professional careers by playing the same game in the field as the humble, uneducated, illegal aliens in Cobden.

I came to the realization, however, that what I had in mind would not clinch my point. I doubt whether such an ephemeral text has ever been preserved. But the problem is not the difficulty of finding such a relic if it still exists. After all, even the first field glossary of an obscure graduate student would serve, as long as it is his or her very first one, raw, before any *re*-writing. The problem is that only a native speaker of the indigenous language in question well-versed in reading the "queer symbols" and diacritics that I imagine were used by Boas, Sapir, and Pike even in their very first scratch notes—only such a reader, I have come to realize, would "get the joke." No one but such a reader would be analogous to the biliterate Latinos who chuckle when they first set eyes on Jacinto's *diccionario*. At the sight of, say, a P where the literate native speaker expects a Q, who else would laugh—or frown?

Nevertheless, my armchair quest for an imagined relic to place beside the Cobden glossaries was not entirely in vain. It invokes an ephemeral yet foundational scene of writing which lives in legend.

> If "the field" is anthropology's version of both the promised land and an ordeal by fire, then field notes symbolize what journeying to and returning from the field mean to us [professional anthropologists]: the attachment, the identification, the uncertainty, the mystique, and, perhaps above all, the ambivalence.[26]

The classroom is a familiar scene of writing, in some ways all too familiar. The field is the opposite. I have interpreted the scene of writing in Cobden as situated in an "institutional no man's land between two legal systems, two economies, two sovereign states, two languages, and, ultimately, between two institutionalized forms of alphabetic literacy."[27] And those who have written about

---

Footnote 25 continued—

chart ought to be *transformed into a diagram, a plan, an exhaustive, synoptic table of cases*" (Malinowski 1961[1922]: 13–14), my emphases. "Finally, he has to apply a number of special methods of *collecting, manipulating and fixing* his evidence" (Malinowski 1961[1922]: 6), my emphasis.

26. Jackson (1990: 33).

27. See p. 77, above.

the "orders and disorders"[28] of their own fieldwork, not as it is in legend, but as it is actually experienced in real life, often describe themselves as writing in a similar space between the borders of legitimacy. Like "illegal aliens," fieldworkers dwell and write in a liminal space where a bit of paper marked with cryptic symbols can indeed come to resemble a holy relic. In her research on field notes as a symbol of professional identity,[29] Jean Jackson interviewed 70 American anthropologists. "Many speak, usually ironically, about their field notes as *sacred*, *'like a saint's bone.'* Some even volunteer that their field notes are fetishes to them. The legends about lost notes and the frequent theme of burning suggest the presence of a mystique."[30]

> For some reflective types, field notes possess a liminal quality, and strong feelings may result from this alone. Field notes are liminal—betwixt and between—because they are between reality and thesis, between memory and publication, between training and professional life . . . They are a "translation" but are still en route from an internal and other-cultural state to a final destination.[31]

Field notes are "neither discourse nor text."[32] They are between emic and etic, between *como de veras se oye* and how it really sounds, between the insider's point of view and the outsider's. They are—like Panchito's JUELLULIB—means for triggering off memories. Jackson asked a colleague, "Are memories field notes?" and the colleague answered, "*I* am a field note."[33] Jackson comments:

> This interviewee's willingness to state "I am a field note" reflects the shifting, ambiguous status of field notes. At times they are seen as "data"—a record— and at times they are seen as "me." I create them but they also create me; insofar as writing them creates and maintains my identity as a journeyman anthropologist.[34]

"Field notes are liminal" + "I am liminal" = "I am a field note."

Field notes are written at the margins of literacy. The fieldworker, like the Mexican migrant worker in the United States, becomes marginal not only to the institutions back home that legitimized the journey across the border into the alien

---

28. Clifford (1990: 51).
29. First presented at the 84th annual meeting of the American Anthropological Association, Washington, DC, December 4–8, 1985.
30. Jackson (1990: 23), my emphasis.
31. Jackson (1990: 14).
32. Sanjek (1990).
33. Jackson (1990: 21), my emphasis.
34. Jackson (1990: 21–22).

culture, but also alien and marginal to the culture whose language he or she is trying to learn. Fieldworkers are, in a nontrivial sense, "illegal aliens" in their "host" communities. They represent themselves as "marginal natives," "professional strangers," "self-reliant loners," and "self-denying emissaries."[35]

> To do fieldwork apparently requires some of the instincts of an exile, for the fieldworker typically arrives at the place of study without much of an introduction and knowing few people, if any. Fieldworkers, it seems, learn to move among strangers while holding themselves in readiness for episodes of embarrassment, affection, misfortune, partial or vague revelation, deceit, confusion, isolation, warmth, adventure, fear, concealment, pleasure, insult, and always possible deportation.[36]

And it is in this liminal situation that fieldworkers jotting down unknown languages from scratch begin by ignoring Sapir's theorem and playing with the values that letters of an alphabet can take. Like the Mexicans in Cobden, they make up hybrid alphabets recording hybrid phonemes whose legitimacy is limited by the liminal scenes of writing in which they are invented, the ambiguous status of the writers who use them, and the ephemeral lifespan of the field notes in which they are temporarily preserved as strange looking strings of letters.

Preliminary field glossaries, and the hybrid alphabets used to construct them, are therefore very private and intimate, and are normally seen only by those who write them and perhaps a close circle of their trusted companions. They may be valued by their author/owner as priceless and life-preserving—but they are primarily of educational value only to the person who wrote them. For they are written by people who, like the Mexicans in Cobden, are learning, by the seat of their pants, by ear, by hook or by crook, to converse with friendly natives in the local language.

Here is Burling's advice to anyone learning a field language from scratch:

> When you hear a new word in a context that leads you to believe that you know what it means (or when you have what seems to be a reliable translation) jot it down on paper with a rough English equivalent. Spell it as best you can. Use familiar letters for familiar sounds and make up symbols for unfamiliar sounds. You will help yourself if you are reasonably consistent and if you try to use the same symbol for the same sound. However, if you think of your notes not as precise transcriptions, but simply as a means for triggering off memories of what you have heard, then the particular

---

35. Van Maanen (1988: 2), quoting Freilich (1970), Agar (1980), Lofland (1974), and Boon (1982), respectively.
36. Van Maanen (1988: 2).

spelling you choose will not be so important at this stage . . . If you keep
the words on a list [i.e., a glossary] you can also use moments of quiet and
solitude (if your field situation allows such a luxury) to work on them some
more and commit them to memory.[37]

Bilingual glossaries are central to the initial stages of linguistic fieldwork. But,
like any other field notes, they can hardly begin by looking the way they will if
and when they finally appear in print, in public. Confronted with the chaos
of a hitherto unwritten language, a fieldworker who decides not to write any of
it down until *after* he or she has analyzed it will never begin learning the
language.

Granted, the linguistically trained fieldworker brings into the field more letters
and more speech-sounds than the amateur (such as Jacinto). But a larger repertoire
does not change the basic structure of the game; rather, it lets the game be played
with more pieces. It's still the same game: this [x] sounds to me almost like [y],
so just for now I'll write it as ʏ to remind me of the resemblance.

No one's first such transcriptions can be systematic: they are always, to begin
with, impressionistic. *Impressionistic*, as a technical term in the discourse of linguists,
does not mean vague: it means *candid*. The descriptive validity[38] of an impressionistic transcription is not necessarily inferior to that of a systematic transcription.
On the contrary, in initial field glossaries, impressionistic transcriptions offer a
more valid description of what the natives really sound like. Systematic transcriptions, in the initial stages, would prematurely *interpret* the data, would, as it were,
cook it before it had even been gathered "raw."[39] No one, I believe, has put this
more clearly than the British phonetician David Abercrombie:

> An impressionistic transcription is distinguished from what is called a
> *systematic* one. These are the two basic classes into which the many different
> types of phonetic transcription all fall. (This is not the familiar division into
> "broad" and "narrow," which are both varieties of systematic transcrip-
> tions.) In a systematic transcription, the symbols do not symbolize with
> reference to the general human sound-types, but with reference to a par-
> ticular language or form of speech only. The symbols are thus used more
> economically, and the classes of sound they represent are established on
> more complex grounds than phonetic similarity—on *phonemic* grounds, those
> who like to use that term could say.
>
> So anything recorded in phonetic notation is not raw material but
> processed material, processed according to known and easily-formulated
> principles if it is a systematic transcription, but processed in a very individual,

---

37. Burling (1984: 29).
38. On descriptive, interpretive and theoretical validity, I follow Maxwell (1992).
39. "Phonetics gathers raw material. Phonemics cooks it" (Pike 1947: 57).

personal, way if it is an impressionistic one. This must necessarily be so: the categories on which an impressionistic transcription is based are *personal* categories. Since they are established on purely phonetic grounds the boundaries between them are inevitably vague and fluctuating, and each transcriber will make them where his experience, and the degree and nature of his training, dictate.[40]

My imaginary quest for an imagined relic was not in vain, for it led me to the realization that the actual texts displayed in Chapters 1 and 2 are already "relics" of the sort I was imagining: ephemeral texts of a sort rarely seen by more than a few eyes, intimate, impressionistic, personal, private field notes, written in improvised scenes of writing by amateur linguistic fieldworkers, playing the same game with the "fluctuating boundaries" of hybrid phonemes that fieldworkers—novices and seasoned professionals—play when they "fudge" Sapir's theorem by using an existing orthographic map to begin charting the topography of alien, exotic, unintelligible speech.

Although the analogy I hoped to prove may not be clinched without further socio-historical analysis of the bilingual glossary as a genre, the above considerations do confirm that interpreting Jacinto's *diccionario* as a student exercise makes less sense than interpreting it as an "intelligently conceived and executed"[41] synoptic table of cases which transforms a mental chart into a real chart by collecting, manipulating, and fixing raw data.

III

How to Legitimize a Hybrid Alphabet: Three Variations on a Genre

In order to understand more deeply how linguists cope with the illegitimacy of hybrid alphabets, we need to undertake genre studies[42] of the social construction of bilingual glossaries coding two (or more) languages in *systematic* alphabetic writing

---

40. Abercrombie (1967[1954]: 110–111), original emphases.
41. See above, p. 72, 80.
42. The methodological literature on which such genre studies can draw is now large and still growing. For present purposes, a couple of quotations may suffice: "The strategic value of generic concepts for Marxism clearly lies in the mediatory function of the notion of a genre, which allows the coordination of immanent formal analysis of the individual text with the twin diachronic perspective of the history of forms and the evolution of social life" (Jameson 1981: 105). "Genres have specific forms and meanings, deriving from and encoding the functions, purposes and meanings of the social occasions [of which texts are a part]. Genres therefore provide a precise index and catalogue of the relevant social occasions of a community at a given time . . . Texts are given form and meaning by discourse and genre. Nevertheless, texts are the product of individual speakers who, as social agents, are themselves formed in discourses through

systems that are hybrid to a greater or lesser degree than that of the Cobden glossaries, with particular attention to the scenes of writing in which such glossaries have been produced, the discourse on letters and sounds by which their legitimacy has been established, the status of those who have produced them, and the "scenes of reading" in which they have made sense to their readers.

For although, as we saw in Chapter 3, there are educational discourses and practices which have trouble making sense of texts such as the Cobden glossaries, there are nevertheless other discourses that do have a "preferred relationship" with the genre to which the Cobden texts belong, and each of these discourses has its institutional and educational projections. Learning environments that favor the adult use of bilingual glossaries differ from the ESL classrooms familiar in the United States. Comparative case studies of these other learning environments will help us understand the difference.

To motivate the need for such genre criticism, and to suggest what it might reveal, I offer a preliminary, impressionistic, thumbnail sketch of three cases in which biliterate glossaries have been used as a genre: (a) by the U.S. Army to teach soldiers, quickly and cheaply, how to converse in foreign languages without having to master the alien writing systems in which such languages are conventionally written; (b) by universities to teach students of linguistics how to represent the phonology and/or phonemics of *whatever* natural language one chooses to study; and (c) by missionaries and revolutionary educators to teach illiterate indigenous peoples in developing nations how to read and write both their native tongue and the national language which offers access to the benefits of modern life. The actual process by which a mere field glossary was turned into a legitimate educational text differs in each of these cases, and should, I believe, repay close study.

Bilingual Glossaries on the Battlefield: Chinese in Your Pocket

During World War II, as part of the war effort, Morris Swadesh produced a handbook called *Chinese in Your Pocket* to teach soldiers, in 15 "sessions," how to "get along" in spoken Chinese. His initial glossary of 17 phrases (see next page) is designed to generate enough sentences to "get you just about anything

---

Footnote 42 continued—

texts, attempting to make sense of the competing, contradictory demands and claims of differing discourses. While social beings share much, they also are, in any one particular instance, on any given occasion divided by differences, of whatever kind. This difference always has linguistic form, and leads to dialogue, and hence to text. Texts are constructed in and by this difference . . . In texts the discursive differences are negotiated, governed by differences in power, and by genre . . . Texts are therefore the sites of struggle, always, and in being the sites of struggle, texts are the sites of linguistic and cultural change" (Kress 1989: 19, 31–32). See also, for example, Bennett (1990), Halliday and Hasan (1989), Hirsch (1967), and Swales (1990).

TALKING UNIT ONE
EXPRESSIONS FOR GETTING ALONG

SECOND SESSION
SEVENTEEN SENTENCES

Here are seventeen Chinese sentences which will get you just about anything you want, provided you use them cleverly and throw in a few gestures.

English	*Chinese*	*Word-by-word*
1. O.K.? *or* Hi!	Hǎu-bu-hǎu	Good-not-good
2. Fine, good	Hǎu	Good
3. Not good	Bù-hǎu	Not-good
4. Go there	Dàu-nǎ-li chyǔ	Reach-there go
5. Come here	Dàu-djə-li lái	Reach-here come
6. Have a look	Kàn-yi-kan	Look-one-look
7. What's this?	Djə-gə shìr shə́m-mə	This be what
8. What're you doing?	Nǐ dzwə̀ shə́m-mə	You do what
9. Don't do that	Byə́ nà-yang	Don't that-manner
10. Do this	Dzwə̀ djə̀-yang	Do this-manner
11. I want this one	Wǒ-yàu djə̀-gə	I-want this-item
12. Give me that one	Gǒi-wǒ nà-gə	Give-me that-item
13. How much money?	Dwə̀-shǎu chyán	Much-little-money
14. Where's Peiping?	Běi-píng dzài-shə́m-mə dì-fang	Peiping located-what place
15. You take me —O.K.?	Nǐ dài-wǒ chyù —hǎu-bu-hǎu	You lead-me go —good-not-good
16. Thanks	Shyə̀-shyə	Thank-thank
17. So long	Dzài-djyàn	Again-see

you want." It is typical of the countless glossaries produced by those involved in the design and delivery of crash courses for soldiers in many different languages.[43]

This is really two glossaries in one. The middle column, in bold face, codifies spoken Chinese "the way it really sounds." The left-hand column[44] offers one kind of English gloss, the right-hand column another. Both kinds of gloss are written in conventional English spelling (not, like Chinese, in a strictly phonemic code). The left-hand column draws its glosses from ordinary colloquial English. The accuracy of the translations is not an issue here: the glosses are just simple gambits of everyday speech and indicate a semantic zone rather than pinpointing what a Chinese adult might really mean by using a particular phrase to encompass a concrete situation. The right-hand column offers a set of "hybrid" glosses that are distinctly "unEnglish." Their ungrammatical word order represents a one-to-one mapping of the combinations and permutations of *semantic* units in the middle column. The inclusion of this "word-by-word" mapping is a hybrid "bridging device." Linguistically, this right-hand gloss is somewhere between English and Chinese, halfway between etic and emic. What a hybrid alphabet does at the phonetic level of speech-sounds, this bridging device does at the semantic level of words and sentences: it offers a peek into the "black box," an X-ray of the linguistic no man's land between the two languages.

Institutional Legitimacy

A triumph of Sapir's theorem in the service of patriotic pedagogy, this phonemic glossary is typical of many that were produced and distributed by the State Department of the United States during World War II:

> Probably [the] most important reason for the success of structural linguistics in the United States is that the American government, early on, found it in its interest, directly or indirectly, to sponsor structuralist research. The special relationship between the government and the profession [of linguistics], which began on the eve of the Second World War, was so vital for the field that it has even been suggested that "American structuralism was shaped in the post-war period by field work experience directed, not toward anthropology, but toward the international involvements of the United States."[45]

---

43. Haugen (1951). For an unflattering portrait of Swadesh as a Stalinist smarty-pants by a bourgeois wartime colleague who heartily disliked him, see Hall (1975).
44. The set of numbers on the far left are for identification purposes only: they are part of the frame.
45. Hymes and Fought (1981: 119), cited in Newmeyer (1986: 51).

In 1941, with $100,000 from the Rockefeller Foundation, the ACLS [American Council of Learned Societies] organized the Intensive Language Program (ILP), and appointed J. Milton Cowan, then secretary treasurer of the Linguistic Society of America, as director. By the summer of 1943, the ILP conducted fifty-six courses, in twenty-six languages, at eighteen universities, for some seven hundred students. When the ILP was terminated at the end of the war, it was estimated that every trained linguist in the United States had been involved in it . . .

Almost immediately after America entered the war, the Army, through the American Council of Learned Societies, turned to the Linguistic Society for professional services. As early as 1942, the journal *Hispania* observed "that the Director [of the ILP, J. Milton Cowan] is constantly called upon for advice on language problems by practically every agency of the Government which has these problems: Office of Strategic Services, Board of Economic Welfare, Department of Justice, as well as the numerous departments of the Army, Navy, and Marine Corps."[46]

The most visible products of the joint government-ACLS-LSA work during the war were "useful" materials: pocket language guides [of which *Chinese in Your Pocket* is typical] and accompanying records in fifty-six languages, and complete self-teaching courses in thirty languages . . . After the war, the Language Training Program of the Foreign Service Institute (FSI) of the State Department filled the void left by the termination of the ILP and other war-connected programs . . . [and] became "one of the major centers of linguistic research in the United States."[47,48]

After the war, some of the best self-teaching language courses, including Morris Swadesh's Chinese course, were made available to the general public on the open market. Swadesh's course was first published in 1948 by Henry Holt & Company under the catchy and accurate title *Chinese in Your Pocket*,[49] and then republished in 1964 by Dover Publications for $3.50 under the title *Conversational Chinese for Beginners*.

Scientific Legitimacy

The strategy used to write Chinese "the way it really sounds" in this glossary is the strictest possible application of the *one letter, one phoneme* rule. This strategy,

46. Graves and Cowan (1942: 490), cited in Newmeyer (1986: 53).
47. Carroll (1951: 182), cited in Newmeyer (1986: 54).
48. Newmeyer (1986: 51–54).
49. Although not quite as cute as the title of Swadesh's *Speak Russian Before You Know It*.

although backed by the authority of the U.S. government, is ultimately legitimized by the authority of science itself—certainly not by whatever authority backs the use of Chinese writing by the Chinese themselves to represent their own language. From a mathematical point of view, arbitrary symbols (e.g., Zapf Dingbats) could have been used to represent the phonemes of spoken Chinese. Instead, letters of the roman alphabet[50] are allowed to take fixed values that differ from English speech-sounds. According to Swadesh and those who shared his faith in the phonemic philosophy of the 1930s, concentrating on phonemes and letting the allophones take care of themselves guarantees that a beginner can articulate the sound distinctions that matter most *to the Chinese ear*. The romanization[51] chosen by Swadesh:

> gives an automatic pronunciation of the consonant sounds. That is, if you read the consonant letters with their usual English values, you make either a sound that is exactly right or something that is *near enough* so that people will have no trouble understanding you.[52]

Swadesh was here telling his "lay" readers what he told his professional colleagues in 1934 in his classic paper on the phonemic principle: "The test of an adequate phonemic writing is that it be possible for one who does not know the meaning of the words to read them off correctly and without serious distortions."[53] (At their meetings in the Village Hall, the producers of the Cobden glossaries were beginning to move in the direction of meeting this criterion; see pp. 44ff, above.)

The residually hybrid moves in the game played with letters and sounds in Swadesh's code is evident in Chao's remark on the values that the letters *p* and *t* can and cannot take: "You can't forget to *un*aspirate your *p*'s and *t*'s if they are written as *b*'s and *d*'s to start with."[54]

The limits of phonemic *purism*, however, are evident in the admission that although those who speak Mandarin will understand you, you will not necessarily understand them.[55] This is in stark contrast to the hybrid mixture of phonemics and phonetics in the Cobden glossaries, whose "impurities" are a direct expression of their authors' determination to *understand* what the local Anglos were saying (not merely to be understood *by* them).

---

50. Plus ə for schwa.
51. Chinese National Romanization, first developed by Yuen Ren Chao.
52. Swadesh (1948: xv). I have italicized the move that "fudges" Sapir's theorem.
53. Swadesh (1934) in Joos (1958: 35).
54. Foreword to Swadesh (1948: vii).
55. "If you talk in the manner explained in this book, you will be quite easily understood by all who speak Mandarin. The chief difficulty comes when you try to understand them" (Swadesh 1948: xiv).

The pre-existing "orthographic map" used to chart the topography of Chinese speech-sounds claims theoretical validity: it claims to be grounded in a scientifically precise representation of the true structure of spoken Chinese. To represent its mapping, this sort of glossary uses a hybrid, although consistent, textual strategy: an etic or "value-free" system for Chinese and an emic or "value-laden" system for the colloquial and the "hybrid" English glosses. This sort of glossary thus maps etic onto emic.[56] The decision to use this hybrid strategy is informed not by scientific, but by educational, considerations.

Educational Legitimacy

This text is typical of glossaries produced by professional linguists not for their professional colleagues, nor for native speakers of the language in question who want to speak English as a second language, but as study guides for ordinary adults who speak only English and want to learn to speak something else as a second language as quickly as possible. This particular glossary proved its educational value "in the field"—that is to say, in the battlefield, not just in the Army classroom. Introducing Swadesh's "pocket-size introduction to Chinese" to the general public in 1948, Chao wrote:

> Dr. Swadesh's experience in organizing rapid courses for various languages right on the field in Burma and in China has resulted in a book of live language with live material for use in live situations. But don't take this for one of those handbooks made up in a hurry for men of supposedly low I.Q. to get a smattering of pidgin Chinese. While the style of exposition may be deceptively informal and colloquial, the stuff behind it is basically the same as what you would learn—or ought to—as part of a more *formal academic course*.[57]

A rapid course for adult learners can afford to put speaking first and writing last.[58] It is presumably easier for an adult to learn to play with new values for letters of a familiar alphabet than to learn an entirely new kind of script, especially one as ancient and unalphabetic as Chinese writing. To make Chao's Chinese National Romanization "still easier for the beginner," Swadesh modifies it in a

---

56. Note that, curiously enough, it is the phonemic system that is etic, the non-phonemic system that is emic.
57. Swadesh (1948: vii), my emphasis.
58. "My conclusion is that the 'army' method is after all the only really natural method, or perhaps I should say it is a properly organized form of the natural method, and as such it is as applicable to civilian as to military situations. It is based on the principle that *daily speech is the real language, the core on which we should concentrate in our teaching*" (Haugen 1972b[1951]: 208).

few small points. For example, he introduces ə "for the slightly varying, but essentially single, sound shown by both *e* and *o*."[59] And to represent the tones, he invents those cute little arrows—icons, mnemonic devices.

Educational goals also determined the *content* of this glossary. It consists of 17 gambits which Swadesh introduces with a characteristically informal gesture: "Here are seventeen Chinese sentences *which will get you just about anything you want,* provided you use them cleverly and throw in a few gestures."[60] These are 17 *generic* speech units. Swadesh's bold claim that, collectively, they empower you to get just about anything you want is grounded in the structure of the glossary as a whole. Items included have satisfied two quite different criteria: (a) they are "expressions for getting along," but also (b) they constitute a *generative set*, such that by recombining and frecreating its elements, you can strategically encompass just about any situation. They could be called *generative words* in Paulo Freire's sense. Granted, they do not "name the world." But if you combine them cleverly and throw in a few gestures, you and your Chinese friends will be able to collectively define "just about" any situation.[61]

Biliteracy

Romanize Chinese but not English is the textual strategy for "being in two languages" exemplified by this glossary. Consequently, to read this glossary calls for a rather peculiar blend of two different kinds of literacy. We can call one kind English literacy,[62] but we can't call the other Chinese literacy. We can call both kinds alphabetic literacy as long as it is clear that they are alphabetic in two very different senses of the term. We can call one English alphabetic literacy, but what can we call the other kind of alphabetic literacy? Generic phonemic literacy? Romanized literacy? Whatever we call it, the way it blends with English literacy to generate this particular glossary, and many others like it, is informed by the constellation of institutional, scientific, and educational values sketched out above. And Swadesh's glossary differs from the Cobden glossaries, not because he is playing a different *game* with letters and sounds, but because, to encompass a different situation, he has chosen a different strategy: phonemic purification.

---

59. Swadesh (1948: xv). Compare my notes on the use of ɛ and o for ə in the Cobden alphabet, p. 38, above.

60. Swadesh (1948: 18), my emphasis.

61. This recalls Freire's calculation that 17 generative words are enough to capture the "phonetic richness" of all the "phonemic families" in Portuguese or Spanish—see above, p. 71. The recurrence of the number 17 in two such different situations is, no doubt, a mere coincidence.

62. Knowing enough of the alphabet to read 17 decontextualized phrases in conventional English spelling—even when, as in the "word-by-word" column, they don't really make sense—certainly used to qualify as "literacy" until about 1970.

Bilingual Glossaries in the University: Ganda Liquids and Squamish Vowels

Let us turn now to a set of paradigmatic glossaries shaped by a different blend of institutional, scientific, and educational values: the 40 or so glossaries in the canonical *Problem Book in Phonology* produced by Morris Halle and G. N. Clements and published by MIT Press in 1983 (with the subtitle *A Workbook for Introductory Courses in Linguistics and in Modern Phonology*).

The use of "half-cooked" field glossaries to teach linguists how to rewrite and purify hybrid transcription systems originated, I believe, with Kenneth Pike. In 1936, just one year after his seat-of-the-pants initiatory fieldwork with Mixtec (armed with nothing more than a 10-day crash course on phonetics "from a person who had never had much training"),[63] Pike was asked by William Cameron Townsend, the founder of the just-born Summer Institute of Linguistics, to write a soundly scientific text book on how to create hybrid orthographies for hitherto unwritten indigenous languages. By the time Pike's classic text, *Phonemics: A Technique for Reducing Languages to Writing*, was published in typescript by the University of Michigan in 1947, the problems in it had been used to train about 1,000 missionaries to write impressionistic field glossaries on strict phonetic principles, to rewrite them on strict phonemic principles, and then to re-hybridize the resulting system so as to make it acceptable to secular authorities who insisted on the rapid transfer of literacy skills from indigenous to national languages. Pike's book consists of a meticulously ordered sequence of over 250 problems: each consists of a short glossary that is to be rewritten according to a particular procedure. Each glossary looks like an authentic field glossary, but all are actually simulations. Some are glossaries of imaginary languages (for interesting glossaries of Sapir's two imagined languages *A* and *B*,[64] see Problems 201–202, p. 156); most are glossaries of actual, but simplified, languages, carefully restricted to illustrate a particular procedural challenge.

In their newly established PhD program in Linguistics, the same method was chosen by Halle and Clements to train professional linguists (who were, presumably, not going to preach the gospel in the vernacular to illiterate natives). Four of the 40 glossaries in their workbook are reproduced on p. 104.

Commentary on Ganda

Here, the left-hand column codifies a language identified as Ganda. The right-hand column is a set of very simple English glosses. The glosses are merely ornamental. They are irrelevant to the problem posed by this text.

---

63. Pike (1981: 183).
64. Sapir (1925) in Joos (1958: 23); see above, p. 86, n. 9.

Ganda Liquids

1. [r] and [l] are in complementary distribution in one variety of Ganda. State the conditions under which each appears.

1.	kola	'do'		11.	wulira	'hear'
2.	lwana	'fight'		12.	beera	'help'
3.	buulira	'tell'		13.	jjukira	'remember'
4.	lya	'eat'		14.	eryato	'canoe'
5.	luula	'sit'		15.	omuliro	'fire'
6.	omugole	'bride'		16.	effirimbi	'whistle'
7.	lumonde	'sweet potato'		17.	emmeeri	'ship'
8.	eddwaliro	'hospital'		18.	eraddu	'lightning'
9.	oluganda	'Ganda language'		19.	wawaabira	'accuse'
10.	olulimi	'tongue'		20.	lagira	'command'

Angas Sonorants

Voicing is predictable in Angas sonorants. State the rule.

1.	muṭ	'to die'		13.	fʷan	'to rain'
2.	nuŋ̊	'to ripen'		14.	tam̥	'bench'
3.	ntaŋzum̥	'wasp'		15.	ŋgak	'snake'
4.	mbaŋga	'drum'		16.	ndarm̥	'bark'
5.	nemʸel̥	[name of village]		17.	pampam̥	'bread'
6.	sir̥	'to forgive'		18.	lɛp	'to send'
7.	li:li:	'slowly'		19.	dondon	'yesterday'
8.	ʔara	'road?'		20.	ʔar̥	'road'
9.	kʷal̥	'joint'		21.	tarwep	'harvest season'
10.	kʷɔnsar̥	'finger'		22.	dɛŋ	'to drag'
11.	mɓɛlm̥	'to lick'		23.	potiŋ	'sky'
12.	nfʷarm̥	'head cold'		24.	zigɔl̥	'Satan'

Squamish Vowels

Show that the phones [eˑ], [e], [ɛˑ], and [ɛy] derive from a single underlying phoneme. State the rules accounting for their occurrence, and indicate any necessary ordering.

1.	ceʔ	'there is'	16.	χɛˑq	'scratch'
2.	q'ɛyt	'be morning'	17.	čeˑλ	'top'
3.	t'eˑqʷ	'cold'	18.	q'eˑχɛyʔ	'become black'
4.	χʷeˑq'ʷ	'be arrested'	19.	tmeˑxʷ	'earth, ground'
5.	χɛypʼ	'get touched'	20.	qḷeˑm	'weak'
6.	ceˑxʷ	'reach'	21.	sq'ɛyʔ	'slices of dried salmon'
7.	tseʔ	'feel cold'	22.	χʷɛyʔ	'be lost'
8.	kʼʷeˑn	'few'	23.	neʔč	'high seas'
9.	weˑɬq'ʷt	'ask'	24.	kʷceʔc	'person with magic power'
10.	teˑ	'this'	25.	sleˑɬ	'bunch of blankets'
11.	nəq'eˑɬos	'wise'	26.	χʷɛˑɬʔ ·	'come out'
12.	xʷaɬɛytn	'white man'	27.	nsqɛynṃ	'rub oil in one's hair'
13.	leˑxʷ	'fall'	28.	stæqtaqɛyw	'horses'
14.	λ'ɛˑq	'arrive'	29.	meˑχæλ	'black bear'
15.	ʔeˑ	'be here'			

Proto-Bantu Voiced Obstruents

The following set of data is from Proto-Bantu—the reconstructed latest common ancestor of the modern Bantu languages spoken in Eastern, Central, and Southern Africa, including Swahili and Ganda. [β, l, ɣ] are in complementary distribution with [b, d, g] respectively. Account for their distribution by postulating an underlying phoneme for each pair and stating the rule accounting for the phonetic forms.

1.	βale	'two'	13.	kiɣa	'eyebrow'
2.	leme	'tongue'	14.	ɣiɣɛ	'locust'
3.	taβe	'twig'	15.	kulu	'tortoise'
4.	pala	'antelope'	16.	oŋgo	'cooking pot'
5.	kondɛ	'bean'	17.	tendɛ	'palm tree'
6.	zɔŋgɔ	'gall'	18.	zala	'hunger'
7.	βeɣa	'monkey'	19.	zɔɣu	'elephant'
8.	βɛmbe	'pigeon'	20.	βele	'body'
9.	limo	'god, spirit'	21.	lɛlu	'chin, beard'
10.	kaŋga	'guinea fowl'	22.	eɣi	'water'
11.	ɣɔmbe	'cattle'	23.	kiŋgɔ	'neck'
12.	lelɔ	'fire'	24.	nto	'person'

In this glossary, a strict application of the *one letter, one phoneme* rule seems to have been used to write Ganda "the way it really sounds." But this turns out to be not quite so. Only 18 letters of the roman alphabet are actually used. Sixteen represent phonemes. Two of them—*l* and *r*—represent allophones of one phoneme. This glossary is carefully designed precisely to help the reader discover this impurity, by induction. To read this glossary correctly is to *rewrite* it, using only 17 instead of 18 letters of the roman alphabet. To do so, all you need to know about Ganda is already encoded in the decontextualized text.

That's why the English glosses on the right-hand side are a mere formality, to preserve the look of a field glossary. Any one or more of the glosses could be arbitrarily changed (e.g., to meaningless ✿)(■ ℔☋)(■℔✦, or to any other short English phrase) without in any way affecting the outcome of the analysis. "It would be possible to group the sounds of a language into phonemes without knowing the meaning of any words."[65]

In short, if Swadesh's pocket glossary of Chinese is "really two glossaries in one," this one is really only half a glossary. It could just as well be a one-column table. The English column is included merely to satisfy the surface conventions of the genre. Each glossary in the workbook uses a *different* code to chart the topography of a different language. This is clearly not "Conversational Ganda for Beginners." These glossaries are not intended to help people who may want to "get along" in Squamish or Proto-Bantu. In contrast to Wallerstein's imagined classroom exercises with the Cobden glossaries, these glossaries are designed precisely to stimulate classroom discussion on "which of various moves in the game is best and why."[66] In the linguistics classroom, the *accuracy* of a codification becomes a central topic in the discourse on letters and sounds, which distinguishes professionals from amateurs and linguists from non-linguists.

If Swadesh's Chinese glossary is a paradigm of *applied* linguistics, Halle and Clements's textbook is (in Kuhn's sense) a paradigm of *pure* linguistics: a canonical set of problems produced by the leaders of the profession to help their professional colleagues pass on a mastery of the discipline to those who seek to become licensed members of the guild.

In one way or another, none of the glossaries in the set is "pure." For educational purposes, each transcription deliberately contains impurities, deliberately mixes two or more phonological levels, representations and/or rules. They do, to this extent, simulate glossaries collected in the field, which are always subject to further systematization. The rules for *rewriting transcriptions* is what these glossaries are really "about."

---

65. This once canonical and oft-quoted principle was first articulated by Daniel Jones (1929). But it wouldn't be possible to group phonemes without knowing that they mark a meaningful distinction.
66. Cf. above, p. 78.

Many of the glossaries use more than the 26 letters of the roman alphabet—see *Angas sonorants* and *Squamish vowels*. The use of the alphabet "as a kind of algebraic notation" is pushed further and further into the realm of purely mathematical formalism. Algebraic formulas and geometric diagrams are implicit in each of the glossaries. The task is to make the mathematics explicit. Once you have done so, you can rewrite the glossary. Each glossary thus represents work in progress. Furthermore, phonological theory is itself still evolving, still work in progress.

Halle and Clements "field tested" these glossaries—not in the field, not with the "natives," but in their classrooms at Harvard and MIT. Insofar as these glossaries claim to be scientifically accurate "pictures of reality," their claims to theoretical and interpretive validity are mediated by the institutional authority of the university, whereas their claims to descriptive validity are ultimately grounded in their origin as impressionistic, handwritten field notes. Many of the original field glossaries were transcribed by Clements himself, in the field, from the lips of competent native speakers of Ganda (etc.). Clements's original field transcriptions were no doubt subsequently rewritten many times, but these rewritings are not to be regarded as affecting the descriptive or empirical validity of the directly observed data.

Working through these classroom exercises teaches you a kind of X-ray vision. To read these glossaries means learning to see through the surface structure of any (eligible, well-formed) transcription to the deep structure. The mathematical enterprise of pure phonology is neatly captured in a deft metaphor by François Dell:

> Since E [= the domain of inquiry] is an infinite set, the linguist can only ever obtain a small part of it by direct observation. He therefore has to proceed by successive extrapolations. He begins by collecting a certain number of sentences from speakers and noting their descriptions: the set A of the descriptions of the well-formed sentences which he has collected. This set A is a finite sample of the infinite set E. Once he has the sample, he can then set himself the following problem: how exactly to define E, knowing A ... See for example, a classic problem in astronomy: having determined through observation a number of points on a planet's orbit, characterize the infinite set of points on this orbit, i.e. find an equation which defines that set.[67]

---

67. Dell (1980: 13). E can be taken as referring to one language at a time. But just as astronomers seek to generalize their equations to define the set of all possible orbits in the universe, so generative phonology seeks to universalize its "domain of inquiry." In other words, in the long run, E refers to all possible vocal productions: "The linguist reduces the infinity of *possible vocal production* to a finite alphabet of phonetic symbols. By this, he is making the hypothesis

The game played with letters and sounds in Halle and Clements's textbook does not merely code "two languages at the same time." In the final analysis, its goal is to code, so to speak, "all languages at the same time"—the way they *all* really sound. To read these glossaries as records of moves made in a game played at such a high level demands the development of a special kind of biliteracy, a kind of mathematical literacy. (Each glossary is elegant in the mathematician's sense of the term.) In the final analysis, what you are meant to learn by working through them is precisely how to write a well-formed "glossary" of whatever language you want, at whatever phonological level you choose: how to construct a representation that is scientifically correct, consistent, and complete. This is why they might justly be called paradigmatic—or, if you prefer, *generative*—glossaries.

Nevertheless, these didactic glossaries differ from the Cobden glossaries, not because Halle and Clements are teaching their students a different game, but because, to encompass a different situation, they have chosen a different strategy: mathematization.[68]

Hybrid Alphabets in the Service of Christ and the Revolution

The Tarascan Project, which took place in 1939 in Cherán, Michoacán, the hometown of the 800 Tarascans who made their way to Cobden in the summer of 1980, deserves a book-length study of its own. For it can be interpreted as prefiguring many, perhaps all, of the motifs—the games, the discourses, the scenes of writing—which characterize the "illegal" Cobden glossaries, as well as the paradigmatic glossaries examined above.

Some might say that the professional game played by Swadesh and Halle and Clements in constructing their glossaries differs substantially from the amateur game played by the authors of the Cobden glossaries. I have preferred to say that, due to the difference in their postures toward institutional legitimacy, they chose different *strategies* to cope with Sapir's theorem. One difference between the official orthography of the Royal Academy of Spain and the writing system which the Mexicans in Cobden referred to as *la ortografía mexicana*[69] lies in the fact that since the 1930s—one might as well say since the Spanish Conquest—Sapir's theorem

---

Footnote 67 continued—

   that the relevant linguistic properties in the pronunciation of *any sentence of any language* can be exhaustively described by using a finite number of parameters, each parameter describing a scale of discrete values, themselves finite in number ... The letters of the phonetic alphabet are just useful abbreviations to designate a set of specifications [in relation to the various distinctive features]" (Dell 1980: 31–34, 35), my emphases.

68. Kortlandt (1972).

69. See p. 21, above.

has been systematically "fudged" in Mexico to create hybrid alphabets for indigenous "native" languages.[70] In the late 1930s, the intellectual labor of producing, disseminating, and institutionalizing these hybrid alphabets in Mexico was shared by Tarascan *indios*, revolutionary educators, professional North American linguists, and Christian missionaries, in close collaboration. The socialists, led by President Lázaro Cárdenas, provided the ideology—*one nation, one alphabet*—and the "proto-Freirean" pedagogy; the linguists, led by Morris Swadesh, provided the professional discourse on phonemics and phonetics; and the Christian missionaries, led by William Cameron Townsend and the young Kenneth Pike, provided the impressionistic field glossaries and the pragmatic defense of hybrid alphabets. Each group had its own preferred discourses, each discourse its own ideological dimensions: what makes the case of the Tarascan Project potentially so interesting is the trade-offs between these discourses and ideologies, trade-offs reflected in the values taken by letters in the finished alphabet. An intense ideological charge was invested in letting the letters of the roman alphabet take the values of both European and Indian speech-sounds *on an equal basis.*[71]

Adult Biliteracy: The More Hybrid, the Better

Adult biliteracy has always been central, not marginal, to the work of Christian missionaries. To be acceptable and useful, a new orthography devised by a missionary for a hitherto unwritten language must maximize its "biliteracy quotient" (i.e., its transferability to the legitimate orthography of the dominant colonial and/or trade language in the region). Impressionistic field alphabets are hybrid by default, but orthographies developed by Christian missionaries (especially by those trained by the Summer Institute of Linguistics) are hybrid by design.

   In his 1959 article aptly entitled "How Shall I Write This Language?" the Rev. William Smalley codified a wealth of experience shared by Christian missionaries grappling with the trade-off between language-specific values and competing educational, social, political, and economic values.[72]

---

70. For a canonical account of adult biliteracy campaigns in Mexico, see Heath (1972b: 99–150). For the Spanish version, see Heath (1972a: 151–222).

71. Precisely how intense the charge was became clear in 1942 when Cárdenas's successor, Avila Camacho, allowed reactionaries and fascists to label as a communist anyone who used (and defended the value of) a hybrid alphabet, and to purge such communists—at gun point if need be—from the Mexican educational system (Kirk 1942; Vejar Vazquez 1944). On the ideology of the *cardenistas*, see Medin (1972).

72. The article was reprinted along with many detailed, fascinating studies of specific cases, in Smalley et al. (1963: 31–52).

Smalley analyzes and lists in order of importance five criteria which govern the production of hybrid alphabets by missionaries:

1. Maximum motivation for the learner, and acceptance by his society and controlling groups such as the government. Occasionally maximum motivation for the learner conflicts with government acceptance, but usually the learner wants most what is considered standard in the area.

2. Maximum representation of speech. The fullest, most adequate representation of the actual spoken language is, by and large, the ideal. There are a few points of exception here . . .

3. Maximum ease of learning. Many writing systems have failed as a missionary tool because they were essentially too complicated for a learner.

4. Maximum transfer. Here we refer to the fact that certain of the alphabet or other written symbols will, when learned, be applicable to the more rapid learning of the trade or colonial languages in the area. Thus, if a new learner learns a certain pronunciation of a certain symbol in his own native language, and if he can use that same pronunciation with the same symbol in the trade or national language, this is a case of transfer. If, however, the same symbol is used with different value in the other writing system, that transfer cannot be made.

5. Maximum ease of reproduction. Typing and printing facilities are a consideration, although they are not of first importance.[73]

Smalley's criteria 1, 3, 4, and 5 can be interpreted as interesting variations on the criterion that I call "fudging" Sapir's theorem.[74]

A Marxist–Christian Dialogue

At the top of Smalley's list is the criterion that he calls maximum motivation, but which might more aptly be described as maximum *legitimacy*. Christian missionaries do not, by and large, devise or advocate orthographies that question or threaten the legitimacy of the dominant power structures in their host countries. (If and when the power structure changes, especially after a revolution, the orthographies thus given to linguistic minorities may then be criticized as

---

73. Smalley in Smalley et al. (1963: 34).

74. Secular and Marxist writers on the production and distribution of orthographies continue to draw on Smalley's five criteria. Smalley et al. (1963) is cited as an authority, for example, by Donaldo Macedo in his doctoral thesis on the phonology and orthography of Cape Verdean Creole (Macedo 1979: 146–165), by Joshua Fishman in a long section on the creation of writing systems (Fishman 1974: 1750–1762), and by Florian Coulmas, along with a detailed commentary (Coulmas 1989: 226–236).

reactionary by the ideologues of the new regime.) This willingness to accept the prevailing ideology of the host government explains the paradoxical and spectacularly successful collaboration between the founder of the Summer Institute of Linguistics, William Cameron Townsend, and the leader of the Mexican socialist reform movement of the 1930s, President Lázaro Cárdenas.[75]

Cárdenas was himself from Michoacán and valued his Tarascan heritage. Under his presidency, the Tarascan Project began its ascent to stardom. In 1936, three young missionaries from the newborn Summer Institute of Linguistics conducted groundbreaking biliteracy campaigns in Mexico, along with their leader Townsend. One was Kenneth Pike, who, among the Mixtec of Oaxaca, began his illustrious career as a phonetician armed with little more than a crash course on vowels and consonants. (Pike recalls with affection "ordering sight unseen" the writings of Sweet and other phoneticians in a Mexico City bookstore.)[76] The other two were Maxwell and Elizabeth Lathrop, who chose Tarascan and settled in Cherán, Michoacán. (In 1980, Tarascans in Cobden, Illinois, would fondly describe "Don Max" to me as an old gringo who had lived in Cherán forever and who—they all agreed—spoke a purer and more correct variety of Tarascan than any indio. He had read the old, old books—the Tarascan–Spanish dictionaries compiled by Vasco de Quiroga at the time of the Conquest. Don Max and his wife translated the entire Bible into impeccable Tarascan.)[77]

The Tarascan Project became the showpiece of adult biliteracy campaigns, first on a national level, and then on an Inter-American (i.e., Latin American) level.[78] When the great Mexican poet, diplomat, and educator Jaime Torres Bodet became the first Director of UNESCO in 1948, he elevated the Tarascan Project to paradigmatic status as a model for how to conduct adult biliteracy campaigns in Third World countries. UNESCO's advocacy of vernacular biliteracy based on the design and dissemination of hybrid alphabets was grounded in values that informed the original Tarascan Project in 1939.[79]

The virtues of Tarascan culture and the poetic "metaphonological awareness" of Tarascan linguistic theorizing[80] would need to be taken into account in a full analysis of the unusual success of this project which simultaneously launched the Mexican adult biliteracy movement and the Summer Institute of Linguistics.

---

75. On the fruitful results of the close personal friendship between Townsend and Cárdenas, see Brend and Pike (1977) and the works cited in Heath (1972a: 154–184, 1972b: 99–150).

76. Pike (1981: 182).

77. Paul Friedrich (one of the very few people qualified to judge) says the Lathrops' Tarascan translation is excellent, and compares their achievement to that of Luther. Personal communication, October 1, 1994.

78. Heath (1972a: 171, 180, 1972: 113).

79. Heath (1972a: 208, 1972b: 139), UNESCO (1953), Stavenhagen (1984).

80. Friedrich (1975, 1986: 46–64).

báses lingуístikas de la enseñánsa

los partidários de los divérsos métodos en són insis-
tiéndo en el balór de un método i negándo balór algúno a los
demás. podémos abaluárlos sin prejuísio, si émpre fiğándonos
en la finalidád de la enseñánsa: el lográr kon rapidés la ka-
pasidád de leér kualkiér kósa kon fasilidád. sabér los nóm-
bres de las létras es de módo ménos importánsia.

el fonetísmo, o sea sabér los sonídos de las létras,es
indispensáble para leér. ántes de tenério es sólo posíble
memoriár kuántos kompléjos o aprendér palábras entéras,en-
tre más fonétika sen la eskritúra, más importánte es el fonetísmo. sólo en una eskritúra nó fonétika, komo la antígua
dína, si ke aprendér tódas las palábras individualménte. una
eskritúra semifonétika, ó seá una ke tiéne irregularidádes,kó-
mo las tiéne dnes la espáñola i modérnas lá inglésa. nese-
síta una kombinasión de la memoriasión de palábras komplé-
tas i del fonetísmo estrikto. lá eskritúra sientífika ke a-
sémos en las lénguas indíjenas nó rekiére ningúna memoriasión.

por ótra párte nó sírbe el método demasiádo analítiko
ke fesdíta de una estríkta aplikasión del onomatopeísmo; no
se les kon fasilidád leér a por létra, sino kombinándo fásil-
ménte las létras en sílabas, i komprendiéndo grúpos entéros
dé sílabas. sikolójika y lingüístikaménte korréktos son los
métodos silábiko i sikofonétiko, porke akostúmbran al alúmno a las kombinasiónes de létras i le permíten sakár un sen-
tído del balór de las létras por un proséso de abstraksión.
es desír, kuándo el alúmno konóse ka ke ki ko ku, desprénde
rá el eleménto komún en éos. pronunsiár una sílaba no pre-
sénta ningúna difikultád, porke korespónde a los ditos lin-
güístikos normáles. pronunsiár sonídos aislados no kofes-

		ala	eje	flor	ojo	uña
		a	e	i	o	u
	béka	ba	be	bi	bo	bu
	čángo	ča	če	či	čo	ču
	dóga	da	de	di	do	du
	fáro	fa	fe	fi	fo	fu
	gáto	ga	ge	gi	go	gu
	jáfo	ja	je	ji	jo	ju
	kása	ka	ke	ki	ko	ku
	lápis	la	le	ll	lo	lu
	máno	ma	me	mi	mo	mu
	nábo	na	ne	ni	no	nu
	pájaro	pa	pe	pl	po	pu
	Fáta	Fa	Fe	Fi	Fo	Fu
	sápo	sa	se	si	so	su
	tása	ta	te	ti	to	tu
	wáje	wa	we	wi	wo	wu
	yábe	ya	ye	yi	yo	yu
	aráña	ra	re	ri	ro	ru
	kañáda	ña	ñe	ñi	ño	ñu

The Tarascan Project has often been written about, by those who participated in it and by others.[81] The most accessible and reliable analysis of its historic importance is Shirley Brice Heath's 1972 doctoral dissertation, published in Mexico as *La Política del Lenguaje en Mexico*, and in the United States as *Telling Tongues*.

The heart of the Tarascan Project was the creation and legitimization of a hybrid alphabet capable of coding two *abecedarios* at the same time: Tarascan and Spanish. The Tarascan Project established once and for all that indios—illiterate indigenous monolingual adults—could learn to read and write both their own language and the metropolitan language in less than a month or two—provided *both* languages were systematically coded in a single alphabet *deliberately designed to be as hybrid as possible, on the principle of one letter, one hybrid phoneme*. Spanish coded in this alphabet did not look the way Castilian was supposed to look. In 1940, Swadesh typed his staff development handbooks in Spanish using the new hybrid alphabet: not "correct" Castilian orthography, but *la ortografía mexicana* (for a sample, see previous page).

Reforming and hybridizing the structures of the national alphabet was (at least until 1942) defended as a small but essential step in the much harder task of reforming and hybridizing the class structure of Mexican society.

The hybrid Tarascan alphabet used in Mexico today is a descendant of the writing system collaboratively designed in 1939 by Swadesh, Lathrop, Pike, and Mexican revolutionary educators. Between 1978 and 1982, I occasionally heard Tarascan spoken in and around Cobden. I even learned a Tarascan song—*líricamente*—and spent two weeks in Cherán, among Tarascans I had met in Cobden. But I didn't see Tarascan in written form until the summer of 1982, when a Tarascan friend in Cobden gave me a small Tarascan–Spanish glossary, called *Frases sencillas* and printed in Cherán by the legendary old gringo, Don Max. (For a sample page from that glossary—which, in 1982, crossed the border from Cherán to Cobden—see p. 115.)

In preparing this book, I went through a phase when I believed I could answer the tantalizing question: Where and how did the Mexicans in Cobden learn to play the game that created their hybrid alphabet? Once the game got started, it spread from person to person along and across social networks. The same could be said of the basketball game that took off in the village park on July 7.[82] Basketball had never before been played in Cobden by mixed teams of locals and Mexicans: yet to those who played it, it was not a new game. Likewise, the game played with letters and sounds was new to Cobden, but it was certainly not *invented* in

---

81. For example, Arana de Swadesh (1975), Barrera-Vásquez (1953), Brend and Pike (1977), McQuown (1941), Stavenhagen (1984), Swadesh (1940, 1941), UNESCO (1953), Wallis and Bennett (1964), and see the wealth of primary and secondary sources cited by Heath (1972a: 154–184, 1972b: 99–150).
82. See p. 2, above.

1980: like basketball, it has been played in other places by other people. Where did the Mexicans learn to play it?

They didn't learn the game from me. I tried, without much success, to learn it from them. I hadn't seen it played before, and I never managed to play it as well as they did. Spanish is my first language, but I am more literate in English than in Spanish.[83] I never seemed able to shake my mind sufficiently free of English literacy to hear English from the outside *como de veras se oye*—the way it sounds to Spanish (let alone Tarascan) ears innocent of English spelling. I was never able to predict which of various possible transcriptions they would choose as the best. Except for some simple monosyllables such as FREND or MACH, I was surprised by the strings of letters that the authors of the Cobden texts actually chose.

As I bring this book to a close, I conceive a companion volume, a history of this "holy relic," an interpretation of this little Tarascan glossary as a record of moves made in a game played—for high political and religious stakes—with letters and sounds in Mexico between 1939 and the present. Such a study might help answer the intriguing question: Did the game played in Cobden in 1980 begin in Cherán in 1939? Or did it begin much longer ago?

---

83. I first heard English spoken in 1948 in Australia when, as a Mexican immigrant speaking only Spanish, I entered first grade at Marrickville Infants School, New South Wales. I spoke no English at all. Back in Mexico, I had learned the *abecedario* of Spanish in kindergarten with the help of my big brother Jorge. Did I perhaps try to write English *como de veras se oye*? I don't remember . . .

sesi jándini	buen tiempo
	ser bonito algún lugar
janini	llover
janikua	nube, lluvia
taɹiáta	aire, viento
tsándini	cuando el sol está alumbrando,
	o calentando fuerte
juɹiata	el sol
emenda	tiempo de aguas
kuarésima	tiempo de secas
pauámbauani	diariamente
šanóata	granizo
pirítakua	relámpago, rayo
šúšuŋäkuɹani	estar verde el campo
kuetéškuɹita (šupakata)	el arco iris
k'aɹíkjándini	estar todo seco
iauakua	hielo
šumu	neblina
sʌuíni	remolino
iéstakua	nevado
t'upuri	polvo
ts'irákuaɹini	hacer frío
apáɹikuaɹini	hacer calor

EPILOGUE

A Game as Old as
the Alphabet?

Are you not somewhat bulgar with your bowels?
—Joyce

If we begin with the premise that all writing systems are socially constructed, it follows that, in particular, alphabets, and the relations between letters and sounds, are not given by Nature, God, or the State. The social practices and discourses of institutions such as the Church or the State or the Academy may reserve the power to bestow legitimacy on some alphabetic writing systems and withhold legitimacy from others. Few of the alphabets that present themselves as candidates for such "canonization" were legitimate when they were first invented. And the genealogy of alphabetic writing systems used in the world today suggests the interesting conclusion that they were all "born hybrid." They are all born hybrid in the sense that the alphabets used by the Mexicans in Cobden and Cherán were born hybrid: the values conventionally assigned to each letter were initially stretched to capture the speech-sounds of a new language that had not before been coded in that particular alphabetic code. In Cherán in 1939, the "new" language was Tarascan; in Cobden in 1980, it was an English vernacular.

Many different alphabetic writing systems are currently in use today around the world. Most alphabets are used to code more than one language: they have crossed over from language to language:

> Cyrillic Serbo-Croatian is on the western edge of a huge Cyrillic alphabet area stretching from Serbia to the Pacific. Roman Serbo-Croatian is on the eastern edge of an even huger Roman alphabet area stretching from Croatia and covering Western Europe, the Americas, most of the Pacific

and Oceania, and a great deal of Africa. The rest of the world falls into three other main script areas: the Chinese area—China itself and some adjoining countries, Taiwan, Japan, South Korea; the Indian area, containing a huge family of scripts both within India and beyond; and the Arabic area, stretching from North Africa to Central Asia.[1]

Furthermore, the ancestral alphabets of each of these script areas (except Chinese) are themselves all descended from a single common ancestor: the proto-Canaanite writing system.[2]

"The most significant developments in the history of writing were achieved whenever a script was borrowed and adapted to a new language across linguistic types."[3] In the family tree of alphabets, each such branch marks a moment when Sapir's theorem was "fudged" for two languages, H and L: the high "parent" language and the low thitherto unalphabetized language:

> Writing systems are adapted to structural peculiarities of the languages for which they are used. To the extent that writing systems are language sensitive, their transfer to new languages is bound to meet with difficulties. In order to cope with them, certain adaptations are necessary.[4]

In each such case, bilingual alphabet makers modified an existing and legitimate alphabet to chart new sound patterns. They restructured an established code to capture new data. "The application of a given writing system to a new language always bears the risk of badly adjusted scripts, because typically scripts are borrowed in a process of 'natural' adaptation rather than on the grounds of linguistic analysis."[5]

"Whenever a script was borrowed and adapted to a language type or language family other than that in whose context it was developed, important changes in the systematic make-up of that script resulted."[6] Start with present-day Roman, Cyrillic, Arabic, or Devanagari alphabets—each of which has spread and bifurcated from language to language—and go back upstream to their common origin, to the "unique and once-and-for-all-invention,"[7] and in each generation of the genealogy you find that right from the start, every alphabet is "always already" born hybrid.

---

1. Mountford (1990: 716).
2. Florian Coulmas (1989) offers a detailed, linguistically informed account of the way adult biliterates have ferried each alphabet over from one language to the next. I draw on his work in this section. He presents genealogical trees for each script area.
3. Coulmas (1989: 167).
4. Coulmas (1989: 89).
5. Coulmas (1989: 45).
6. Coulmas (1989: 162).
7. Illich (1987: 10).

The proto-Canaanite writing system, ancestor of all alphabets now in use around the world, was itself a strategic political and economic response to multilingualism, a hybrid writing system. In the second half of the second millennium, the region inhabited by the western Semitic peoples who invented (i.e., constructed) the first alphabet was:

> at the international crossroads of influences from powerful and flourishing adjacent cultures. The trading ports at the eastern Mediterranean coast were in contact with Egypt, Crete, the Aegean islands, Anatolia and also with peoples further east. The ensuing cultural multiplicity, the many languages that came into contact with each other, as well as the knowledge of the existence of different [non-alphabetic] writing systems such as Egyptian, Assyrian and Hittite must have created the ideal conditions for experimenting with new possibilities and simplifications. The many new forms of writing that evolved in Syria, Palestine and Sinai bear witness to the prolific cultural development of this region in the second millennium.[8]

In the final analysis, the alphabet that works for all languages is the one that lets each letter take many sounds. Each single letter represents sounds in many languages, which, to save the appearances, are treated as if they were all one and the same sound, although "in fact"—etically or emically—they are not. Each letter thus comes to stand for a socially constructed "meta-sound," a "generic phoneme."

Each actually existing alphabet has "impurities." But these are not necessarily imperfections. They may be the price it pays for being in the world: a compromise, a trade-off between competing incommensurate value systems, between converted and unconverted communities, between emic and etic values.

Between the theoretical principle of one-phoneme-per-letter and the "field" practice of two-phonemes-per-letter lies the little gap that separates a pure phoneme from a hybrid phoneme. A hybrid phoneme is (at least) two phonemes in one: some of its allophones belong to one language, some to another. A hybrid phoneme is born when two sounds that are "phonetically similar" mate and fuse into one sound. This hybrid sound can be conceptualized in theory as either the union or the intersection of the two sounds: as either containing both its "parent" phonemes, and therefore belonging naturally to both languages, or else as an illegitimate half-breed bastard, born in "the field," wandering in the structural no man's land between the two (legitimate) parent languages, but belonging to neither. A pidgin, creole, mestizo phoneme: a source of pollution, noise, interference. An undocumented alien sound illegally crossing the linguistic border to "pass" for a legitimate sound of a language to which it doesn't "really" belong.

---

8. Coulmas (1989: 138).

For how we imagine hybrid phonemes may depend, in the final analysis, on our attitudes to purity and pollution. These attitudes shape the way the topic of hybrid phonemes is, implicitly or explicitly, conceptualized and talked about— or passed over in silence. If we think that pure is better than hybrid, then we will tend to think of pure phonemes as "occurring in nature," gathered in the field by scientists, and we will tend to think of hybrid phonemes as unnatural noise, pollution, a symptom of "outside influences," of foreign powers acting at a distance. Normally, people don't stretch a phoneme into a second language, because "normal" people are monoglot natives.

If, on the other hand, we think that normal people speak more than one language, we will tend to think that hybrid phonemes thrive in their natural habitat, in the speech of so-called "bilinguals." (I say "so-called" because if it is normal to speak more than one language, then it is only in artificially "pure" circumstances —where people are reduced to monoglossia, speaking with only one tongue— that hybrid phonemes will degenerate into merely "pure" phonemes.)

Uriel Weinreich imagined hybrid phonemes as "actual sounds" dwelling in the "structural no man's land" between structured languages.[9]

But Einar Haugen, who maintained an ecological attitude of "phonetic realism," imagined hybrid phonemes as naturally occurring patterns of sounds actually spoken by people.[10] Empirically, such patterns can be observed only in the speech of bilingual individuals when they are perceived as speaking two languages at the same time (or as speaking something perceived as neither one language nor the other). These kinds of data, so precious to the work of Einar Haugen, are invalidated by the methodological criteria of linguists whose object of study is the pure phonemes of monolingual, preferably illiterate, native speakers.

Empirically, very little separates a hybrid phoneme from either of its pure parent phonemes. This little gap can be made to appear so small as to be negligible. Or it can be pulled open to deconstruct the professional discourse on phonemic alphabets, to demystify the premature ideological closure, the ideological mirage that makes the little gap vanish even in theory.[11]

Some historians now point out that the phoneme was not an innovation of the 1930s or even of twentieth-century linguistics. The 1930s and 1940s presented as new something that is actually as old as the alphabet, nothing new:

> Transcriptions which record only those distinctions that serve to distinguish one word from another *within a given language* were not only the basis of the original reduction of languages to writing but were perfectly familiar

9. Weinreich (1953: 14).
10. See above, p. 87, n. 12.
11. "The appropriate object of study emerges only when the appearance of formal unification is unmasked as a failure or an ideological mirage" (Jameson 1981: 56).

in the theoretical study of language as well, rather than the innovation many writers on phonemic theory in the 1930s and 1940s claimed.[12]

The phonemes that are as old as the first alphabet are perhaps as much the hybrid phonemes that serve to distinguish one word from another *in two different languages* as the pure phonemes that serve for only one language. The game recorded in the Cobden glossaries was played every time an alphabet "fudged" Sapir's theorem by crossing the no man's land between two languages.

The question of whether a letter represents one pure sound, or an impure mixture of two or more, may seem like a storm in a teacup. But so may the question of whether a person represents one pure race, or a mixture of two or more. It's the same teacup. And the same storm.

---

12. Anderson (1985:173), my emphasis. Roy Harris, however, objects that "it is far from clear, to say the least, that the inventors of the alphabet were inspired by anything like modern phoneme theory" (Harris 1986: 104).

Commentaries

OPTING FOR THE VERNACULAR

Peter Elbow

University of Massachusetts—Amherst

It still bothers me—what those impressive immigrant workers did in Cobden Illinois in 1980. I'll start with my sadness—a sadness that I explored a few years ago in my *Vernacular Eloquence.*[1] That sadness came back strongly as I revisited *Illegal Alphabets* to write this little essay. But I'll go on to describe some completely different reactions I had during this recent writing—and finally my perplexity at feeling whipsawed between contradictory reactions.

So my sadness? Even though few of those Mexicans had much schooling, they somehow allowed *writing*—silent alphabetized text—to trump *hearing* and *speaking*. They allowed the *eye* to trump the *ear* and the *mouth*. When Panchito wanted to ask the pretty young Anglo girl where she lived, he was given a spoken answer: "Where do you live?" But he wasn't satisfied; he wanted a written equivalent. He wrote down JUELLULIB. Maybe he practiced *saying* these sounds over and over—tuning his mouth and his ear and his memory—sounds that his tongue was not used to making. We never hear about this kind of mouth and ear practice—only about writing.

Why did these Mexicans work so hard to produce all those *written codes* for how to say English words—producing, indeed, a small dictionary? One might say they weren't *just* interested in speech, they were interested in writing itself. My whole career has been devoted to trying to get people interested in writing. Yet the writing they developed would be of no use if Panchito wanted to write a note to the girl or to anyone else. And, of course, this transliteration of English wouldn't help them write a note to a Spanish speaker. As someone remarks of JUELLULIB, "It's not English and it's not Spanish." How wonderful to have devised

---

1. Elbow (2012: 359–362).

their *own* form of writing or literacy, yet what kind of literacy is that? One obvious answer to my wet blanket response—and true enough—is that they wanted a visual aid to memory, and a visual code they could pass along to a friend who hadn't *heard* how to say the words. True enough, but I don't think that's the whole answer. I want to bring in a story told by Ivan Illich.

He tells of how Nebrija—a learned grammarian—came to Queen Isabella of Spain in 1492. Nebrija told her that if she wanted empire and if she wanted a lasting reputation, she needed to impose her language, Castilian, on the people in her kingdom, many of whom spoke a variety of different languages. "Language has always been the consort of empire, and forever shall remain its mate," he wrote to the Queen.[2] She was skeptical at first. She wondered why Castilian speakers needed help to speak their own native language. But Nebrija won her over—like another good rhetorician who came to her in 1492.

As a result of the grammarian's success, schools began for the first time to teach children "correct" Castilian. So thanks to the insight of a grammarian who thought all language should be regularized with a grammar like that of Greek and Latin, and the power of a strong queen, we now take for granted something that Illich and Sanders insist is new under the sun: that children and adults cannot be trusted to speak their native language properly unless they get help from professionals—that is, grammarians and school teachers. And that help will characteristically involve writing.

Outside of those societies that we now call Modern European, no attempt was ever made to impose on entire populations an everyday language that would be subject to the control of paid teachers or announcers. Everyday language, until then, was nowhere the product of design; it was nowhere paid for and delivered like a commodity. And while every historian who deals with the origins of nation-states pays attention to the imposition of a national tongue, economists generally overlook the fact that this taught mother tongue is the earliest of specifically modern commodities, the model of all "basic needs to come."[3]

> Henceforth, people will have to rely on the language they receive from above, rather than to develop a tongue in common with one another. The switch from the vernacular to an officially taught mother tongue is perhaps the most significant—and therefore least researched—event in the coming of a commodity-intensive society . . . Formerly, there had been no salvation outside the Church; now, there would be no reading, no writing—if possible, no speaking—outside the educational sphere . . . Both the citizen

---

2. Illich (1981: 33). Nebrija's *Grammatica Castellana* was printed in Salamanca just 15 days after Columbus sailed; it is available online—search for Nebrija. And see Ofelia García in the next commentary, p. 87, n. 7.
3. Illich (1980: 47).

of the modern state and his state-provided language come into being for the first time—both are without precedent anywhere in history.[4]

As a result of the exceptional events that Nebrija and the queen set in motion, few people in our almost worldwide culture of correct literacy feel they can operate safely not just in writing but in their own *spoken* language. When people learn that they can't trust the words that come naturally out of their mouths—the tongue they learned from their mothers—we see the seeds of a deep distrust of the self. Even literate "cultured speakers"—perhaps especially cultured speakers—tend to worry about whether they make "mistakes" in using what is their mother tongue.

But how does this story pertain to the migrant workers in Cobden, Illinois in 1980? Yes, they might have thought their spoken Spanish was often "wrong," but in the project Kalmar describes in *Illegal Alphabets*, they were aggressively *ignoring* any worries about correctness. They didn't care about correct English writing: they wanted to write everyday vernacular *spoken* English. Yet, I'd argue that they inherited the distrust of mouth and ear and memory that Nebrija helped set in motion—the idea that they needed *writing* to get a handle on speech. They inherited the *allure* of written words and literacy—only written words have genuine authority. (It wasn't until the twentieth century that linguists figured out that the main authority for a language is the native speaker. For understanding any language, linguists consult the not-thought-out-intuitions of native speakers. Linguists have been remarkably uninterested in writing.)

James Gee tells a very different story to explain why the migrant workers didn't trust their mouth, ear, and memory. He posits the universal operation of what he calls "Discourse"—with a capital D: "A Discourse is a sort of 'identity kit' which comes complete with the appropriate costume and instructions on how to act, talk, and often, write so as to take on a particular social role . . . 'Discourse', as I am using the term, does not involve just talk or just language."[5]

Discourse as identity. So even without much schooling in Mexico, these workers could not help breathing in the air of the Discourse or culture of literacy. They came to own—or, as Gee would say, *be owned by*—a "Discourse." They had been inducted into membership in a group that unconsciously considered the *written* word to be the most real form of language.

But even at their best, visual letters are not a good way to represent spoken sounds (and Spanish letters are more trustworthy than English for representing sounds). The Mexicans worked hard at their task—often in serious discussion with each other. Yet with only half the effort alone and communally, they would have learned to speak the English words more accurately and fluently and

---

4. Illich (1981: 36). I develop the story of Nebrija and the queen in Elbow (2012: 183–185).
5. Gee (1990: 142). See above, p. 57, n. 5, and see Gee's commentary below, "Ways with letters and sounds."

comfortably than they did. Teachers of second languages almost universally avoid *writing* until the students get spoken words carefully and accurately in their mouths and ears. Some teachers use the old-fashioned method of starting with writing and grammar, but they tend to condemn their students to permanent strong accents.

Note that is, it doesn't take schooling to be inducted into a culture of literacy that distrusts spoken language. I recently read an account of a young educated man helping an older poor man with various aspects of his life. The older man admitted with shame that he couldn't read. Finally, he blurted in a moment of exasperation, "I have no *words!*" I feel his words like a kick in the stomach. It's not just that he was running over with words; the story made it clear that he was *more eloquent* than the young man helping him. But he didn't *feel* he had any words because he felt that spoken words don't count.

When I described this line of thinking to my wife—and when I tried out a draft version of it on my writing group—they were all suspicious of my reactions. Of course, we all learn to discount the doubts of a spouse, but the doubts that came from my two close and trusted friends in my writing group: they make me sit up and listen. Indeed, they confuse and perplex me. They said things like this:

- "But Peter, you ought to *like* what those migrant workers did."
- "They're using invented spelling instead of feeling oppressed by any obligation to spell words right. They are doing it for their own purposes instead of feeling a need to do literacy the 'right' way. And they have an understandable pragmatic reason for their form of writing. They want a code that will help them remember how to say the words after they have forgotten the sounds in their ears—sounds that are alien to their mouths. They want to be able to show a friend how to say these English sentences—friends who never heard the words spoken in English. Isn't that the kind of thing you've been fighting for?"
- "They're using *literacy* and making literacy fit them and serve their own needs. We thought that's what you liked. Indeed, they insist on *owning* their own language."
- "Can it be? You seem to be saying, 'They are writing *wrong.*' How is your reaction any different from that of the conservatives who criticize you, saying, 'You're bad to invite students to use invented spelling or to write in African American English or other nonstandard dialects. No one will accept writing like that or even understand what they write. This kind of writing is useless and will give them misleading ideas about writing.'"

Have I perhaps fallen into the white liberal trap? Is my sadness based on saying, "I *want* them to be free, but to get there, they should follow my directions." As teachers, we all love it when students come into our classroom already excited about our subject—already willing to work hard on strong personal goals. Yet their own goals and motivation often lead them to ignore our directions for what we consider the most effective way to learn. Am I really driven by a need for them to use writing the way I approve of, which, in this case, paradoxically means *not use* writing?

These doubts lead me to look again at a piece of my behavior that I've long noticed but not quite questioned. When I'm in church and someone reads from the Old Testament and then from the New, I tend to pick up the program where these readings are printed. I tend to follow along from the text. And it's not as though the sound system garbles the reading (as in some churches), and often enough the reader reads clearly. Why must I use my *eyes* on a *visual text* for words that my ear can get perfectly well? It's as though the spoken words don't fully *register* with me unless I read the silent writing.

Perhaps I'm just driven by obsession. I acknowledge that it took eight years of obsession to write *Vernacular Eloquence*; maybe that is now clouding my thinking. The fact is that I'm downright *angry* at the culture of literacy and how it makes almost everyone distrust speech and feel that only writing has authority. My wife can testify that I'm an obsessive champion of spoken language.

So do I have to give in to those voices from others, and even now from myself, that say, "Give it up Peter. Your original reactions are just wrong."?

I feel stuck. But I'll end by availing myself of another of my obsessions that says contraries don't always have to be reconciled; one point of view or argument doesn't always have to win. (See my book, *Embracing Contraries*, and my essays on binary thinking and the believing game.)

For I'm not willing to "give it up." In truth, as a white liberal—what else can I call myself?—I have really learned a lot about this matter of speech and writing—ear and eye. I have gathered some wisdom. I'm not willing to discount my knowledge about this—even if it's partly driven by obsession.

And here's one way to end, to bring a kind of resolution. In fact, I'm *not* tempted to *make* those Mexican workers do things my way. For example, I have sometimes had students who try to refuse my teacherly suggestions and assignments; they try to insist on taking their own path. My approach has tended to be to try to persuade them of the value of my assignments; but if I fail (again, like a wishy-washy liberal), I tend to give them their head and follow their own path. So if these migrant workers were in my classroom and wanted to use writing the way they want to use it—for their purposes—I'd try to persuade them of the value of giving more primacy to their mouths and ears and memories and not give such a *monopoly* to visual text. But if I couldn't persuade them, I'd let them follow their path. (Of course, I couldn't do this if I had them in a required first-year writing class. One of the things I love about teaching outside an institutional setting is that I don't have to serve the needs and assessment requirements of an institution.)

So, in my defense, I'm *not* a conservative who wants to *make* them do things my way. In the end, I'll give primacy to their remarkable initiative for taking language and literacy in their own hands. How can I not admire their creativity for figuring out a way to use literacy in a way that is almost unique? No, my main response is *sadness* at the way the culture of literacy has taken over all our minds—perhaps since Nebrija. And I'm sad also when I notice how deeply my mind has been taken over by the culture of literacy. I have no memory; my ear may be pretty good because of how much music I do, but I'm still crippled by a need to take in language by way of text. Those migrant workers had a better chance to develop a better relationship with spoken language. Certainly, their memories for language are far better than mine—and I suspect their mouths and ears are better. How sad for me to see them not trust and exploit those strengths.

Works Cited

Elbow, P. (2009) The believing game or methodological believing, *Journal for the Assembly for Expanded Perspectives on Learning*, 14 (Winter): 1–11.

—— (1986) *Embracing Contraries: Explorations in Learning and Teaching*, Oxford: Oxford University Press.

—— (1993) The uses of binary thinking, *Journal of Advanced Composition*, 12(1) (Winter): 51–78. Reprinted in *Everyone Can Write: Essays Toward a Hopeful Theory of Writing and Teaching Writing*, New York: Oxford University Press, 2000, pp. 48–80.

—— (2012) *Vernacular Eloquence: What Speech Can Bring to Writing*, Oxford: Oxford University Press.

Gee, J. P. (199) *Social Linguistics and Literacies: Ideology in Discourses, Critical Perspectives on Literacy and Education*, London & New York: Routledge.

Illich, I. (1980) Vernacular values, *Co-Evolution Quarterly*, Summer: 1–49, available at: www.preservenet.com/theory/Illich/Vernacular.html. These essays were the basis of most of Illich's book *Shadow Work*, Marion Boyars, 1981.

Illich, I. and Sanders, B. (1989) *The Alphabetization of the Popular Mind*, New York: Random House.

TRANSLANGUAGING AND *ABECEDARIOS ILEGALES*

Ofelia García

The Graduate Center, City University of New York

Language-minoritized bilingual communities throughout the world are always required to perform linguistically in the dominant language according to a standardized variety imposed by the majority language community. They are treated as if their bilingualism was invisible and as if only their performance in the dominant language was valid. Often, that monolingual performance, rendered through the speaker's bilingual system, is different from that of monolinguals and evaluated as deficient. This is especially so in the context of schools, instruments of nation-states that impose one way of using language, *un alfabeto, un abecedario y un discurso*.

Tomás Kalmar's *Illegal Alphabets precisamente y no sólo líricamente*, turns this position upside down. Instead of considering bilingual performances from the perspective of the dominant majority and schools, Kalmar adopts the perspective of Spanish-speaking workers who pick manzanas and peaches in orchards around Cobden, Illinois, and, in so doing, also pick up *sonidos del inglés*. But there's more than just Spanish sounds and English sounds going on here; there are intermingled sounds, just like in the old corridos that the men from Los Altos de Jalisco sing and that Kalmar documents in his book.

Kalmar describes the old traditional style of the corridos—"two men sing in such close harmony and with such complete recall of the entire text that you cannot tell who is leading and who is following, which is *la primera voz*, which *la segunda voz*—which is the first voice, which the second" (p. 2). This is precisely what is happening as the workers pick up English. Their voices in what is considered to be Spanish and then English *comienzan a interpenetrarse*, so that you can't tell anymore which is *la primera voz*, which *la segunda voz*. Their home language practices start to be simultaneously accompanied by language practices that some call English. To the speakers themselves, however, these practices do not constitute separate languages, external to them and relating to nation-state systems. These practices become part of their integrated language repertoire, of one semiotic system of meaning. Thus, to the world, and especially to schools, the language practices of bilingual speakers can be assigned to one language system (English) or another (Spanish). Although both practices are *bueno* to communicate, they are not *correcto* according to the imposed monolingual norm by which they are judged. The bilingual speech is considered not *correcto* English; but neither is it judged *correcto* Spanish, now intermingled with other words, other voices. To the bilingual speaker, however, these practices are not either *una primera voz* or a first language, and *una segunda voz* or a second language. They are not only *bueno*, but also *correcto*. They are simply the complex bilingual practices that are easily observable among all bilingual speakers.

The intermingling of voices in a corrido is not unlike the counterpoint of Bach's music, where there is a melodic interaction between several independent lines of music sung simultaneously, thus producing something interdependent and new. The counterpoint/*contrapunteo* between tobacco and sugar, with the aroma of the *cafecito con azúcar* and the *humo del tabaco* intermingled with pleasure and sweat in consumption/production is the topic of the monumental study of the Cuban ethnologist, Fernando Ortiz, *Contrapunteo cubano del tabaco y del azúcar*.[1] In the prologue to this work, Bronislaw Malinowski explains Ortiz's concept of *transculturación* as referring to "a process in which *a new reality emerges*, compounded and complex; a reality that is not a mechanical agglomeration of characters, not even a mosaic, but a new phenomenon, original and independent."[2]

Just as in *transculturación*, bilingual speakers engage in multiple and discursive practices taken up simultaneously in order to make sense of their bilingual worlds. I have referred to this simultaneous and integrated rendering of two voices as *translanguaging*,[3] a concept that has much to do with the transliteracies that Kalmar describes in his book.

Translanguaging, just as transliteracies, takes as its starting point the language practices of bilingual people as the norm, and not the practices of monolinguals. Kalmar's hybrid alphabet was first developed in Su Casa Grocery. In the same way, translanguaging and transliteracies are practices created *en su casa bilingüe*, a *casa* that is a "No man's land," as Kalmar titles the first chapter of his book. Mexicanos and gringos meet in that no man's land that they make *su casa*, and it is there that *la lengua* was *doblada*. Kalmar quotes one of the men, Alfredo, as saying, "*La lengua tiene que doblarse donde uno la maneja*" (p. 6). But to the translation provided by Kalmar of "your tongue has to fold the way you tell it to," we can add other meanings of *la lengua doblada*. The language that Alfredo craves is like that of Gloria Anzaldúa, "neither eagle nor serpent, but both. And like the ocean, neither animal respects borders."[4] "Doblar" *en español* has a sense of "to double."

---

1. Ortiz (1978[1940]).
2. Ortiz (1978[1940]: 4), my translation and emphasis.
3. García (2009), García and Li Wei (2014).
4. Anzaldúa (1997: 84).

By incorporating language practices from Anglos, Alfredo is doubling his capacity to speak, his voice rings and echoes further, as in *doblar campanas*, the bells which ring wildly. But *"una lengua doblada"* also has meanings as a language dubbed or translated. When Alfredo picks up sounds of English, it is as if his voice in Spanish is being dubbed in English—in no way substituted, but simultaneously present. Spanish starts to *doblar*, to change directions, as it responds to many more voices and interlocutors with different histories and ideologies. *En esa casa bilingüe, la lengua y la escritura* are released from the historical and academic constraints to which they have been subjected as "Spanish" or "English" in order to ensure *doblar* in other directions, so that other ideologies, visions, and realities are included. Alfredo is claiming agency for himself as an emergent bilingual and demanding a different direction from that offered in the traditional government ESL classes that Kalmar so well describes. Alfredo is, in many ways, taking a translanguaging epistemological stance *al demandar que* JUELLULIB be seen for its *significado* in the life of Panchito, *pero también al amplificar una voz bilingüe* that incorporates different *historias è ideologías*, thus forging new possibilities and a new political reality for Mexican workers.

Throughout *Illegal Alphabets*, Kalmar keeps raising the same question in different ways: "What is this word? *Es inglés? Es español?* Both? Neither?" (p. 18). "In which language is JUELLULIB written?" (p. 41). This stance is also reflected in some of the reactions of some teachers of English as a Second Language Kalmar cites: "This isn't English, it isn't Spanish, it's nothing, it's worse than nothing, it's not bilingual, it's zero-lingual." The reason why this is an impossible query is because it stems from a belief that there is such a thing as *a* language.

The concept of a language is closely linked to the construction of the nation-state. In a convincing book, Makoni and Pennycook argue that the concept of a language *es una invención Europea, producto of colonialismo* and of a Herderian nineteenth-century nationalist romanticist ideology that insisted that language and identity were intrinsically linked.[5] Languages do not exist on their own, *y todas las lenguas están en contacto con otras*—being influenced by others, and containing elements *de otras*. National "languages" are constituted from resources *de diversos* places and times.

Likewise, Jørgensen argues that it doesn't make sense to talk of "a language" per se, although he defends the concept of "language." Languages are constructs that cannot be counted or categorized. Jørgensen claims that language in itself consists of human behavior between people by which we form and shape our social structures. He convincingly argues that "the concept of *a* language is thus bound in time and space . . . and it is not part of our understanding of the human concept of language. Features are, however. Speakers use features and not languages."[6]

---

5. Makoni and Pennycook (2007).
6. Jørgensen (2008: 166), my emphasis.

For Spanish, it was the publication of Antonio de Nebrija's *Gramática de la Lengua Castellana* in 1492 that constructed what we learned to call *castellano/español*. Nebrija dedicates the grammar to Queen Isabella by saying: *"Siempre la lengua fue compañera del imperio."* A single "Spanish" language was needed to rule subjects and to build *el imperio*.[7] The standardization of language as carried out by grammarians, linguists and language academies in conjunction with politicians has played an important role in the construction of nation-states and ethnic identities. It is this construction of a standardized way of using words that we call today "language."

If we take this position, then the "illegal" alphabets of the *mexicanos* in Cobden, Illinois, are *doblando* the linguistic border between what is known as *español y* English and acquire legitimacy and authority. What is being produced is, as Anzaldúa writes, "neither eagle nor serpent, but both" (1999, p. 84) because it is also neither. Su Casa Grocery acts as a Thirdspace:

> a space of extraordinary openness, a place of critical exchange where the geographical imagination can be expanded to encompass a multiplicity of perspectives that have heretofore been considered by the epistemological referees to be incompatible, uncombinable. It is a space where issues of race, class, and gender can be addressed simultaneously without privileging one over the other.[8]

The space and process that Kalmar describes invigorates languaging, and traditional *abecedarios*, with new possibilities from a site of both creativity and power. As Li Wei and I have said in describing translanguaging: "Going *beyond* language refers to transforming the present, to intervening by reinscribing our human, historical commonality in the act of languaging."[9] Translanguaging, as well as the transliteracies that Kalmar describes, is a creative process that is the property of the speakers' way of acting in interactions and in their literate lives, rather than belonging to the language or *alfabeto* system itself.

As Kalmar shows, transliteracy practices are not new and are not unusual. Translanguaging in writing has been common from ancient times to today.[10] We have evidence of bilingual texts, as well as transliterated texts and "mixed-language" texts where writers use different language conventions and scripts as far back as the early Roman Republic. Today, some languages, such as Wolof, Pular, and Manyika, are written in either Arabic or Roman scripts or a combination of the two, depending on writers and audience.[11] The Dominican-

---

7. García (2011). And see Peter Elbow's commentary above, p. 126, n. 2.
8. Soja (1996: 5).
9. García and Li Wei (2014: 25).
10. Adams (2003).
11. Makoni et al. (2012).

American Junot Díaz, the 2008 Pulitzer winner for his novel *The Brief Wondrous Life of Oscar Wao*, describes what he calls his "mash-up of codes", which includes no way to privilege one or another way of speaking by focusing on linguistic simultaneity: "By keeping the Spanish as normative in a predominantly English text, I wanted to remind readers of the fluidity of languages, the mutability of languages. And to mark how steadily English is transforming Spanish and Spanish is transforming English."[12]

Today, more than ever, new technologies have enabled the production of more fluid language texts.

In presenting Latino migrants as gamers, as creators of new realities and from a position of power, and not from that of undocumented brown immigrants to which they are often relegated, Kalmar portrays the human ability to be creative and critical, and the ways in which people resist the constraints of standardized ways of speaking and writing. Kalmar reminds us that the men in this community are involved in the same kind of fieldwork done by missionaries and linguists. In rendering words *como de veras se oye* (and not with conventions imposed externally from the top), these men are operating in the "margin of literacy," a literacy standardization that has been constructed to privilege some and exclude others. The Mexican workers in Kalmar's book are operating, as are all field-workers, anthropologists, linguists, and ethnographers, using their creativity and intelligence, fudging, solving the puzzle as in a *rompecabezas*. The writing practices of these workers, as they make sense of sounds that they hear, are in no way "illegal." What should be illegal is using language and literacy to undermine the ways in which those who have been marginalized by society use their own resources to *romper el círculo de opresión*.

JUELLULIB will never be accepted in school and will not be made part of the Common Core State Standards that are so much part of the educational discourse today. But it was, as Kalmar makes evident, transformative in the life of Panchito. The game in which Panchito engaged enabled him to make sense of the English sounds that he needs in society and to make contact with someone else. It transformed his life because it gave him the ability to speak, to voice, to make human contact. The question for educators who hold onto traditional views on language and literacy is: What is more important? Is it more important to teach narrowly the conventions of English writing or to give many like Panchito the ability to speak, and also the ability of the English-speaking Martha to hear Panchito's words? So what if it is fudging? Isn't that what linguists documenting languages do? So what if it doesn't fall within institutionalized forms of writing? Hasn't that standardization also been a game? Which games count? What are the games for?

---

12. Díaz, cited in Ch'ien (2005: 204).

These are all *preguntas importantes* for all of us who are interested in language and education. The answer for me, as I think for Kalmar, is clear—*tenemos que doblar*/bend and turn in order to *doblar*/double and amplify the voices of those who have been robbed of the ability to speak. A translanguaging/transliteracy approach gives us ways to make this *desdoblamiento* possible and to let the multiple simultaneous voices of the *corridos* take the due course that is also their due.

Works Cited

Adams, J. N. (2003) *Bilingualism and the Latin Language*, Cambridge: Cambridge University Press.

Anzaldúa, G. (1997) *Borderlands/La Frontera. The New Mestiza*, 2nd ed., San Francisco, CA: Aunt Lute Books.

Ch'ien, Evelyn Nien-Ming (2005) *Weird English*, Cambridge, MA: Harvard University Press.

García, O. (2009) *Bilingual Education in the 21st Century: A Global Perspective*, Malden, MA & Oxford: Wiley-Blackwell.

García, O. (2011) Planning Spanish: nationalizing, minoritizing and globalizing performances, in Manuel Díaz-Campos (Ed.), *The Handbook of Hispanic Sociolinguistics*, Malden, MA & Oxford: Wiley-Blackwell, pp. 665–685.

García, O. and Li Wei (2014) *Translanguaging: Language, Bilingualism and Education*, Basingstoke: Palgrave Macmillan.

Jørgensen, J. N. (2008) Polylingual languaging around and among children and adolescents, *International Journal of Multilingualism*, 5(3): 161–176.

Makoni, S., Makoni, B., Abdelhay, A., and Mashiri, P. (2012) Colonial and postcolonial language policies in Africa: historical and emerging landscapes. In B. Spolsky (Ed.), *The Cambridge Handbook of Language Policy*, Cambridge: Cambridge University Press, pp. 523–543.

Makoni, S. and Pennycook, A. (2007) *Disinventing and Reconstituting Languages*, Clevedon, UK: Multilingual Matters.

Ortiz, F. (1978[1940]) *Contrapunteo cubano del tabaco y el azúcar [Tobacco and Sugar: A Cuban Counter Point]*, Caracas: Biblioteca Ayacucho.

Soja, E. W. (1996) *Thirdspace: Journeys to Los Angeles and Other Real-and-Imagined Places*, Malden, MA & Oxford: Blackwell.

WAYS WITH LETTERS AND SOUNDS

James Paul Gee

University of Wisconsin at Madison

Illegal Alphabets and Adult Biliteracy represents an important and innovative contribution to an area now sometimes referred to as "New Literacies Studies."[1] New Literacies Studies starts with a rather paradoxical claim: If you want to understand how reading and writing work, don't look at them directly and in and of themselves. Rather, look directly at specific social practices in which specific ways of writing and reading are embedded. Furthermore, look at how these specific ways of reading and writing, within these social practices, are always integrally connected to specific ways of using oral language; specific ways of acting, interacting, thinking, believing, valuing, feeling; and specific ways of using various sorts of objects, tools, technologies, symbols, places, and times. All these "ways with words, deeds, and things" allow people to do certain things (and not others), to mean certain things (and not others), and to be certain kinds of people (and not others).[2]

Thus, there are as many literacies as there are ways in which written language is recruited within specific social practices to allow people to enact and recognize specific socially situated identities (being a certain kind of person) and specific socially situated activities (doing a certain kind of thing). That's why New Literacies Studies often uses the word *literacy* in the plural, *literacies*. The graffiti of a Latino gang member in Los Angeles are different from those of an African-American gang member in Los Angeles, and both, in turn, are different from tagging carried out by often multicultural tagging crews in Los Angeles. Each of these groups of people are being different kinds of people doing different kinds

---

1. This commentary originally served as the Foreword to the first edition of this book.
2. For programmatic statements, see Barton (1994), Gee (1996), and Street (1995).

of things when they write graffiti or tag a freeway overpass. Neo-Darwinian adaptationist biologists write up research results differently for a professional journal than they do for a popular science magazine,[3] and both, in turn, differ from how biochemists write up their results in either case. Each of these groups of people are being different kinds of people doing different kinds of things when they write as professional scientists for their colleagues or as popularizers for more general audiences. Nor can we really detach how these people write or read as professionals from how they talk to their colleagues or operate with their instruments and instrumental procedures.[4]

A second central claim of New Literacies Studies is this: Literacy is not first and foremost a mental possession of individuals. Rather, it is first and foremost a social relationship among people, their ways with words, deeds, and things, and their institutions. Literacy is primarily and fundamentally out in the social, historical, cultural, and political world. It is only secondarily a set of cognitive skills, skills that subserve literacies as social acts in quite diverse ways in different contexts.

What does it mean to say that literacy is a social relationship among people, their ways with words, deeds, and things, and their institutions? Consider, as an example, a young girl in first grade, named Shanti, who is "reading" a book using "multiple cues"; that is, she is using her knowledge of letter-sound correspondences, the syntax of English, plausible meanings at word, phrase, and text levels, her recognition of words as larger shapes, and predictions she can make from pictures in the book, singly or together at different points in the text, to recognize words and give meaning to the book. One teacher or researcher, who has allegiance to "Whole Language," says the child is "really reading" and is "a reader." Another teacher or researcher, who has allegiance to a strictly psycho-linguistic view of reading as a process in which people first recognize words only by letter-sound decoding and only then use other sorts of cues to check on this recognition, says the child is not "really reading" (because she is using multiple cues for word recognition and not just word checking) and is still an "emergent reader."

In this case, *who* the child is (a "reader," an "emergent reader") and *what* she is doing ("really reading," "not really reading") are not in the child's head or the teacher's or researcher's. Rather, they are in the set of relationships that are being set up among the child, the book, the teacher or researcher, theories, social practices, and institutions. Does it matter? It surely does, because in each case the child gets captured or recruited into different "discourses" or "ways of being in the world."[5]

---

3. Myers (1992).
4. Latour (1999).
5. Varenne and McDermott (1998).

To take another example—one that shows how the child can be differently "captured" in different situations—consider that the child's teacher writes in her notebook: "Shanti is reading by using multiple cues." This sentence and this act of writing mean quite different things if they are part of a journal kept by a Whole Language teacher or part of an assessment instrument carried out by a psycho-linguistically driven teacher, in the sense discussed above. In the first case, the sentence constitutes an acknowledgment of the student's progress; in the second case, it constitutes a possibly negative evaluation of the student's progress. The first teacher is liable to recommend more books, the latter more phonics. Apart from the social practice of which it is a part, the teacher's sentence means just nothing, or nothing much. Within a specific social practice, connected to specific social groups and their institutions, the sentence is part of the ways in which student and teacher enact and recognize specific identities and activities.

Now these examples are not, of course, innocent. They remind us of the current reading wars, the battles between advocates of Whole Language, and related movements, people who stress immersion in multiple reading and writing practices, and the advocates of direct phonics and direct, scripted instruction, people who stress early and direct instruction on the letter-sound code, often with "decodable books." In this battle,[6] opponents of New Literacies Studies often say that things such as phonics and the letter-sound code are surely not social practices or importantly embedded in them, but merely mental "skills." Surely, these people say, the letter-sound code has not much to do with people's "socially situated identities." *Illegal Alphabets and Adult Biliteracy* very much shows otherwise.

In this book, for the first time, someone shows how something as seemingly simple as the letter-sound code, something that seems so clearly instantiated merely as a mental skill, is profoundly embedded in social practices, in the formation and transformation of people's identities, in the pursuit of their political projects, in the trajectories of institutions, and in the ways in which cultures have sought to meet (for better and worse) across borders and boundaries. Kalmar moves deftly between fieldworkers doing linguistics as part and parcel of their very survival, their politics, and their transformation of society, on the one hand, and the historical workings of the field of professional linguistics constructing and construing languages and cultures, language variation and language universals, on the other hand. In between and at both poles are language and culture, not as stable "objective" phenomena, but as always "temporal, emergent, and disputed."[7] This book is, I believe, destined to become a classic of New Literacies Studies.

---

6. In which, by the way, I don't accept either side or that there are just two sides—see Gee (1999).

7. Clifford (1986: 19), Hopper (1998: 156).

Works Cited

Barton, D. (1994) *Literacy: An Introduction to the Ecology of Written Language*, Oxford: Blackwell.

Clifford, J. (1986) Introduction: partial truths, in J. Clifford and G. Marcus (Eds.), *Writing Culture: The Poetics and Politics of Ethnography*, Berkeley, CA: University of California Press, pp. 1–26.

Gee, J. (1996) *Social Linguistics and Literacies: Ideology in Discourses*, 2nd ed., London: Taylor & Francis.

—— (1999) Reading and the New Literacy Studies: reframing the National Academy of Sciences Report on Reading, *Journal of Literacy Research*, 31(3): 355–374.

Hopper, P. J. (1998) Emergent grammar, in M. Tomasello (Ed.), *The New Psychology of Language: Cognitive and Functional Approaches to Language Structure*, Mahwah, NJ: Lawrence Erlbaum Associates, pp. 155–175.

Latour, B. (1999) *Pandora's Hope: Essays on the Reality of Science Studies*, Cambridge, MA: Harvard University Press.

Myers, G. (1992) *Writing Biology: Texts in the Social Construction of Scientific Knowledge*, Madison, WI: University of Wisconsin Press.

Street, B. (1995) *Social Literacies: Critical Approaches to Literacy in Development, Ethnography and Education*, London: Longman.

Varenne, H. and McDermott, R. (1998) *Successful Failure: The School America Builds*, Boulder, CO: Westview.

THE POWER OF THE SINGLE CASE

Hervé Varenne

Teachers College, Columbia University

In the age of "big data," what is the point of the single case, historically unique, now lost in the past of most participants—except perhaps for the recorder or analyst who writes a book about it? What can a few Mexican men who met for a few weeks 30 years ago in Southern Illinois tell us about language, literacy, migration, life in Mexico and the United States?

They can tell us about otherwise unimaginable possibilities of the human spirit.

As Tomás Kalmar reminds us, he does not write about a mass event, repeated in a similar fashion among millions, or even thousands, of Mexicans when confronted with the need to make themselves understood by potential employers in the United States. He writes about something that *can* happen. He writes about an often-discounted potentiality: people can teach each other a language none of them speak, and they can do this without special schooling. He knows it because he observed how some men did this, as they were doing it, with little prodding on his part except for asking them to explain how they were doing it. As the men perform it, this is serious and purposeful work. It is also an occasion for joking and fun. It is, as some anthropologists now would say, "deep play" with potentially serious consequences. Kalmar also tells us that similar, though different, encounters happened, in other times and places when other peoples confronted other linguistic puzzles, for other purposes, whether religious, political, or scholarly.

Eventually, Kalmar writes about an analytic, theoretical, and yet very practical intelligence that can be triggered in the most unlikely of places, among the most unlikely of people, and that can produce complex analyses of local conditions—and not only about linguistic conditions. He gives us a wonderful example of how we can gain further systematic knowledge about a general truth fundamental to human history. And, by doing so, he illustrates, again, the kind of knowledge that "big data" cannot produce and that anthropology has been building up to offer: knowledge about the deliberate production of culture in all sorts of circumstances and for all sorts of reasons. The Cobden Abecedario is unique. The possibility that something like that might be produced is ubiquitous.

For any number of reasons, anthropology is not widely known for producing this very knowledge about cultural production even though it can be argued that this is where the discipline started and made its major contribution. Over much of its history, anthropology encouraged its audiences to transform "culture" into one of the conditions that shape people and limit what they can do. Culture would be something that was learned early in life by individuals, and that, then, handicapped or disabled them unless special institutions helped them deal with the difficulties. But anthropology did not quite start with such a set of assumptions. Anthropology, I offer, started with the sense that if one looked carefully in places far away in time or space, one found that human beings are much more productive in constituting, or designing, lives for themselves than most theories of humanity could imagine, even when the theories are supported by a large amount of data. What anthropological research across the globe demonstrated was that it is easy for those who would measure humanity not to notice that they easily miss much that is fundamental—including the altogether surprising flexibility of human beings as they keep adapting to hostile environments—whether the hostility is geographical or sociopolitical. Human beings left the plateaus of East Africa tens of thousand years ago, and now can survive on the moon. They probably started in small bands with limited institutional specialization, and now continue to dispute who should regulate and in what ways, sexuality, reproduction, marriage, inheritance, birth privilege, etc. They started moving across landscapes, and they keep moving, across such inhuman (if one thinks socio-biologically, or humanistically) boundaries as international frontiers that are, of course, the fully human, in a cultural sense, product of history.

Illegal Alphabets is one of the many works of the past quarter century that recaptures the excitement of the time when Boas, Rivers, Malinowski, Mead, and others brought back evidence that, in the nooks and crannies of islands, mountains, deserts, human beings were doing wonderful things. By the end of the twentieth century, the nooks and crannies are most often found in urban centers, migrant camps, or refugee centers, but the excitement is the same. Down the street and around the corner, up or down this way or that, some people are doing what most theories of the impact of late modernity, complex industrialization, neoliberalism, etc., cannot imagine they are doing. They may even teach themselves a language none of them can speak! They can do so by analyzing what they hear, in context, and then by assessing whether their hypothetical analysis corresponded both to what might work interactionally, and to the representations that the target language uses. They do this, "against the odds"—as calculated by social statisticians who do not have the tools to reveal the powerful unique. People do this by getting together, figuring out their resources, deliberating, that is, in my summary term,[1] "educating" themselves while producing something new, fleeting, and unique—for example, the Cobden Abecedario.

Kalmar discusses extensively how the *possibility* of such processes of joint deliberation about language and its organization or representation is *not* unique. There are many examples of people conducting such analyses, though they are easy to miss when they are not the product of "experts" with esoteric knowledge. Kalmar lists some of those. Another powerful example can be found in the many cases of Africans, enslaved in the United States, teaching themselves how to read English.[2] It is probable that we would have more examples if we had paid closer attention to the language about language that is produced by the non-expert in the course of their lives. Many years ago, Roman Jakobson had affirmed that "metalanguage is not only a necessary scientific tool utilized by logicians and linguists; it plays also an important role in our everyday language."[3] Ofelia García has been drawing the consequences by writing about what she terms "languaging";[4] that is, the process by which new languages (and literacies) emerge in and through interaction whether in the more local of familial contacts or through various forms of global media.

Kalmar, like García, is writing about the linguistic activities of the non-expert, in settings not directly controlled by the state—and certainly not for the purposes to which they are being put. He is writing about what has been called "informal" education, or "community education," though these words do not capture the fundamental or general character of the activity. For this is work that precedes and follows the work of those who may be granted by some corporation or state the special status of analyst, writer, curriculum developer, assessor. It is work that encompasses the work of the specialist even if the specialist loses sight of the political processes that constitute the status. Jacques Rancière has explored how this blindness has been induced through the history of European philosophy, from Plato onwards,[5] and how it has prevented experts from noticing and acknowledging the education that the "ignorant" give each other.[6] Kalmar, with many others, has shown that this philosophical critique of philosophy has much empirical evidence to back it. It is time for us to make our colleagues pay attention, and policymakers draw the practical consequences.

---

1. Varenne (2007).
2. Gundaker (2008).
3. Jakobson (1985: 354).
4. García (2013).
5. Rancière (2004[1983]).
6. Rancière (1999[1987]).

Works Cited

García, O. (2013) Informal bilingual acquisition: dynamic spaces for language education, in D. Singleton, J. A. Fishman, L. Aronin, and M. O. Laoire (Eds.), *Current Multilingualism: A New Linguistic Dispensation*, Berlin: Mouton de Gruyter, pp. 99–118.

Gundaker, G. (2008[2007]) Hidden education among African Americans during slavery, in H. Varenne and E. Gordon (Eds.), *Anthropological Perspectives on Education*, Lewiston, NY: The Edwin Mellen Press, pp. 53–74.

Jakobson, R. (1985[1956]) Meta language as linguistic problem, in S. Rudy (Ed.), *Roman Jakobson, Selected Writings, VII*, The Hague: Mouton, pp. 113–121.

Rancière, J. (1999[1987]) *The Ignorant Schoolmaster: Five Lessons in Intellectual Emancipation*, translated by K. Ross, Palo Alto, CA: Stanford University Press.

—— (2004[1983]) *The Philosopher and His Poor*, translated by J. Drury, C. Oster, and A. Parker, Durham, NC: Duke University Press.

Varenne, H. (2007) Difficult collective deliberations: anthropological notes towards a theory of education, *Teachers College Record*, 109(7): 1559–1587.

ETHNOMETHODOLOGY AND *MESTIZAJE*

The Cherán Connection

Luis Vázquez León

*Centro de Investigaciones y Estudios Superiores en
Antropología Social de Occidente*

Forty percent of the 2,000 pickers in Cobden were bilingual Tarascans from
Cherán, Michoacán. Why did they choose Cobden? It seems they followed a
migration route first established by pioneer biblical missionaries of the Summer
Institute of Linguistics who lived for many years in Cherán—ever since the birth
of the 1940 Tarascan Project. Kalmar asks, "Did the game played with letters
and sounds in Cobden in 1980 begin in Cherán in 1939? Or did it begin much
longer ago?"[1] In the light of what is happening in Cherán today, this provocative
connection is worth serious investigation and reflection.

I have long urged Kalmar to publish his research on private correspondence
written in 1941 in Swadesh's *alfabeto lójiko* by newly biliterate participants in the
Tarascan Project. The professional game played by Swadesh's colleagues and native
informants for high political stakes prefigures the textual and communicational
strategy adopted by Kalmar's amateur linguists to cope with life in Cobden, Illinois.
Swadesh's *alfabeto lójiko* is a grandparent of the *abecedario mojado* which so baffled
the American teachers who saw in it a Spanish deformation of English. What
those teachers didn't realize was that the "illegal" authors of the biliterate
diccionarios were accustomed to situations of analogous linguistic interactions in
tierra de nadie—or, as Kalmar puts it, in "no man's land." Back in Mexico, they
were already biliterate in that peculiar way.

The legacies of literacy are not confined to the historical transition from
premodernity to modernity, to the advent of printing, of schools, and the rest.
They also point to continuities and discontinuities arising in the long history of
literacy itself. In the Tarascan case, this can take us all the way back to the writing
of codices before the sixteenth century, and then to the colonial linguistics used

---

1. This volume, p. 114.

in the spiritual conquest of Mexico, including the past century's revolutionary bilingual education.

The fact that, in 1980, new *abecedarios* were being devised to represent English speech *como de veras se oye* shows that, far from being obsolete as objects of study, such legacies are sustained by a socio-historical context that is still active. Those of us whose profession relies on a presentist discourse on literacy must admit that much of our attention has centered on transnational migrant communities— what, in Michoacán, we call *comunidades extendidas*. The occasions of linguistic interchange Kalmar studies and the dialogue sessions and scenes of writing they turn into are as ephemeral as the seasonal passage of the workers through Cobden: barely a few months, before they continue their migratory cycle and head for labor camps in Florida. And yet the situation in Cobden illuminates the context in which life unfolds when, after successfully crossing the national border, unauthorized migrants undertake to then cross the linguistic and cultural border. Kalmar does not spell out the thrust of phrases such as *the law doesn't protect us* (spoken when a fellow worker was killed) or *huelga* (uttered in the first meeting at the town hall). But he does explicate the inability of American teachers to truly engage in Paolo Freire's pedagogy of the oppressed. Confronting unauthorized migrants from whom it is necessary to learn (and with whom they must interact), they condemn the systematic use of this "illegal" phonetic/phonemic notation system as a corruption of English. The lack of understanding that appears in these social situations has deep roots in attitudes to purity and impurity—and not just to linguistic purity and impurity, either. The dangerous myth of racial purity was already at stake in the police chief's reaction to the migrants' interacting with the town's Anglos playfully—and seriously—in public spaces.

Kalmar's Freirean legacy converges with disturbing perceptions gained through the microsociology of Erving Goffman, and, above all, with the discoveries made by applying ethnomethodology to educational research in which the subject of inequality plays a major role. Whether in Church, State, or Academy, the issue of power underlies even the deliberate use of such illegal alphabets. Kalmar takes care to stress that the strategy of reducing English speech to an impressionistic phonetic notation not only is theoretically valid, but has its own forgotten lineage—witness the case of the Kassel glossary in the ninth century, when the efforts of an unknown community of readers aimed to make Vulgar Latin intelligible through the use of a Germanic language resembling Anglo-Saxon. For monolingual Anglo teachers in most ESL programs, however, the Cobden glossaries are *desautorizados*—unauthorized, devoid of authority. As one of them says, in a canonical fit of indignation, "I'd never be allowed to let my students get away with this sort of thing."[2] Read with a prejudice fostering the inequality

---

2. This volume, p. 20ff.

of one language in asymmetrical contact with another, such glossaries, under the most extreme construction of illegality, are experienced as a source of contamination. Even Kalmar's Freirean colleagues prove prone to invoking the authority proper to the teacher's position, and to imagining that Kalmar was responsible for his students' decision to write this emic/etic way.

But in Cobden, the encounters of linguistic exchange were totally informal, outside any classroom, lacking any formal recognition. They began in the basement of a store with a group of migrant workers and locals trying to understand each other in their incommensurable languages. Over time, these encounters led to the imperative of appropriating the Anglos' way of talking by alphabetizing their speech-sounds—a project that, right from the start, engages the distinction between emic and etic frames. Kalmar addresses the slipperiness between the socially constructed frames of the actors' own lifeworld and the metalanguage of social scientists. This emic *versus* etic debate first arose among academics. But it extends into the practices and beliefs of the actors who are the object of anthropological study. This "mutual interpretative interplay between social science and those whose activities compose its subject matter"[3] is what Anthony Giddens means by the double hermeneutic. It is what has given Mexican anthropology so much of its appeal as a popular genre.

A part of the social unease that this interaction provoked is that the Anglos in Cobden—relatively close in social status to their illegal counterparts—accepted the role of informants for the amateur linguists. The border being crossed was no less dangerous for being symbolic. Today, we know that such situations of face-to-face interaction have led to the emergence of creoles and pidgins among monolingual workers brought together on plantations. The Cobden glossaries, however, do *not* represent the *pachuco* or *pocho* Spanish used in Arizona and parts of southern California. What these Tarascan workers were trying to do was similar to what anthropologists and linguists do when they write field notes. And Kalmar himself has a field day with this, providing illuminating linguistic passages that bring his analysis straight back to the connection between Cobden 1980 and the Tarascan Project in Cherán 1940. He thus throws light on biliteracy campaigns and bilingual education promoted by revolutionary teachers and Christian missionaries in Mexico in the past century.

Cherán Today: The Revitalization of Ethnicity

What happened in Cherán in 1940 and what happened in Cobden in 1980 contrast with what is happening in Cherán today. To illuminate this contrast, I now consider recent data on biliteracy and the current politics of bilingual identity in Mexico. In 1997–1998, there were, in the town of Cherán, no less than 257 teachers in

---

3. Giddens (1984: xxxii, 348).

30 schools, teaching preschool, elementary, middle and high school students. At present, there is also a technical college and a teacher's college. Even the few monolingual Tarascans who still speak only the indigenous language are now literate. Meanwhile, the Americanization of Tarascans who managed to become "legal" in Illinois has already had unexpected results. In Cherán, a contradictory variety of cultural revitalization is underway. It aims to undo the biliterate education programs that formerly led to such successful integration. Census data for 1990 and 1995 show that use of an indigenous language has been fading notably. The census in Mexico (unlike in the USA) recorded use of an indigenous language from which to deduce the person's indigenous status. Starting in 2000, ethnic affiliation has been recorded, with paradoxical results comparable to those experienced in the recent U.S. census when given the option of identifying as "Hispanic race." In 1990, out of a total of 5,024 people in Cherán, 90 percent spoke Spanish. Five years later, due to the effect of emigration, the population fell to 4,765, of whom 98 percent spoke Spanish. In the same period, monolingual Tarascan speakers shrank from 5.5 percent to only 0.7 percent of the total municipal population.[4]

Those who speak an indigenous language now *decline* to choose any ethnic group. Meanwhile, those who do *not* speak an indigenous language choose to identify themselves as members of some ethnic group. The 2010 census, behind the facade of widespread bilingualism, managed to capture the population that "does not speak but does understand an indigenous language," and in Michoacán this focused on the municipalities of the Tarascan Plateau, including Cherán.[5] Significant differences have since been observed in these municipalities: the highest percentage of native speakers are now located in neighboring Charapan and Nahuatzen; those who "do not speak but do understand" the language are concentrated in Cherán, Tzintzuntzan, and Erongarícuaro.

Cherán, Charapan, and Chilchota stand out among those municipalities whose population identify themselves as indigenous.[6] For many years, these very places were the canonical paradigms of the most hybrid, the most *amestizados*—that is to say, the most *acculturated* communities. This loss of native language use has put the political and educational elite of the county seat on their mettle. Cherán had been, for many years, the host of the Centro Coordinador Indigenista of the Instituto Nacional Indigenista, dedicated to promoting the acculturation of the regional indigenous population. In 2003, that center was dissolved to make way for the new Comisión Nacional para el Desarrollo de Pueblos Indígenas [National Commission for the Development of Indigenous Peoples]. This was rooted in the new policy of multicultural recognition. Its orientation was thus the opposite

---

4. Instituto Nacional de Estadística y Geografía (2000). For detailed critique, see Vázquez Léon (2010), esp. pp. 85ff.
5. Instituto Nacional de Estadística y Geografía (2011: 52–53).
6. New Parangaricutiro is also prominent. Instituto Nacional de Estadística y Geografía (2011: 53).

of its predecessor: acculturation was no longer the point. Now, the aim was to revitalize ethnicity.

Except that in response to the evident loss of the indigenous language—which, in Mexico, has long meant the loss of *indigenidad*—in Cherán, the revitalization of ethnicity has turned into a radical traditionalist reaction. The small town of Cherán has ceased to be the county seat. It used to include Tanaco, many tiny villages and *rancherías*. Cherán has changed into an urban community governed by *usos y costumbres*, an assembly of neighborhoods. Tanaco and the neighboring little villages have been recast as sources of conflict, regarded as shelters for organized crime.

Cherán has become a legal anomaly: of the 113 municipalities in Michoacán, it is the only one that is not a *municipio*. It has been dissolved by a major reorganization of state power, which has been taken away from mayors and from the interim governor accused of complicity with a criminal organization. Under these conditions, the entire municipal police force has disappeared, government councils by direct vote have been imposed, and federal funds are now channeled through a Security Commissioner with more power than the mayors and the governor himself.

Legally, in short, Cherán is now no man's land. Whereas, for example, in Oaxaca the establishment of local governments *por usos y costumbres* first required the Bill of Rights of Indigenous Peoples and Communities enacted in 1998, there is, on the contrary, no such law in Michoacán. Instead, local governments by *usos y costumbres* invoke what their lawyer Aragón calls their "right to insurrection"[7] based on arms. So, in the middle of a War on Drugs unilaterally declared by the President of Mexico, the new community leaders have formed the first paramilitary guard (subsequently expanded as self-defense militias in Michoacán), which has now, via check-points, closed off all access to the town. A special corps of sappers, also heavily armed, has formed to protect the mountains.

Cherán has been not just the pioneer in paramilitarization: its stealthy accession to Michoacán's Consejo General de Autodefensas y Comunitarios exemplifies a true "working out of Durkheim's Aphorism"[8] on the concreteness of social facts since it has no real insurrection in mind, but only intends to strengthen the security of the state precisely where its monopoly on violence falls short.

Ethnomethodology and *mestizaje*

Does this qualify as a new ethnomethod in Garfinkel's sense of the term? What we witness here is a resounding reversal of what happened in Cobden in 1980 when authentic ethnomethodology helped immigrants integrate into American

---

7. Aragón (2013).
8. Garfinkel (2002).

society. In Cobden, the mojados managed to cross not just the national, but also the ethnic border, and to negotiate their settlement on the other side of it. So it is striking that, in Cherán, ethnic borders have now been reinforced to the point of rejecting other Tarascans or Purepechas who had formerly been their neighbors and even their relatives. Now they are enemies, an ambivalent representation that can only be understood as a result of the War on Drugs.

Put in Garfinkel's terms, ethnomethods provide evidence of being "locally produced, naturally accountable phenomena of order, logic, reason, meaning, method, etc."[9] Ethnomethods are "procedures that the members of a social form use to produce and to recognize their world and to make it familiar as they assemble it."[10] We can understand the effort made by the mojados in Cobden to produce their *diccionario mojado*: it was, to begin with, an (ethno)method to adapt themselves to American society, contradicting Huntington's notion that high immigration tends to retard the assimilation of immigrants.

I realize many people still believe in the hoary Sapir–Whorf thesis on the emic incommensurability of languages and cultures. Some[11] still believe in cultures as entelechies, monads immune to any modifying interactions.[12] We anthropologists label these theories of identity "primordialist" or "essentialist" since they tend to rely on assumed origin myths and biased feelings which can pose as patriotism and nationalism rather than racism. But for a diffusionist anthropologist to speak nowadays of worldwide circles of cultural diffusion is revolutionary. Implicit in the theory that cultures can be transmitted across long distances from certain points of origin is the principle that any other group, nation, or society can assimilate the transmitted patterns without losing its own cultural patterns. Today, this notion of hybrid cultural change is less acceptable because it implies cultural interbreeding, pollution, *mestizaje: la pensée métisse*.[13]

Every age produces its conservative thinkers. In the name of cultural, racial, or ethnic purity, there will always be interests to protect. Fortunately, common sense and practical reason can always resist the dangerous illusion of having to live under an enclosure as protection against strangers. This was the situation Kalmar found in Cobden. The whole social situation there was predisposed to provoke a "clash of civilizations," a strange outcome for a community shaped by pioneer immigrants. There was indeed some violence. But it was far from being an army of the night.[14] The strangers did not come to Cobden to stage a *reconquista*.

---

9. Garfinkel (2002: 169).
10. Coulon (1995: 49).
11. Huntington (2004).
12. Of course, the idea of culturally self-contained emic worlds of life goes back much further than the development by German and American diffusionist theories in the late nineteenth century and the first third of the twentieth century of the dating method of seriation. In fact, the idea was used by the Greek thinkers to refer to the "barbarians."
13. Gruzinski (1999).
14. Buchanan (2002).

What they did was culturally something truly innovative: they behaved like professional linguists without being more than rural workers. An ethnomethodology that would have fascinated Harold Garfinkel.[15]

Indigenous educators and academics who appoint themselves the intellectuals of ethnicity, in order to elevate their mother tongues to the status of creations as emically incommensurate as their indigenous cultures now turn to anthropological linguistics for a light to guide them through etic intercultural spaces in the search for practical and discursive meanings. But Kalmar bypasses the prejudicial framework of linguistic purity and impurity, of the superiority and inferiority of one language to another. He shows that using hybrid phonemes to represent mixed sounds of two different languages inevitably mixes the emic and etic levels of analysis.

For us members of Mexican society, this raises a crucially political—and disquieting—question: Should indigenous education in Mexico continue to be bilingual as well as intercultural? Before we segment ourselves within our respective emic worlds, as if all of us were foreign to one another, it would be appropriate to look at the illegal alphabets from Cobden—if only to remind ourselves that an ignored group of amateur Mexican linguists, without any power beyond their desire to understand, relying on their rudimentary biliteracy as a legacy of official revolutionary bilingual education, crossed the no man's land separating the point of view of the foreign outsider from the point of view of the native insider. Thanks to their modest teaching, we can see that being inside or outside, foreign or native, is more a question of positioning in a situation than of a tradition constraining all social interaction.

Works Cited

Aragón Andrade, O. (2013) El derecho en insurrección: El uso contrahegemónico del derecho en el movimiento purépecha de Cherán, *Estudos e Pesquisas sobre as Américas*, 72: 37–69.

Buchanan, P. J. (2002) *The Death of the West: How Dying Populations and Inmigrant Invasions Imperil Our Country and Civilization*, New York: St. Martin's Press.

Coulon, A. (1995) *Ethnomethodology*, Thousand Oaks, CA: Sage.

Dresch, P. and Skoda, H. (2012) *Legalism: Anthropology and History*, New York: Oxford University Press.

Garfinkel, H. (2002) *Ethnomethodology's Program: Working Out Durkheim's Aphorism*, Lanham, MD: Rowman & Littlefield.

Giddens, A. (1984) *The Constitution of Society: Outline of the Theory of Structuration*, Cambridge: Polity Press.

Gruzinski, S. (2000) *El pensamiento mestizo*, Barcelona: Paidós Ibérica.

Huntington, S. P. (2004) *¿Quiénes somos? Los desafíos a la identidad nacional estadounidense*, Barcelona: Paidós Ibérica.

---

15. Coulon (1995), Garfinkel (2002).

Instituto Nacional de Estadística y Geografía (2000) Tabulados de la muestra censal. Cuestionario ampliado. XII Censo general de población y vienda, Aguascalientes.

—— (2011) Panorama sociodemográfico de México, Censo de Población y Vivienda 2010, Aguascalientes.

Vázquez León, L. (2010) Niveles étnicos bajo el fin del indigenismo y la nueva proletarización de la población indígena: El caso de los jornaleros tarascos, Multitud y distopía, Ensayos sobre la nueva condición étnica en Michoacán, México, UNAM-Programa Universitaro México Nación Multicultural.

PANCHAAN

Karen Velasquez

Antioch College

Immigrants such as Jacinto, Cipriano, and Alfonso in *Illegal Alphabets* continue migrating to the United States, despite the hardships of physically demanding and time-consuming labor, the dangers of possessing an undocumented legal status, frequent discrimination, and the challenges of having a limited knowledge of English. Still in high demand for the low cost of their labor, Latinos move across towns and cities in the U.S., helping each other to survive and finding ways to share and express their experiences through language, no matter how that language looks or sounds. This is the important element of voice that is captured in Kalmar's work that encourages us to listen and take seriously the language conventions people develop for themselves and teach each other.

Communicative practices are multimodal: whether they are gestures, printed text, or shiny images on smartphone screens, language practices are increasingly restless and defiant. As language media spread and transmit messages across new spaces and populations, these constant shifts create new problems that each generation of immigrants must solve. As immigrants move in search of work, they will have to make sense of new linguistic and cultural environments in order to make a living. Labor migration brings people together with a broad range of experiences that should be valued, regardless if they are considered skilled or unskilled, educated or uneducated. Today's workers continue to develop their own communities of practice and autonomous language forms without needing to pursue paths to legalization or go through formal language education or vocational training.

Kalmar's research has inspired scholars and researchers of language and culture to seek out how these autonomous language forms develop among diverse populations in unique, previously unexplored places. His case history brings us close to the people of Cobden and the practices that matter to them. We are able to observe the resilience and strength of Mexican immigrants coming together and expressing solidarity and the ability to overcome difficult experiences. As a text that encourages ethnographic exploration, Kalmar's writing has also inspired my own research into the difficulties Latino immigrants continue to encounter in the United States today. As a daughter of Colombian immigrants who settled in Queens in search of a better life, I grew up with firsthand experience of the struggles felt by my own family and other immigrant families in New York City. As a result, the challenges that undocumented Latinos experience in the United States, and the resilience they exhibit amid difficult situations, have been a central focus of my studies in education and cultural anthropology. I have been exploring how immigrant adults from different parts of the world living in New York City work together and invent strategies for survival as undocumented employees in the service sector economy. My principal location of interest has been the borough of Queens, New York—the most diverse borough in the United States of America, where over 138 known languages are spoken. For decades, Latino immigrants have arrived in Queens in search of employment, much like the Mexicans in Cobden who went to Illinois for the opportunity to earn some money to support families in Mexico. Amid this diversity, I have tried to understand how immigrants develop ways of communicating together while going along their daily business of trying to make a living in the United States. Here, I will recount one of my first experiences with improvised language in the field, where I got a glimpse of a complex "no man's land between languages."

In Queens, I grew interested in a population of undocumented Latino immigrants employed in ethnic neighborhoods of Queens and Manhattan, particularly Koreatown. In K-town, immigrants from Mexico, Guatemala, Ecuador, and elsewhere are hired by Korean immigrants to perform service labor, especially in the food and restaurant industries (bussing tables, cleaning kitchens, prepping food, stocking aisles, etc.). Intrigued by the opportunity to understand how Latinos and Koreans communicate at work despite linguistic and cultural boundaries, I moved to the Koreatown area of Flushing, Queens. Getting to know Latino immigrants employed in Korean businesses was challenging, but I soon befriended Andres, a Mexican employee in a Korean supermarket, who invited me to join him and his two male coworkers (one Korean immigrant and another Mexican) at a Korean barbeque restaurant in Flushing. In many ways, this experience was an important introductory moment, just as the initial meeting between Anglo reporters and Mexican farmworkers broke the ice and opened conversation in *Illegal Alphabets* (pp. 10ff).

The Korean restaurant—known for its plentiful *panchaan* (Andres's spelling for the Korean word for appetizer or side dishes) and lack of air conditioning even in the hottest summer months—was buzzing and filled with customers at 9:00 p.m., and it smelled overwhelmingly of thinly sliced meat cooking on table grills. (As I stared at the meat-loving crowd, I knew that the end of my vegetarian diet was near.) Once seated, I watched Korean servers deftly swerve around tables, speaking in Korean with the clientele, scribbling down or memorizing food orders, and bringing them back to the kitchen, where I could see and hear Latinos working next to Koreans, preparing food and washing dishes, occasionally coming out of the back to clear plates off tables. At first, there was little conversation in our group of four, and I felt my presence was the culprit of our awkwardness, so I asked Andres, in Spanish, if his friends knew anything about me. Andres tried to translate my academic language for his friends so he could explain my strange anthropologist profession (to no avail), but they were more curious about my relationship with Andres (which they assumed to be romantic in nature). The Korean male, affectionately called "El Chino" by his Latino friends,[1] shrugged off the confusion and wasted no time ordering our first bottle of Soju, a staple Korean rice liquor, the potency of which is craftily masked by its sweetness.

As a newcomer, I could barely hold my chopsticks (especially so after multiple rounds of Soju), but I knew my initiation into Koreatown would be incomplete without at least some humiliation to serve an instructive purpose about the order and sequence of things. Soon after our shot glasses had been filled, and refilled, the three coworkers started to have a conversation in three languages; and I chimed in mostly with confused laughter, which was when I realized I had absolutely no idea what was going on. There we were, smiling, laughing, and intermittently using English and Spanish words, mixing in Korean in seemingly random fashion (Andres would later call this an example of an *ensalada de lenguajes*, a mixed language salad). From what I could gather, Andres was playfully accusing El Chino of being *chandory* (his Spanish pronunciation of the Korean word for "cheap") and too old to date any of my single friends (about whom El Chino asked multiple times). Pointing and waving his chopsticks around, El Chino dismissed Andres's accusations, and then instructed me on what order to combine and sample, one by one, the 15 appetizer dishes lavishly laid out in front of us, including at least four kinds of kimchi. Over the course of the evening, the three coworkers seemingly repeated the same words and phrases they knew in common, but in different combinations, and were perfectly satisfied to have conversations and entertain one another that way. In the midst of trying to decipher the order of conversation and appetizer eating rituals, I also began to listen carefully to our Latino waiter. He approached our table and—in Spanish—asked Andres what main entrees we would like to order for the table. Then, to my amazement, he began speaking Korean effortlessly with El Chino. The other Mexican at our table simply continued eating his food nonchalantly beside me, expertly dipping his chopsticks into Korean food as though he had eaten it countless times before. The waiter committed our food order to memory and relayed it back to the kitchen staff in Korean. As I observed these exchanges, I asked Andres if this was

1. "El Chino," literally "the Chinese man," is a term frequently used by many Spanish speakers to describe Koreans and other Asian people, although it is also used affectionately when referring to a child of any ethnic/racial group.

normal and he explained that, indeed, many Latinos learn to speak Korean—to varying degrees—over the course of their time as employees in Korean establishments. In the following weeks, I approached our Latino waiter, José, and asked him to talk to me about his experience working at the restaurant. One evening, armed with a field notebook, a pen, and a voice recorder, I followed him to one of his preferred restaurants, a Korean–Chinese fusion restaurant down the street from his workplace. I learned he was 30 years old, from Veracruz, Mexico, and married to a Korean woman (a former waitress at his restaurant), and that he now considers himself a part of the family of Korean coworkers. I showed him a glossary of Korean vocabulary words with their Spanish translation assembled by Andres.

Sample of Korean words (left) and their Spanish translation (right) written by Andros, 25, Mexican immigrant worker in Koreatown

KOREAN	SPANIHS [sic]
TELLY	GORDO
QUENCHANA	ESTABIEN
TOKATE	IGUAL
CHANDORY	CODO
MUIAIGO	QUE ES ESTO?
CHOCON	POCO O POQUITO
PIOA	QUEDO, O TODAVIA QUEDO
PIOAISEHO	QUEDO TODAVIA
MOSHISOO	SABROSO
AROA	SABES, CONOCES
ARAAYOO	USTED SABE, CONOCE
KERAAN	HUEVO
PANCHAAN	LOS APERITIVOS
PIOA SUCHEUO	NECESITO EL RESTO DE LA ORDEN
KALBI	HANA SUSHEOU
IGOO	ESTE

One by one, he corrected them according to his criteria of pronunciation and use. Using his own linguistic knowledge developed through 10 years of work experience with Koreans, he attempted to transform Andres's words into more formal Korean, mindful of the important role of honorifics in Korean culture—

words, expressions, and gestures that convey respect and indicate awareness of social hierarchies.

As a result of our dinner outing, I was educated in multiple, contested versions of what counts as proper language and pronunciation, much like the glossaries debated in Cobden. But I was also educated on how language fits into the broader context of restaurant life, Korean food, and Latino–Korean employee relationships in New York City. The emergence of these language practices differs depending on the social context, but through fieldwork it is possible to see how contemporary multilingualism in the American workforce is growing at a faster pace than ever. And it is important to remember that ordinary spaces such as grocery stores and small businesses are just as capable of supporting the transformation of languages as powerful multimillion-dollar global corporations or policy-driven educational development initiatives.

Careful analysis of these spaces, inspired by the work of scholars such as Kalmar, enables us to understand how immigrants transform and improve their work and living conditions in the US while using language in unexpected ways that challenge our assumptions about what counts as competent language and legitimate forms of language education. As educational historian Lawrence Cremin stated many years ago, education is not synonymous with schooling; it happens in everyday situations and in unexpected ways that often surprise us and challenge our assumptions about the ways people live, work, and play together. To study education outside the classroom is to pay attention to moments where people develop creative solutions to the constraints they encounter on a daily basis, to see people not as reproductions or mirrors of their cultures, but as active participants in a world that presents often-unpredictable situations, as well as abundant opportunities for learning.

AFTERWORD

Tomás Mario Kalmar

Tamen quae sine anima sunt vocem dantia sive tibia sive cithara nisi distinctionem sonituum dederint quomodo scietur quod canitur aut quod citharizatur. Etenim si incertam vocem det tuba quis parabit se ad bellum . . . Tam multa ut puta genera linguarum sunt in mundo et nihil sine voce est. Si ergo nesciero virtutem vocis ero ei cui loquor barbarus et qui loquitur mihi barbarus.

And even things without life giving sound, whether pipe or harp, except they give a distinction in the sounds, how shall it be known what is piped or harped? For if the trumpet give an uncertain sound, who shall prepare himself to the battle? . . . There are, it may be, so many kinds of voices in the world, and none of them is without signification. Therefore if I know not the meaning of the voice, I shall be unto him that speaketh a barbarian, and he that speaketh shall be a barbarian unto me.

—I Corinthians 14: 7–11 (KJV)

There is irony in the fact that biliteracy, although marginal to the culture of the United States, is of increasing importance everywhere else. The ever-expanding globalization of English as a universal international medium of communication means that in the decades to come, more and more people worldwide will speak and write English, and will therefore become, by one definition or another, biliterate. Nevertheless, it is safe to predict that within the United States, biliteracy, no matter how sophisticated its definition, will, for the foreseeable future, continue to challenge the monolingual mainstream and will therefore remain an essentially contested contribution that Latino and other linguistic minorities claim to make to the culture of the United States.[1]

---

1. This and the next three paragraphs are reproduced, by permission, from Kalmar (2005).

The history of the English word *literacy* starts with the simplest possible kind of code: a one-to-one correspondence between a finite set of letters and a finite set of sounds. Codes that are occult to outsiders but well known to insiders continue to be at the center of all redefinitions of literacy. The story of 100 years of literacy in the United States is a story about the power of gatekeepers to define and redefine "codes" as criteria by which to close and open the gates that admit people into full civil citizenship. Redefining literacy is, and has always been, right from the start, a way of redrawing the line between "us" and "them," between those who know the chosen code and those who don't. Conservative (re)definitions seek to close that gate, to exclude as illiterate those formerly permitted to pass, while progressive (re)definitions seek to open that gate, to legitimize the literacy of those formerly denied entry.

The functional approach redefined literacy as the ability to read codes other than the alphabet. The sociocultural approach unpacked the metaphor of coding and decoding to ask what counts as a code in the first place, who has the power to encode and decode what, and who has the authority to answer questions such as these. The radical version of literacy therefore seeks to unmask and undermine the gatekeeper's role. From a radical or Freirean point of view, the powerless are struggling to express their own lived experiences in their own voice. The voice of the powerless has been strategically redefined by the powerful as illiteracy. To draw the line dividing "us" from "them," to determine when to permit the powerless to cross that line, and when to keep them out, the powerful administer their literacy tests.

Biliteracy is more like a strategy or style of play than like a function in an algorithm. Biliteracy events are more like jam sessions or dramas than like programs. It is as if biliteracy initially crosses borders without asking permission from institutional gatekeepers. Ecologically speaking, biliteracy is born in the no man's land between languages, and develops by playfully switching and mixing bits and pieces of code proper to more than one cultural, economic, or social system. Those who practice biliteracy, even in its simplest alphabetic form, share the knowledge that one code can be used to transcribe two languages the way they sound, that tokens in that code can be assigned variable rather than constant values, that new tokens must sometimes be coined and circulated, that, after all, letters and sounds are only pieces in a game; in short, that we can agree to change the rules of the game and still use the same pieces. In the decades to come, we can expect to see lively debates over more sophisticated redefinitions of biliteracy to include a knowledge of how to play with codes in general, how to switch them, how to mix and match them, how to create new rules for hybrid linguistic, cultural, and political "games."

That is why I did my best (as I said in the Prologue) to construct this case history as a parable. Perhaps every good case history is also a good parable. What you find in it reflects back what you bring to it. What you think the point is tells you who you are. For what it's worth, I now want to say, frankly, what I myself find in this parable. It's not that I want to have the last word. I don't. As you will see below, I want you, dear Reader, to have the last word—if there is ever to be a last word.

The point of this story of letters and sounds is a mystery, like the mysterious point of the parable of the Laborers in the Vineyard: all ages are immediate to God, and the spiritual experience of those who enter into the spirit of the game at the last moment is in communion with, and of no less value than, the spiritual experience of those who were in it from the start:

> For the kingdom of heaven is like a landowner who went out early in the morning to hire laborers for his vineyard. After agreeing with the laborers for the usual daily wage, he sent them into his vineyard. When he went out about nine o'clock, he saw others standing idle in the marketplace; and he said to them, "You also go into the vineyard, and I will pay you whatever is right." So they went. When he went out again about noon and about three o'clock, he did the same. And about five o'clock he went out and found others standing around; and he said to them, "Why are you standing here idle all day?" They said to him, "Because no one has hired us." He said to them, "You also go into the vineyard." When evening came, the owner of the vineyard said to his manager, "Call the laborers and give them their pay, beginning with the last and then going to the first." When those hired about five o'clock came, each of them received the usual daily wage. Now when the first came, they thought they would receive more; but each of them also received the usual daily wage. And when they received it, they grumbled against the landowner, saying, "These last worked only one hour, and you have made them equal to us who have borne the burden of the day and the scorching heat." But he replied to one of them, "Friend, I am doing you no wrong; did you not agree with me for the usual daily wage? Take what belongs to you and go; I choose to give to this last the same as I give to you. Am I not allowed to do what I choose with what belongs to me? Or are you envious because I am generous?" So the last will be first, and the first will be last.
>
> —Matthew 20: 1–16 (NRSV)

Is the Laborers in the Vineyard merely about grape pickers selling their daily labor on a street corner?

Is my parable merely about letters and sounds?

Do you, dear Reader, have ears to hear?

¿GUARIYUSEI?

LIST OF CONTRIBUTORS

Peter Elbow
University of Massachusetts—Amherst

Ofelia García
The Graduate Center, City University of New York

James Paul Gee
University of Wisconsin at Madison

Hervé Varenne
Teachers College, Columbia University

Luis Vázquez León
Centro de Investigaciones y Estudios Superiores en Antropología Social de Occidente, Guadalajara, México

Karen Velasquez
Antioch College

REFERENCES

Abercrombie, D. (1967) *Elements of General Phonetics*, Edinburgh: Edinburgh University Press.
—— (1989) Phoneme, the concept and the word, reprinted in Abercrombie (1992), pp. 22–26.
—— (1992) *Fifty Years in Phonetics*, Edinburgh: Edinburgh University Press.
Agar, M. (1980) *The Professional Stranger*, New York: Academic Press.
Anderson, S. R. (1985) *Phonology in the Twentieth Century: Theories of Rules and Theories of Representations*, Chicago, IL: University of Chicago Press.
Arana de Swadesh, E. (1975) La Investigación de las Lenguas Indígenas de México, in E. Arana de Swadesh et al. (Eds.), *Las Lenguas de México*, Mexico: INAH, pp. 6–16.
Arana de Swadesh, E. et al. (Eds.) (1975) *Las Lenguas de México*, Mexico: INAH.
Asher, R. E. and E. J. A. Henderson (Eds.) (1981) *Towards a History of Phonetics*, Edinburgh: Edinburgh University Press.
Ashton-Warner, S. (1986) *Teacher*, New York: Simon & Schuster.
Barrera-Vásquez, A. (1953) The Tarascan Project in Mexico, in UNESCO (1953) *The Use of Vernacular Languages in Education*, Paris: UNESCO, pp. 77–86.
Barton, D. (1994) *Literacy: An Introduction to the Ecology of Written Language*, Oxford: Blackwell.
Bennett, T. (1990) *Outside Literature*, London: Routledge.
Boas, F., Goddard, P. E., Sapir, E., and Kroeber, A. L. (1916) *Phonetic Transcription of American Indian Languages: Report of Committee of American Anthropological Association*, Smithsonian Institution, Publication 2415.
Boon, S. A. (1982) *Other Tribes, Other Scribes*, Cambridge: Cambridge University Press.
Boyarin, J. (Ed.) (1993) *The Ethnography of Reading*, Berkeley, CA: University of California Press.
Brend, R. M. and Pike, K. L. (Eds.) (1977) *The Summer Institute of Linguistics: Its Works and Contributions*, The Hague and Paris: Mouton.
Burke, K. (1962) *A Grammar of Motives and a Rhetoric of Motives*, Cleveland, OH and New York: The World Publishing Company.

—— (1973[1941]) *The Philosophy of Literary Form*, 3rd ed., Berkeley, CA: University of California Press.

Burling, R. (1984) *Learning a Field Language*, Ann Arbor, MI: University of Michigan Press.

Carroll, J. B. (1951) *The Study of Language*, Cambridge, MA: Harvard University Press.

Chao, Y.-R. (1934) The non-uniqueness of phonemic solutions of phonetic systems, *Bulletin of the Institute of History and Philology, Academia Sinica*, 4(4): 363–397. Reprinted in Joos (1958).

Clifford, J. (1986) Introduction: partial truths, in J. Clifford and G. Marcus (Eds.), *Writing Culture: The Poetics and Politics of Ethnography*, Berkeley, CA: University of California Press, pp. 1–26.

—— (1990) Notes on (field)notes, in R. Sanjek (Ed.), *Fieldnotes: The Makings of Anthropology*, Ithaca, NY: Cornell University Press.

Collinge, N. E. (Ed.) (1990) *An Encyclopedia of Language*, London: Routledge.

Connolly, R. (1981) Freire, praxis and education, in R. Mackie (1981).

Cottom, D. (1989) *Text and Culture: The Politics of Interpretation*, Minneapolis, MN: University of Minnesota Press.

Coulmas, F. (Ed.) (1984) *Linguistic Minorities and Literacy: Language Policy Issues in Developing Countries*, Berlin: Mouton.

—— (1989) *The Writing Systems of the World*, Oxford: Basil Blackwell.

Davis, H. G. and Taylor, T. J. (Eds.) (1990) *Redefining Linguistics*, London and New York: Routledge.

Davis, R. (1970) Education for awareness: a talk with Paulo Freire, *Risk*, 6(4). Reprinted in Mackie (1981).

Dell, F. (1973) *Les Règles et les Sons*, Paris: Hermann.

—— (1980) *Generative Phonology*, English translation by C. Cullen of Dell 1973, Cambridge: Cambridge University Press.

de Tal, F. (1988) *Even in My Own Tongue*, Lawrence, MA: Lawrence Literacy Coalition Working Paper #2.

Elcock, W. D. (1960) *The Romance Languages*, New York: The Macmillan Company.

Entwistle, W. J. (1953) *Aspects of Language*, London: Faber & Faber.

Fishman, J. A. (1974) The sociology of language: an interdisciplinary social science approach to language in society, in T. A. Sebeok (Ed.), *Current Trends in Linguistics*, 12: 1829–1784.

Freilich, M. (1970) *Marginal Natives*, New York: Wiley.

Freire, P. (1965) *Educação como Prática da Liberdade*, Rio de Janeiro: Editoria Paz e Terra.

—— (1968) *Extensión y Comunicación*, Santiago: Institute for Agricultural Reform.

—— (1971) *Pedagogy of the Oppressed* (translated by M. B. Ramos), New York: Herder & Herder.

—— (1975) *Pedagogia do Oprimido*, Lisbon: Afrontamento/Porto.

—— (1983) *Education for Critical Consciousness* (translated by L. Bigwood and M. Marshall), New York: Continuum.

Friedrich, P. (1975) *A Phonology of Tarascan*, Chicago, IL: University of Chicago Press.

—— (1986) *The Language Parallax: Linguistic Relativism and Poetic Indeterminacy*, Austin, TX: University of Texas Press.

Garton, A. and Pratt, C. (1989) *Learning to be Literate: The Development of Spoken and Written Language*, Oxford: Basil Blackwell.

Gee, J. (1990) *Social Linguistics and Literacies: Ideology in Discourses*, London: Falmer Press.

—— (1991) What is literacy?, in Mitchell and Weiler (1991: 3–12).

—— (1992) Socio-cultural approaches to literacy (literacies), *Annual Review of Applied Linguistics*, 12: 31–48.

—— (1996) *Social Linguistics and Literacies: Ideology in Discourses*, 2nd ed., London: Taylor & Francis.

—— (1999) Reading and the New Literacy Studies: reframing the National Academy of Sciences Report on Reading, *Journal of Literacy Research*, 31(3): 355–374.

Graves, M. and Cowan, J. M. (1942) Excerpt of *Report of the First Year's Operation of the Intensive Program of the American Council of Learned Societies, Hispania*, 25: 490.

Haas, M. (1975) Problems of American Indian philology, in Paper (1975: 89–109).

Hall, R. (1975) *Stormy Petrel in Linguistics*, Ithaca, NY: Spoken Languages Services.

Halle, M. and Clements, B. N. (1983) *Problem Book in Phonology: A Workbook for Introductory Courses in Linguistics and in Modern Phonology*, Cambridge, MA: MIT Press.

Halliday, M. A. K. (1975) *Learning How to Mean: Explorations in the Development of Language*, London: Edward Arnold.

—— (1978) *Language as Social Semiotic: The Social Interpretation of Language and Meaning*, London: Edward Arnold.

—— (1989) *Spoken and Written Language*, Oxford: Oxford University Press.

Halliday, M. A. K. and Hasan, R. (1989) *Language, Context, and Text: Aspects of Language in a Social-Semiotic Perspective*, Oxford: Oxford University Press.

Harris, R. (1980) *The Language-Makers*, London: Duckworth.

—— (1981) *The Language Myth*, London: Duckworth.

—— (1986) *The Origin of Writing*, LaSalle, IL: Open Court Publishing Company.

—— (1987a) *Reading Saussure*, London: Duckworth.

—— (1987b) *The Language Machine*, London: Duckworth.

—— (1988) *Language, Saussure and Wittgenstein: How to Play Games with Words*, London and New York: Routledge.

Haugen, E. (1942) Facts and phonemics, *Language*, 18: 228–237. Reprinted in Haugen (1972b).

—— (1950) The analysis of linguistic borrowing, *Language*, 26: 210–231. Reprinted in Haugen (1972b: 161–184).

—— (1951) Directions in Modern Linguistics, Presidential Address to Linguistic Society, Chicago, December 19, 1950, *Language*, 271: 211–222. Reprinted in Haugen (1972b: 186–198); also in Joos (1958).

—— (1954a) Review: U. Weinreich, Languages in Contact, *Language*, 30: 380–388. Reprinted in Haugen (1972b: 241–250).

—— (1954b) *Problems in Bilingual Description, Monograph No. 7*, Report of the Fifth Annual Round Table Meeting, Washington, DC: Georgetown University Press. Reprinted in Haugen (1972b: 277–284).

—— (1955) The Phoneme in Bilingual Description, Paper read at the General Phonetics section of MLA, December 27, 1955. Reprinted in Haugen (1972b).

—— (1956) *Bilingualism in the Americas: A Bibliography and Research Guide*, Publication of the American Dialect Society Number 26, University of Alabama Press.

—— (1972a) *The Ecology of Language*, Palo Alto, CA: Stanford University Press.

—— (1972b) *Studies by Einar Haugen: Presented on the Occasion of His 65th Birthday—April 19, 1971*, edited by E. S. Firchow, K. Grimstad, N. Hasselmo, and W. O'Neil, The Hague: Mouton.

Headland, T. N., Pike, K., and Harris, M. (Eds.) (1990) *Emics and Etics: The Insider/Outsider Debate*, Newbury Park, CA: Sage.

Heath, S. B. (1972a) *Telling Tongues: Language Policy in Mexico Colony to Nation*, New York and London: Teachers College Press.

—— (1972b) *La Politica del Lenguaje en Mexico de la Colonia a la Nación*, Mexico: Instituto Nacional Indigenista.

—— (1983) *Ways with Words: Language, Life and Work in Communities and Classrooms*, London: Cambridge University Press.

Henderson, E. J. A. (Ed.) (1971) *The Indispensable Foundation: A Selection from the Writings of Henry Sweet*, London: Oxford University Press.

Herzog, G., Neman, S. S., Sapir, E., Haas, M., Swadesh, M., and Voegelin, C. F. (1934) Some orthographic recommendations, *American Anthropologist*, 36: 629–631.

Hirsch, E. D., Jr. (1967) *Validity in Interpretation*, New Haven, CT: Yale University Press.

Hopper, P. J. (1998) Emergent grammar, in M. Tomasello (Ed.), *The New Psychology of Language: Cognitive and Functional Approaches to Language Structure*, Mahwah, NJ: Lawrence Erlbaum Associates, pp. 155–175.

Hymes, D. and Fought, J. (1981) *American Structuralism*, The Hague: Mouton.

Illich, I. (1987) A plea for research on lay literacy, *Interchange*, 18(1/2): 9–22, The Ontario Institute for Studies in Education.

Illich, I. and Sanders, B. (1988) *ABC: The Alphabetization of the Popular Mind*, San Francisco, CA: North Point Press.

Jackson, J. E. (1990) "I Am a Fieldnote": fieldnotes as a symbol of professional identity, in Sanjek (1990).

Jameson, F. (1981) *The Political Unconscious: Narrative as a Socially Symbolic Act*, Ithaca, NY: Cornell University Press.

Jones, D. (1929) Definition of a phoneme, *Le Maître Phonétique*, 3(7): 43–44.

Joos, M. (1958) *Readings in Linguistics: The Development of Descriptive Linguistics in America since 1925*, New York: American Council of Learned Societies.

Kalmar, T. M. (1983) *The Voice of Fulano: Working Papers from a Bilingual Literacy Campaign*, Cambridge: Schenkman.

—— (1988a) *Do We Need a Linguistic Minority Task Force?* Lawrence, MA: Lawrence Literacy Coalition Working Paper #3.

—— (1988b) *A Five Year Literacy Plan for the Lower Merrimack Valley*, Lawrence, MA: North East Consortium of Colleges and Universities in Massachusetts.

—— (1988c) *Who Requests ESL? A Preliminary Study on Linguistic Minority Applicants to Community Colleges in Northeastern Massachusetts*, Boston, MA: Commonwealth of Massachusetts Board of Regents of Higher Education.

—— (1992) Drawing the line on minority languages: equity and linguistic diversity in the Boston Adult Literacy Initiative, *Adult Basic Education: An Interdisciplinary Journal for Adult Literacy Educators*, 2(2).

—— (1994) ¿GUARIYUSEI?: adult biliteracy in its natural habitat, in Spener (Ed.) (1994).

—— (2005) s.v. "Literacy," in I. Stavans (Ed.), *Encyclopedia Latina*, 2: 443–449, Grolier.

Kirk, B. (1942) *Covering the Mexican Front: The Battle of Europe Versus America*, Norman, OK: University of Oklahoma Press.

Kortlandt, F. H. H. (1972) *Modelling the Phoneme: New Trends in East European Phonemic Theory*, The Hague: Mouton.

Kozol, J. (1981) Preface to Mackie (1981).

Kress, G. (1989) *Linguistic Processes in Sociocultural Practice*, Oxford: Oxford University Press.

Latour, B. (1999) *Pandora's Hope: Essays on the Reality of Science Studies*, Cambridge, MA: Harvard University Press.

Lofland, J. (1974) Styles of reporting qualitative field research, *American Sociologist*, 9: 101–111.

Macedo, D. P. (1979) *A Linguistic Approach to the Capeverdean Language*, Doctoral thesis, Boston University School of Education.

Mackie, R. (Ed.) (1981) *Literacy and Revolution: The Pedagogy of Paulo Freire*, New York: Continuum.

McQuown, N. (1941) Linguistics contributes to native education, *International Science*, 1(1): 2–6.

Malinowski, B. (1961[1922]) *Argonauts of the Western Pacific: An Account of Native Enterprise and Adventure in the Archipelagos of Melanesian New Guinea*, Prospect Heights, IL: Waveland Press.

Marchot, P. (1895) *Les Gloses de Cassel: Le Plus Ancien Texte Réto-Roman*, Fribourg.

Maxwell, J. A. (1992) Understanding and validity in qualitative research, *Harvard Educational Review*, 62(3): 279–300.

Medin, T. (1972) *Ideología y Praxis Política de Lázaro Cárdenas*, Mexico: Siglo xxi.

Mendoza, V. T. (1984) *Lírica Narrativa de México: El Corrido*, Mexico: Instituto de Investigaciones Estéticas Universidad Nacional Autónoma de México.

Mitchell, C. and Weiler, K. (1991) *Rewriting Literacy: Culture and the Discourse of the Other*, New York: Bergin & Garvey.

Mountford, J. D. (1990) Language and writing systems, in Collinge (1990).

Myers, G. (1992) *Writing Biology: Texts in the Social Construction of Scientific Knowledge*, Madison, WI: University of Wisconsin Press.

Newmeyer, F. (1986) *The Politics of Linguistics*, Chicago, IL: University of Chicago Press.

Paper, H. H. (Ed.) (1975) *Language and Texts: The Nature of Linguistic Evidence*, Ann Arbor, MI: University of Michigan Press.

Pike, K. L. (1938) Practical suggestions toward a common orthography for Indian languages of Mexico for education of the natives within their own tongues, *Investigaciones Lingüísticas*, Vol. 1.

—— (1947) *Phonemics: A Technique for Reducing Languages to Writing*, Ann Arbor, MI: University of Michigan Press.

—— (1967) *Language in Relation to a Unified Theory of the Structure of Human Behavior*, The Hague: Mouton.

—— (1972) *Selected Writings*, The Hague: Mouton.

—— (1981) An autobiographical note on phonetics, in Asher and Henderson (1981: 181–185).

—— (1982) *Linguistic Concepts: An Introduction to Tagmemics*, Lincoln, NE: University of Nebraska Press.

Pullum, G. K. and Ladusaw, W. A. (1986) *Phonetic Symbol Guide*, Chicago, IL: University of Chicago Press.

Robbin, F. (1992) Foreword to Watts (1992).

Robinson, D. F. (1969) *Manual for Bilingual Dictionaries*, Santa Ana, CA: Summer Institute of Linguistics.

Sanjek, R. (Ed.) (1990) *Fieldnotes: The Makings of Anthropology*, Ithaca, NY: Cornell University Press.

Sapir, E. (1925) Sound patterns in language, *Language*, I: 37–51.

—— (1949) *Selected Writings of Edward Sapir in Language, Culture, and Personality*, Ed. D. G. Mandelbaum, Berkeley, CA: University of California Press.

Smalley, W. A. (1959) How shall I write this language? *The Bible Translator*, 10.2 (Apr. 59): 49–69. Reprinted in Smalley et al. (1963: 31–52).

Smalley, W. et al. (1963) *Orthography Studies: Articles on New Writing Systems*, London: United Bible Societies.

Smith, F. (1988) *Joining the Literacy Club: Further Essays into Education*, Portsmouth, NH: Heinemann.

Spener, D. (Ed.) (1994) *Adult Biliteracy in the USA*, Englewood Cliffs, NJ: Prentice Hall Regents/Center for Applied Linguistics.

Stanley, M. (1972) Literacy: the crisis of a conventional wisdom, *School Review*, 80(3).

Stavenhagen, R. (1984) Linguistic minorities and language policy in Latin America: the case of Mexico, in Coulmas (1984: 56–62).

Stocking, G. W., Jr. (1976) *Selected Papers from the American Anthropologist: 1921–1945*, Washington, DC: American Anthropological Association.

Street, B. (1995) *Social Literacies: Critical Approaches to Literacy in Development, Ethnography and Education*, London: Longman.

Swadesh, M. (1934) The phonemic principle, *Language*, 10: 117–129. Reprinted in Joos (1958).

—— (1941) *La Nueva Filología*, Mexico: El Nacional.

—— (1948) *Conversational Chinese for Beginners*, New York: Dover.

—— (1948) *Orientaciones lingüísticas para maestros en zonas indígenas: una serie de conferencias*, Mexico: Departamento de Asuntos Indígenas.

Swales, J. M. (1990) *Genre Analysis*, Cambridge: Cambridge University Press.

Sweet, H. (1877) *A Handbook of Phonetics Including a Popular Exposition of the Principles of Spelling Reform*, Oxford: Clarendon Press.

—— (1884) The practical study of language, *Transactions of the Philological Society 1882*, 4: 577–599. Reprinted in Wyld (1913: 34–56).

—— (1888) *A History of English Sounds from the Earliest Period with Full Word-Lists*, 2nd ed., Oxford: Clarendon Press.

Titz, K. (1923) *Glossy Kasselske*, Prague.

Tyler, S. (1987) *The Unspeakable: Discourse, Dialogue and Rhetoric in the Postmodern World*, Madison, WI: University of Wisconsin Press.

UNESCO (1953) *The Use of Vernacular Languages in Education*, Paris: UNESCO.

Van Maanen, J. (1988) *Tales of the Field: On Writing Ethnography*, Chicago, IL: University of Chicago Press.

Varenne, H. and McDermott, R. (1998) *Successful Failure: The School America Builds*, Boulder, CO: Westview.

Vejar Vazquez, O. (1944) *Hacia una Escuela de Unidad Nacional*, Mexico: Ediciones de la Secretaria de Educación Publica.

Wallerstein, N. (1983) *Language and Culture in Conflict: Problem-solving in the ESL Classroom*, Reading, MA: Addison-Wesley.

Wallis, E. E. and Bennett, M. A. (1964) *Two Thousand Tongues to Go: True-life Adventures of the Wycliffe Bible Translators Throughout the World Today*, New York: Harper & Row.

Watts, A. C. (1992) *Bibliography of the Summer Institute of Linguistics*, Dallas, TX: SIL.

Weinreich, U. (1953) *Languages in Contact: Findings and Problems*, New York: Pub. of the Linguistic Circle of New York.

Wrenn, C. L. (1946) Henry Sweet, *Transactions of the Philological Society*, 1946: 177–201. Reprinted in Wrenn (1967: 150–169).

—— (1967) *Word and Symbol: Studies in English Language*, London: Longmans, Green & Co.

Wyld, H. C. (Ed.) (1913) *Collected Papers of Henry Sweet*, Oxford: Clarendon Press.

AUTHOR INDEX

SUBJECT INDEX